INTRODUCTION TO SOCIAL AND COMMUNITY SERVICES

Introduction to Social and Community Services

Sixth Edition

W. E. Baugh

MACMILLAN

First edition 1973
Second edition 1975, reprinted 1976
Third edition 1977, reprinted (with revisions) 1979
Fourth edition 1983, reprinted 1985 (twice)
Fifth edition 1987, reprinted 1988
Sixth edition 1992

Published by
THE MACMILLAN PRESS LTD
Houndmills, Basingstoke, Hampshire RG21 2XS
and London
Companies and representatives
throughout the world

Copy-edited and typeset by Cairns Craig Editorial, Edinburgh

ISBN 0-333-57603-9 hardcover
ISBN 0-333-57604-7 paperback

A catalogue record for this book is available
from the British Library

Printed and bound in Great Britain by Mackays of Chatham PLC, Chatham, Kent

To Joyce, Vivien and Richard

Contents

Contents

Preface to the Sixth Edition

This edition, as with previous editions, attempts to provide an introductory but comprehensive survey of the main social and community services. It gives a brief history of each of the services, their current operation and some of the problems facing them.

The Conservative Party, which came to power in 1979, was influenced by the writings of Milton Friedman, with his belief in a strict control of the money supply. Its economic and social policies challenged the economic and social doctrine of previous governments, both Labour and Conservative, which had been influenced by the writings of John Maynard Keynes.

Whilst policy changes normally take place to meet changing circumstances, the application of the Conservative Government's policies in the social and economic sphere has been very radical indeed, although in the economic sphere some policies have been modified. In the social sphere it has meant that virtually all the social services have undergone important changes with the possible exception (so far) of the Probation and After-Care service. In the case of the Health and Education services, the changes are revolutionary. I have tried to make an assessment of the major changes in each of the services, bearing in mind the different viewpoints to them.

Again I express my indebtedness to all the distinguished academics, journalists and politicians who have written or spoken on the social services, and to the public servants who have answered my queries, but I must emphasise that mistakes and wrong judgements are my own.

As in previous editions, I have given some assignments to encourage students to find things out for themselves although I appreciate teachers have their own ideas on what assignments to give.

Although many excellent books mentioned in the reading lists are now out of print, they will be available in public and some college libraries.

W. E. BAUGH

Acknowledgement

The author and publishers are grateful to the Controller of Her Majesty's Stationery Office for permission to quote statistics from the 1991 edition of *Social Trends*.

Abbreviations

ACAS	Advisory, Conciliation and Arbitration Service
AHA	Area Health Authority
CBI	Confederation of British Industry
CEDP	Committee for the Employment of Disabled People
CEGB	Central Electricity Generating Board
CHC	Community Health Council
CNAA	Council for National Academic Awards
CIU	Central Office of Information
CPAG	Child Poverty Action Group
CSE	Certificate of Secondary Education
CTC	City Technical College
DAS	Disablement Advisory Service
DES	Department of Education and Science
DHA	District Health Authority
DH	Department of Health
DSS	Department of Social Security
DHSS	Department of Health and Social Security
DMA	Diploma in Municipal Administration
DMT	District Management Team
DRO	Disablement Resettlement Officer
EPA	Educational Priority Area
ETS	Employment Training Scheme
FE	Further Education
FHSA	Family Health Services Authority
FIS	Family Income Supplement
FPC	Family Practitioner Committee
GCE	General Certificate of Education
GCSE	General Certificate of Secondary Education

GNP	Gross National Product
GP	General Practitioner (Medical)
HMI	Her Majesty's Inspectors
ITB	Industrial Training Board
MSC	Manpower Services Commission
NAB	National Advisory Body for Public Sector Higher Education
NCVQ	National Council for Vocational Qualifications
NSPCC	National Society for the Prevention of Cruelty to Children
NHS	National Health Service
NSTO	Non-Statutory Training Organisation
OPCS	Office of Population Census and Surveys
PAC	Public Accounts Committee
PCFC	Polytechnics and Colleges Funding Council
RAWP	Resource Allocation Working Party
RGN	Registered General Nurse
RHA	Regional Health Authority
SEC	Secondary Examinations Council
SERPS	State Earnings-Related Pension Scheme
SRN	State Registered Nurse
SSAC	Social Security Advisory Committee
SSP	Statutory Sick Pay
TECs	Training and Enterprise Councils
TOPS	Training Opportunities Scheme
TUC	Trades Union Congress
TVEI	Technical and Vocational Education Initiative
UBO	Unemployment Benefit Office
UGC	University Grants Committee
YMCA	Young Men's Christian Association
YOP	Youth Opportunity Programme
YTS	Youth Training Scheme
YWCA	Young Women's Christian Association

1 The Social Services

DEFINITION

It is difficult to give a definition of a social service to which one can refer for precise guidance on whether a service is, or is not, a social service. But a social service can be defined as a service provided by the community to help those in need – need not necessarily being need of money. A state with many statutory social services can be called a *welfare state*. (For other definitions of a welfare state see William A. Robson, *Welfare State and Welfare Society: Illusion and Reality* (1976), and also Norman Furniss and Timothy Tilton, *The Case for the Welfare State* (1979), ch. 1.)*

The Main Social Services

1. *National Insurance*, which is compulsory and which provides partial cover against loss of earnings during a person's lifetime.
2. *Income Support*, which is a payment made to a person not in full-time work whose income is below what is considered necessary for the person's requirements. The actual payment is the difference between the person's income and his or her requirements. It includes a Social Fund to meet special needs.
3. *Child Benefit*, which is a cash payment to families with one or more children.
4. *Family Credit*, which is a cash payment made to poor families where the wage-earner is working and there is at least one dependent child.
5. *Miscellaneous Benefits*, including Housing Benefit.
6. *Redundancy Payments*, which are cash payments given to workers as compensation for being made redundant.
7. *National Health Service*, which provides a comparatively free health service for everyone. It has three branches:
    (a) Family (personal) practitioner services (doctors, dentists, pharmacists, opticians)
    (b) Hospital services
    (c) Community health services.

---

* Fuller references to works cited in this book can be found in a reading section at the end of chapters.

8. *Local welfare services*, now better known as *personal social services*, run by local authorities and voluntary organisations and including services for children in need of care and protection.
9. *Education service* provided by the state (although there is a large private sector as well), which includes the education of disabled children.
10. *Youth service*, which covers all kinds of youth work run by voluntary organisations and local authorities.
11. *Employment services*, which include not simply help in getting a job but training for a job and special services for the disabled and the young and special schemes for the unemployed.
12. *Housing*, which is included as a social service because an adequate home is considered a basic human need.
13. *Planning*, which is concerned with making our environment as pleasant as possible, bearing in mind all the human needs which have to be satisfied.
14. *Probation and after-care service*, which, among other things, is concerned with looking after an offender who is put on probation instead of being sentenced, and the after-care of prisoners released from prison.

Administration

The main social services are provided by the state working through central government departments, local authorities and *ad hoc* boards, but important social services are also provided by voluntary organisations, and there is a much smaller but growing private sector of health and welfare services. All were pioneered in the first place by voluntary effort.

THE AIM OF THE BOOK

The aim is to give the basic facts about the above social services – how they operate, how they developed and some of the current problems in relation to each of them.

ASSIGNMENTS

1. List the statutory social services in your area and, against each one, the administrative body responsible for it and the address of its main local office.

2. List as many as possible of the voluntary organisations in your area. Which, in your opinion, are providing a social service? Give their official titles and the services they provide. (The names of many voluntary bodies can be obtained from your local library.) Find out from the Chief Executive's department of your local authority which of the voluntary bodies receive financial help from the local authority.

3. What would you say are the main criteria for deciding whether a service is or is not a social service?

READING

Jonathan Bradshaw, 'The Concept of Social Need', *New Society*, 30 March 1972.

D. V. Donnison and Valerie Chapman, *Social Policy and Administration* (Allen & Unwin, 1965), ch. 2.

Norman Furniss and Timothy Tilton, *The Case for the Welfare State* (Indiana University Press, 1979), ch. 1.

Julian le Grand and Ray Robinson (eds), *Privatisation and the Welfare State* (Allen & Unwin, 1984), ch. 2 by Alan Walker.

David C. Marsh, *The Future of the Welfare State* (Penguin, 1964), ch. 1.

William A. Robson, *Welfare State and Welfare Society: Illusion and Reality* (Allen & Unwin, 1976).

2 The Historical Background

Over the past 250 years Britain has developed from a comparatively poor country into a comparatively rich country. This has been due to the introduction of power-driven machinery producing goods previously made by hand, to better farming methods and to a greatly improved system of transport, all of which have led to a much greater output of food and goods at lower costs. Britain was the first country in the world to pioneer the new industrial techniques, and she became the richest country in the world and remained so until the end of the nineteenth century. But after 1870 her relative position in the world began to decline and has been declining ever since. At the beginning of the twentieth century the USA and Germany were beginning to overtake her in *per capita* income and, since 1945, she has slipped even further down the league-table of wealth. This is not to say that since 1870 Britain has been getting poorer. On the contrary, Britain is richer than she has ever been. It simply means that other countries have been getting richer at a faster rate (see Aldcroft, 1978, ch. 5).

The new machinery came first to the textile industry in the late eighteenth century and, to begin with, was powered by water, but, later, steam power was used. Coal was needed to make the steam power and so industry moved to the areas of the coalfields, leading to a drift of population to the north. In the twentieth century there has been, and still is, a drift of population to the south due to the fact that the development of electricity as a source of power has made possible the location of new and expanding industries in the south, while the older, basic industries around the coalfields in the north – textiles, heavy engineering, shipbuilding, iron and steel, coal – have contracted. And in recent years, the growth of the computer industry and the resultant development of information technology have, from an employment viewpoint, benefited the South more than the North.

Parallel with the developments of the new industrial and farming techniques there was a rapid rise in population. For England and Wales the population figures (to the nearest million) are as follows: 1801 – 9 million; 1851 – 18 million; 1911 – 36 million; 1961 – 46 million; 1981 – 49 million. This rapid growth of population (it quadrupled in just over 100 years) led to the rapid growth of towns and gave rise to problems of public health (now called environmental health), especially in the industrial areas where,

4

as well as the natural population growth, there was an influx of people from the countryside seeking work.

The new industrial system was initially resented by most working people. Previously goods were made in people's homes or in small workshops attached to the home, and this domestic system of industry was usually combined with a little farming. Although the home worker normally worked for a middleman who provided materials and sometimes tools, and although working hours were long and piecework paid poorly, at least there was a feeling of being one's own boss. But the new power-driven machinery was too big to be used in the home and had to be housed in buildings called mills or factories. In the factory, even though more money could be earned, workers had to work hard in humid conditions under strict discipline. They lost their sense of independence. To mitigate some of the worst evils of the factory system, especially child labour, Factory Acts were passed in spite of much opposition from most of the factory owners. But they did not become of general application or reasonably effective until the latter half of the nineteenth century. Those people who carried on with domestic industry had to accept less and less for what they produced because they had to compete with the machine-made product, which was cheaper. Is it any wonder that many workers hated the new textile machinery and some of them (e.g. the Luddites) went round in gangs smashing it up?

On the land the new farming methods led to a speeding up of enclosures because it was only by having all the land in one compact holding that farmers could please themselves how they farmed and introduce new farming methods. Under the ancient open-field strip system farming was done communally and an individual farmer could only bring in a new farming technique if all the other farmers agreed. In the main, enclosures were forced through against the wishes of the majority of working people. They were resented because much of the common land was enclosed and people of the village could no longer use it, and those people who lived on it had to seek shelter elsewhere. Many small farmers could not afford the cost of enclosure – the fencing, the ditching, the legal fees – and sold up and became farm labourers or sought work in the towns. On the other hand, enclosures eventually made possible a much greater output of food, of great importance in view of the rapidly rising population.

Thus the industrial and agricultural changes upset a way of life that had been settled for centuries. Changes brought insecurity; insecurity made people think afresh about their lives and their position in society. As a result, many people became sympathetic to the ideas of the French Revolution which broke out when these changes were beginning to have some impact on British society. It is from this period that the history of the modern working-class movement begins. The working class campaigned for political rights, but at the same time practised self-help by forming friendly societies, trade unions and, later on, co-operative societies. After 1850 both the trade-union movement and the co-operative movement had become well established, but it was not until 1867 that the first categories of working men received the vote. In 1918 all working men over 21 and all women over 30 received the vote. In 1928 women, like men, received the vote at 21. But it was not until 1948 that we had 'one man, one vote', when the business vote and university vote were abolished.

By 1850 the main economic changes had been completed – railways were established, the new farming methods introduced in the seventeenth and eighteenth centuries, and others introduced later, were in general use and the mechanisation of the major industries was well under way. People began to get the benefit of these new industrial and farming techniques, and living standards for those in work, between 1850 and 1900, rose fairly rapidly. Apart from the period between 1900 and 1914, when prices rose faster than wages, living standards have been rising ever since, especially since 1945. The firms that produce and distribute the much greater output of goods have grown greatly in size, many of them operating on an international scale, especially since the railway and the steamship opened up the continents of the world to commerce from around 1870 onwards.

In spite of much greater wealth and higher living standards there is still much poverty in Britain, although what is called poverty today is a higher living standard than what was called poverty in the inter-war years. Put another way, the poverty line is higher than it was then.

In accounting for the origin of the welfare state the sociologist emphasises the impact of technological change on the family. Thus before the Industrial Revolution society was less complicated. The family worked together as a unit and a person in need looked first to the family, and as a last resort to the local Parish for help. But the new industrial society led to a much greater division of labour, the family ceased to be the unit of production and more of its members sought work away from home, many in distant parts. The role of the family as provider and sustainer diminished. The state had to take over part of the sustaining role previously done by the family.

On the other hand, the political scientist, in seeking the origins of the welfare state, emphasises the growing role of the state in the nineteenth century, made necessary, in spite of the prevailing theory of *laissez-faire*, to mitigate the evils created by the new industrial society which the private enterprise system left untouched. Thus from almost the beginning of the nineteenth century Factory Acts had been passed to control working conditions in the factories, to be followed later in the century by Acts regulating working conditions in mines. From 1848 the state was very much concerned with public health legislation to combat the insanitary conditions of the rapidly growing towns. A state system of education was introduced in 1870 to give support to the private system of education. By the end of the nineteenth century state interference to help the weaker members of the community (quite apart from the Poor Law, which had been in operation since the sixteenth century) was accepted, and in the first decade of the twentieth century the state ceased to play simply a regulatory role but developed a more positive and constructive role in relation to its citizens. The development of an efficient civil service and local government service after 1870 made this increasing state role workable. From state interference in the nineteenth and early twentieth centuries on behalf of the poorer members of society, there developed in the 1930s, because of the world-wide depression, state interference on behalf of the harassed businessman.

Between 1945 and 1973 economic growth and living standards increased at a faster rate than at any previous time in our history. During these years unemployment averaged only 2 per cent and inflation was kept as low as 3 per cent for most of the period. Influenced by the teachings of John Maynard Keynes, both Labour and Conservative governments practised the management of demand which aimed, by the judicious use of public expenditure, interest rate and taxation policy and, where appropriate, incomes policy, to influence demand in order to maintain near to full employment and improve the working of the market system. But, in the late 1960s, inflation began to take off. In the early 1970s it reached 10 per cent and, helped by the big rise in the price of oil 1973–4, reached 25 per cent by 1975. Critics of Keynesian demand management blamed the extravagant use of public expenditure. Espousing pre-Keynesian economics (later to be popularly known as monetarism), they argued that the quantity of money had increased at a much faster rate than output and thus stoked up inflation. The rising amount of public expenditure on the social services was a particular target for the critics. Influenced to some extent by monetarist arguments and battling with high inflation, the Labour government 1974–9 abandoned Keynesianism and introduced monetary targets. But it was the Thatcher government, elected in 1979 which accepted monetarism in its purity, by making the reduction of the money supply and a progressive reduction of public expenditure the two main weapons in its economic strategy for fighting inflation and making the economy sound. But Keynesians argue that the money supply, at any given time, only reflects what is happening in the economy; it is not therefore necessarily the cause of inflation but is a reflection of the underlying causes of which production costs and wages are key factors.

Experience was to show that governments cannot directly control the amount of money in the economy; all they can do is to influence the demand for money by, for example, varying the interest rate, the use of higher purchase controls and controls over bank lending – the latter two being unacceptable to both the Thatcher and Major governments. The Thatcher government had to modify its monetarist stance. But it held to other policies associated with monetarism. Thus it kept a tight hold on public expenditure yet, in spite of this, public expenditure continued to rise. In its belief that a free market ensures the most efficient allocation of resources, it privatised state industries (denationalisation), weakened the power of trade unions, encouraged private medicine and the privatisation of local authority services and encouraged private finance to supplement public endeavour. It approved the growing inequalities associated with a free market system, believing that trends towards equality lead to economic stagnation.

SUMMARY

Britain has developed in the last two hundred and fifty years from a comparatively poor country to a comparatively rich country due to the introduction of power-driven machinery and better farming methods and a greatly improved system of transport. By 1900 she had become the richest country in the world. In the twentieth century other countries, having adopted many of Britain's industrial methods and having developed their own, have become richer than Britain, though Britain is today richer than she has ever been, supporting a population six times greater than it was 200 years ago and in much greater comfort.

The industrial and agricultural developments created social problems – sanitation problems in the rapidly growing towns, long hours of work and child labour in the factories, embittered relations between employer and worker – leading successive governments in the nineteenth century to pass regulatory legislation to try to mitigate these problems. In the meantime the workers had developed trade unions, co-operative societies and political organisations as a form of self-help.

Positive government assistance to help the weaker members of society, leading to the modern welfare state, began at the beginning of the twentieth century and was a natural development from the regulatory legislation of the nineteenth century. The reduced role of the family as a provider for its members in need, due to its fragmentation by increased division of labour, made this new positive role of government very necessary. Because of high inflation in the 1970s there was growing criticism of Keynesian economics and the propagating of alternative policies known collectively as monetarist which led to the broad consensus on economic strategy between the political parties being shattered. Hence the future of the welfare state is more uncertain than at any time since 1945.

ASSIGNMENTS

1. Briefly trace the development in your local area or geographical region of one of its major industries.
2. What do you understand by the phrase 'Victorian *laissez-faire*'? How do you reconcile it with increasing government intervention in social matters from the 1830s onwards?
3. What is meant by the Thatcher Revolution?

READING

Derek H. Aldcroft, *The European Economy 1914–1970* (Croom Helm, 1978), ch. 5.
Paul Barker (ed.), *Founders of the Welfare State* (Heinemann, 1984).
N. F. R. Crafts and Nicholas Woodward (eds), *The British Economy since 1945* (Clarendon Press, Oxford, 1991).
Ronald Fletcher, *The Family and Marriage in Britain*, 3rd edn (Penguin, 1973), ch. 2.
Denis Healey, *The Time of my Life* (Penguin Books, 1990), ch. 18.
C. P. Hill, *British Economic and Social History*, 5th edn (Arnold, 1985).
Martin Loney (ed.), *The State of the Market, Politics and Welfare in Contemporary Britain* (Sage Publications, 1987), ch. 13, 'The Weakening of Social Democracy'.
J. E. Meade, 'Can we learn a "Third Way" from the Agathotopians?', *The Royal Bank of Scotland Review*, No. 167, September 1990.
A. P. Thirlwell, 'Keynesian Employment Theory is not Defunct', *Three Banks Review*, September 1981.

3 The Origins of Social Security

THE POOR LAW

In the nineteenth century there were two main sources of help for the poor – the state system of poor relief dating from the sixteenth century, and charity provided by voluntary organisations.

The administration of the state system of poor relief in Victorian times was based on the 1834 Poor Law Amendment Act. The country was divided into Poor Law unions, each administered by locally elected Guardians of the Poor, who worked within a framework of regulations laid down by a central authority. But the central authority often found it difficult to enforce its decisions, due partly to the Victorians' dislike of the growing encroachment of central government into local affairs, an encroachment made necessary by the social problems created by the Industrial Revolution. Until 1847 this central authority comprised three Poor Law Commissioners, after which it was replaced by a Poor Law Board responsible to Parliament. In 1871 the Local Government Act set up a new department of state called the Local Government Board which, among other things, took over the work of the Poor Law Board. In 1919 the newly created Ministry of Health took over the work of the Local Government Board and remained the central authority until the Poor Law was officially abolished in 1948.

The assumption behind the Poor Law Amendment Act was that if you were fit and a pauper then it was your own fault. Hence fit paupers, including a male pauper's wife and children, were to be given relief in the workhouse where conditions were to be 'less eligible' than those of the lowest-paid worker outside. In this way it was thought that poverty among the able-bodied would be abolished because, rather than go into a workhouse, the able-bodied pauper would get a job. Even so, in a few Poor Law unions material living standards were better than those of some farm workers.

Men, women and children were kept separate, which meant wives were separated from their husbands, and even children (except babies) from their mothers. Sick paupers could obtain relief outside the workhouse and, in fact, out-relief was never completely abolished even for the able-bodied and their dependants, but usually before relief was given in such cases so many hours' labour had to be done – breaking stones, for example. The administration varied in this respect between one union and another. For example in parts of Lancashire and the West Riding, where workers' opposition to the workhouse was most bitter, out-relief continued to be given in many areas without a commitment to do work in return. This was partly a recognition by the authorities that relief for these industrial workers was a temporary measure to tide them over a period of recession. Some unions continued to give out-relief to the able-bodied because they found it cheaper than keeping paupers in the workhouse. (Derek Fraser, *The Evolution of the British Welfare State* (p. 52), quotes statistics from the annual reports of the Poor Law Commissioners, and reveals, rather surprisingly, that between 1840 and 1870 the proportion of paupers receiving indoor relief was never greater than fifteen and a half per cent.)

The 1876 Metropolitan Poor Act and the 1869 Poor Law Amendment Act empowered local Boards of Guardians to build separate hospitals for the sick poor. But even as late as 1900, in some workhouses, sane and insane shared the same facilities. However, by 1870, the central authority had approved the boarding out of children should a Poor Law union desire it.

The Changed Attitude to Poverty

In the last quarter of the nineteenth century there was a growing realisation that poverty, even among the able-bodied, was not necessarily the individual's fault.

The heavy unemployment Britain experienced for the first time between 1873 and 1896, when Britain ceased to be the 'workshop of the world', brought home to many people the fact that impersonal economic forces could be the cause of poverty.

Many old people were seen to be poor yet known to have worked hard all their lives. In the 1890s the Poor Law authorities reported that 40 per cent of the working class over 65 were on poor relief.

There was also growing evidence that poverty was on a much wider scale than realised. This was due to a number of causes:

1. Education was made compulsory in 1880, and for the first time all the nation's children were on view to the authorities. Many were seen to be badly clothed and fed.

2.   Strikes by unskilled workers in the 1880s gave publicity to their low wages.

3.   Writers like Dickens, Kingsley and Disraeli had hinted at a vast underground sea of poverty, and Henry Mayhew in the 1850s had given detailed descriptions of it. But it was the social investigations of the Reverend Andrew Mearns, Charles Booth and Seebohm Rowntree in the last two decades of the nineteenth century that had the greatest impact and brought home to people the terrible poverty in their midst, especially Mearns's pamphlet *The Bitter Cry of Outcast London*, published in 1883. Booth confirmed Mearns's findings on the extent of poverty in his great work *The Life and Labour of the People of London*, the first volume of which was published in 1889. The main causes of poverty, Booth reported, were unemployment and old age. About a third of the people of London were poor, and of these 28 per cent had not sufficient food and clothing to maintain physical efficiency and the remainder 'live under a struggle to obtain the necessaries of life', but with some of these 'it may be their own fault'. Rowntree made his first survey into poverty in York in 1899, and, using a more precise method than Booth of assessing a minimum income needed to keep a person above the poverty line, found that 28 per cent of the people were poor due mainly to low wages; 10 per cent of the people had such a low income that it was impossible for them to keep physically fit; and 18 per cent were in secondary poverty in that, although in want, they could with more 'careful' spending have maintained an income to buy the bare necessities to maintain physical efficiency.

4.   The final confirmation of widespread poverty came with the outbreak of the Boer war, in 1899, when about a quarter of the volunteers had to be rejected because they were medically unfit.

But the changed attitude to poverty was not simply due to an appreciation of its cause and extent but to its injustice, especially in the midst of so much wealth. The point was driven home by middle-class socialists, trade unionists, working-class socialists, radical parsons and certain academic philosophers, and they all looked to the state to do something about it. To the prevailing *laissez-faire* philosophy that any increase in state activity would diminish individual liberty, Oxford philosopher Thomas Hill Green replied that liberty was not simply freedom from restraint but 'doing what one desires' (John Stuart Mill's definition). State activity could actually increase liberty by removing the obstacles to doing what one desires. One of the obstacles was certainly poverty and the state should therefore get rid of it. Green saw the general role of the state as providing an environment within which the individual could make the most of his abilities. Here was the theoretical justification for a welfare state.

The 1867 Reform Act and the 1884 Representation of the People Act, by giving the vote to a large section of the working class, made its coming inevitable.

The Poor Law Becomes Less Harsh

By the end of the nineteenth century old people were receiving help from the Poor Law Guardians in their own homes and those old people still in workhouses were receiving little luxuries like tea and tobacco; more and more pauper children were sent to ordinary boarding schools or boarded out with foster parents; workhouse hospitals began to compare with the voluntary hospitals and working-class people were using them. The 1885 Medical Relief (Disqualification Removal) Act permitted people receiving poor relief for medical reasons to vote, but other paupers remained disenfranchised until the 1918 Representation of the People Act. The 1894 Outdoor Relief (Friendly Societies) Act authorised Poor Law Guardians to ignore sums of up to 5 shillings a week from a friendly society received by an applicant for relief.

THE RISE OF SOCIAL SERVICES OUTSIDE THE POOR LAW

The foundations of the modern welfare state were laid by the Liberal governments of 1905–15. The assumption behind the social services they created was that poverty was not necessarily the fault of individual people and that society had an obligation to help them. The Poor Law was an unsuitable means of help because of its deterrent principle, being based on the assumption that poverty among the able-bodied was the individual's fault. Before these governments, attempts had been made to provide public-work schemes for the unemployed, and the 1905 Unemployed Workmen Act (passed by a Conservative government) authorised financial assistance to local distress committees which provided jobs for the workless. But these public-work schemes were not a success.

The Liberal Government's main social services legislation
The 1906 Education (Provision of Meals) Act permitted local authorities to introduce school meals in elementary schools. Although parents were supposed to pay a contribution towards them, meals were not withheld

from children whose parents could not afford to pay. This was done outside the Poor Law and was, in fact, the first breach in the Poor Law. In 1914 it was made obligatory for local authorities to provide school meals.

The 1907 Education (Administrative Provisions) Act introduced medical inspection of schoolchildren in elementary schools. Under the Act it was obligatory for local authorities to ensure medical inspection of schoolchildren at least three times during their school career. But it was not until the 1918 Education Act that it was made obligatory for local authorities to provide facilities for treatment. This Act also extended medical inspection to secondary schools. Treatment could be charged for, but payment for treatment was eventually abolished by the 1944 Education Act.

These Education Acts arose from the report of the Inter-Departmental Committee on Physical Deterioration. Because of large number of army volunteers for the Boer war who failed the fitness test, this Committee was set up in 1903 to investigate whether the nation was deteriorating physically.

Local authorities received financial help from the Central Government for providing the meals and the medical services for schoolchildren and this dependence of local authorities on Central Government for money to help pay for services they were given to administer continued to grow as the century progressed.

The 1907 Probation of Offenders Act laid the foundations of the Probation and After-Care Service by providing for the creation of probation officers by the courts to look after offenders put on probation instead of being sentenced.

The 1908 Children Act abolished imprisonment for children under 16 and introduced juvenile courts to keep children away from criminals. It also introduced remand homes to prevent children from going to prison while awaiting trial.

The 1908 Old Age Pensions Act gave pensions, paid for out of taxation, to people over 70. There was a means test and the maximum pension per person was 5 shillings (25p) a week. Since the social investigations in the last century had revealed much poverty among the old, schemes for preventing their 'falling into the clutches of the Poor Law' had been put forward. Because of the need for speed, there was no time to create the administrative machinery for a contributory scheme.

The 1909 Labour Exchanges Act inaugurated a system of labour exchanges, later called employment exchanges, throughout the country to help overcome local unemployment. The first statutory ones were those set up by the London boroughs in 1902. Some voluntary ones were in existence prior to that.

The 1909 Trade Board Act gave the government powers to set up boards to fix minimum wages in 'sweated trades' – mainly tailoring and box-making and later mining. This Act was part of a developing pattern of legislation to protect the worker which began in the first half of the nineteenth century with the Factory Acts. The 1911 Shop Act continued this protection for shop assistants. It established half-day closing once a week.

The 1911 National Insurance Act, which introduced health insurance and unemployment insurance, was the most important social legislation of the Liberal governments. All workers earning less than £160 a year (and all manual workers whatever their pay) had to be in the health insurance scheme (£160 was chosen because it was the limit for exemption from income tax). It provided:

(a)   sickness benefit of 10 shillings (50p) a week – 7s 6d (37½p) for women – for 13 weeks and 5 shillings (25p) for the following 13 weeks

(b)   disability benefit not covered by any time limit and which began when sickness benefit ended

(c)   maternity benefit

(d)   the right to treatment in a TB sanatorium

(e)   payment of the doctor's fee including the prescription charges. Health insurance was administered and benefits paid out by insurance companies, friendly societies and trade unions, collectively known as *approved* societies.

Part 2 of the Act gave compulsory unemployment insurance to workers in seven occupations particularly vulnerable to the ups and downs of trade. A minimum of 26 weeks' contributions qualified a person for 15 weeks' unemployment pay within a period of 12 months at 7 shillings (35p) a week. The benefits were paid at labour exchanges.

The cost of the benefits for both parts of the Act were paid for by the contributions from workers, employers and the government. But the benefits were only to supplement private effort. They were not intended to be sufficient to live on.

The purpose of the state insurance scheme was to cover those workers not covered by private insurance.

Lloyd George and Winston Churchill were the ministers chiefly responsible for the Acts (Lloyd George, health insurance; Churchill, unemployment insurance). Both had previously visited Germany and had been much impressed with its state insurance scheme for pensions and health. Britain, however, was the first country to have unemployment insurance.

The Royal Commission on the Poor Law

This Commission was set up in 1905 before the Liberals came to power, but it reported during the Liberals' term of office in 1909. The two main reasons for setting it up were the Poor Law Board's strong objection to relief being given outside the Poor Law and the increasing cost of the Poor Law per head of the population. There was a Majority and a Minority Report. The Majority Report wanted the Poor Law to continue but it was not against the Liberal government's policy of developing other forms of aid outside the Poor Law, but it preferred such aid to be organised mainly by voluntary bodies, with a more humane Poor Law taking care of those that voluntary action could not deal with. The Minority Report wanted the Poor Law abolished and the various categories of need to be dealt with by appropriate specialised public agencies. For example, it was against separate facilities run by the Poor Law for the sick pauper, and wanted all sick people, whether paupers or not, to be helped by the same administrative body. It felt that specialised public agencies should be committees of the local authorities. But the unemployed (i.e. the able-bodied poor) should be dealt with by a department of central government. Both reports recommended that local authorities should take over the administration of the Poor Law, and this was eventually enacted in 1929.

The Relief Regulation Order 1930 officially ended the principle of deterrence, which both reports had opposed, by instructing local authorities to adopt a more constructive approach to the needy.

DEVELOPMENTS IN SOCIAL SECURITY IN THE INTERWAR YEARS

Health Insurance

In 1919 the income maximum for compulsory health insurance (Part 1 of the 1911 Act) was raised to £250. By 1939 it had been raised to £420, which, in effect, meant it covered the vast majority of workers. Inflation was the main reason for the rise in the income limit, but not entirely – the real income limit had been raised to some extent.

In the depressed 1930s there were special arrangements made for the unemployed who could not keep up with their contributions.

The weakness of the health insurance scheme in the interwar years was that workers' dependants were not covered. Thus married women who did not go out to work (and most of them did not in those days) had to pay for their medical treatment. This was not remedied until the creation of the National Health Service after the Second World War.

Unemployment Insurance

The 1920 Unemployment Insurance Act extended unemployment insurance to virtually all workers except certain categories who were considered to be in stable employment, though some of these, like farm workers and domestic servants, were included in the 1930s. The 1921 Unemployed Workers' Dependants Act introduced unemployment benefits for dependants. In 1921 the unemployment benefit period was extended from 15 weeks to 47 weeks.

Payments outside the Unemployment Insurance Scheme

In the interwar years unemployment rarely averaged less than 10 per cent of the working population. In 1932, the worst year, it averaged 23 per cent. Many workers continued to be out of work beyond the expiry of the benefit period. Long-term unemployment on such a large scale had not been anticipated when the 1911 Act was drawn up. However, instead of forcing the unemployed worker to seek Poor Relief after the expiry period, extra payments were made, beginning with payments to returning soldiers during the First World War. The 1927 Unemployment Insurance Act, based on the Report of the Unemployment Insurance Committee (the Blanesburgh Committee), made these payments of unlimited duration and called them *transitional benefit*. For those claiming transitional benefit, the 1931 National Economy Act introduced a household means test to be administered by the public assistance committee of the local authorities, which had taken over the administration of the Poor Law from the Boards of Guardians in 1929. A household means test meant that the income of the whole family was taken into consideration and not just the income of the applicant. This means test was one of a number of economy measures introduced because of the financial crisis in 1931. It was abolished in 1941.

The Unemployment Assistance Board

A Royal Commission on Unemployment Insurance (the Gregory Commission) set up at the end of 1930 made its final report in 1932. In order to stop the drain on the insurance fund, it recommended that transitional payments should be financed by the Treasury. The government accepted this recommendation (it had, in any case, been the practice since 1930) but not the recommendation that transitional payments should continue to be administered by local authorities. Instead it gave the administration of transitional benefit under the 1934 Unemployment Act to a specially created Unemployment Assistance Board.

In setting up a special board to administer transitional payments the government was influenced by the fact that certain public assistance committees had been, in its view, over-generous. A national board would make for efficiency and standardised treatment. The fact that the board was not subject to parliamentary questions, in connection with its discretion in applying the standard benefits approved by Parliament, meant that the details of its administration were taken out of the political arena.

Contributory old-age-pensions

After the war pensions were raised to take account of inflation. The 1925 Widows, Orphans and Old Age Contributory Pensions Act introduced contributory insurance for old-age pensions, including pensions for widows. Those who paid national health insurance were, in the main, covered. The basic pension was 10 shillings (50p) per week to the insured or his widow at 65, but, on reaching the age of 70, a person receiving a contributory pension transferred to the 1908 non-contributory pension then payable to people reaching 70 without a means test. The Act also gave a pension to the guardian of each motherless orphan child of an insured man until the child reached the age of 14.

The increasing cost of the non-contributory scheme was one reason for going over to a contributory scheme. The increasing cost was mainly due to the increasing proportion of old people in the population. (This proportion will continue to increase up to the late 1980s and is due to a fall in the birth rate from the 1880s onwards plus medical advance.) But many people argued that a contributory scheme was a good thing in itself as pensioners would feel more self-respect in receiving something they had paid for.

A large number of widows had been created by the disasters of the First World War and it was realised that, if over a certain age, it would be difficult for them to find work and hence they were brought into the contributory scheme.

DEVELOPMENTS IN SOCIAL SECURITY, 1939–48

The creation of the National Assistance Board

Because of the price rise during the Second World War, older people could not live on their pensions alone and, at the beginning of the war, it was supplemented, subject to a means test, by the public assistance committee of the local authorities. The 1940 Pensions Act introduced a nationally financed and administered scheme of supplementary pensions which took them out of the hands of local government and gave them to the Unemployment Assistance Board, now renamed the Assistance Board. This Act also reduced the age a woman could receive a pension under the Contributory Acts from 65 to 60. Local government continued to administer the Poor Law, which still included workhouse relief. The Poor Law was officially abolished in 1948, when the National Assistance Act set up the National Assistance Board with duties which included those of the previous Assistance Board and the Poor Law.

The Beveridge Report

In June 1941 the government appointed a committee under the chairmanship of Sir William Beveridge 'to undertake, with special reference to the interrelation of the schemes, a survey of the existing national schemes of social insurance and allied services, including workmen's compensation and make recommendations'. Beveridge's famous *Report on Social Insurance and Allied Services* (Cmd 6404) was published in November 1942. It was a best-seller!

The Report recommended a unified system of social insurance to replace 'the tangled maze and administration' of the then existing social insurance.

The system should be comprehensive in that all should be insured, including the self-employed.

All should pay the same flat rate contribution and all should receive the same flat-rate subsistence benefits.

The Report presupposed full employment, a national health service and a system of family allowances if, as it stated, the five 'giants' of 'ignorance, squalor, disease, idleness and want' were to be slain.

The principles underlining the Beveridge Report were:

1. The benefits should be given against contributions, thus supporting the insurance principle and avoiding any humiliation in accepting benefit as one could accept it as of right.
2. The benefits should be enough to live on at subsistence level without any other source of income. Obtaining an income above this level was the individual's responsibility.
3. Everyone should pay the same contributions and receive the same benefits.

4. Those people who had not paid sufficient contributions to qualify for subsistence benefits or who were not covered at all by insurance should have their income supplemented to subsistence level by national assistance.

But it was expected that as the insurance benefits were to be at subsistence level and all workers had to be insured as well as the self-employed, only comparatively few people would have to seek national assistance and their number would diminish. In other words, national assistance was seen as a safety-net only for the minority not covered or not covered adequately by national insurance.

The legislation embodying most of the ideas in the Beveridge Report was passed within three years of the conclusion of the war.

The 1945 Family Allowances Act provided weekly payments for each child beyond the first until such time as the child commenced work.

The 1946 National Insurance Act and the 1946 National Insurance (Industrial Injuries) Act, operative from 1948 provided, on a compulsory basis, insurance against loss of earnings and gave, among other things, unemployment, sickness and disablement benefit and old-age pensions.

The 1946 National Health Service Act introduced a virtually free health service for everyone, operative from 5 July 1948.

The 1948 National Assistance Act abolished the Poor Law, and hence workhouses, and set up a National Assistance Board to provide payments to people over 16 not at school or in work whose income was below the level considered necessary to meet that person's requirements.

At the same time the government had committed itself to a full-employment policy made possible by a revolution in economic theory largely due to the writings of a famous British economist, John Maynard Keynes (1883–1946).

The failure of National Insurance
If one takes the Beveridge principles as the criteria for success, then the national insurance scheme has failed.

The benefits have never been sufficient to live on without any other source of income, and thus a large number of people, dependent solely on insurance payments, had to seek national assistance (later renamed supplementary benefit and now called income support). And because of means testing, many people (especially pensioners, with memories of the Poor Law and means-tested transitional payments in the 1930s) did not claim it. Others failed to claim because of ignorance. However, it depends what is meant by 'sufficient to live on'. National Insurance benefits today are above Beveridge's basic minimum. Hence by his standards they are more than enough to live on without any other source of income. The reason is that general living standards have risen rapidly since 1945 and, over the years, increases in national insurance benefits have meant that, in spite of inflation, benefits are higher in real terms than they were in 1945. But, at the same time, the poverty line, as denoted by the income support level, has been raised because of increases in the rate of income support, and national insurance benefits have remained below income support payments when housing benefit (previously referred to as housing allowance) is taken into consideration. Hence we still say that people living solely on national insurance benefit have not enough to live on (see Carter and Wilson, 1980, p. 26). Even so, it is still correct to speak of the failure of national insurance because, as originally intended by Beveridge, national insurance benefit was supposed to be equal to the basic minimum, whatever that was considered to be, to avoid people having to undergo a means test. In other words, Beveridge envisaged security against want without a means test and a rising poverty line.

The finance of the Insurance Fund was undermined right from the start due to the government agreeing to a full pension to those reaching pensionable age after only ten years' contributions, and to give full pension to existing pensioners. Beveridge intended that only a full subsistence pension should be given to a person who had made the required number of contributions over a period of twenty years. Others should receive a pension appropriate to their contributions and have it made up to subsistence level from national assistance.

And far more people are outside the insurance scheme than Beveridge envisaged. For example, Beveridge never planned for a big rise in one-parent families, nor a return to mass unemployment. Thus payments have had to be made outside the insurance scheme to help certain categories of people with special needs. Finally, the government contribution to the Insurance Fund has not been as generous as Beveridge originally envisaged.

The abandonment of the Beveridge principles
Beveridge's principles of the same contribution from everyone and the same benefit for everyone have been abandoned. There are two main reasons for this:

1. Living standards have improved considerably since 1945, and for a person to go from the income he has been used to down to a near-subsistence income was considered too big a drop. Hence,

as well as the flat-rate scheme, graduated (i.e. earnings-related) schemes were introduced, whereby those who earned more paid more but received bigger benefits. (These earnings-related schemes were modified by the 1986 Social Security Act.)

2.   As living standards have risen and continue to rise, the subsistence level of benefit is considered too low, but, in order to increase it, the employee's and employer's shares of the contributions have to be increased. But the poorer employee paid the same flat-rate contribution as the richer employee and hence there was reluctance to increase the flat-rate contribution to provide larger benefits because of the financial burden this placed on poorer people. In other words, the flat-rate contribution had to be set at a level the lower-paid worker could afford and this was not high enough to give the income from contributions to provide adequate benefits, although those on very low earnings pay no contributions. Inflation aggravated the problem.

SUMMARY

The legislation of the Liberal governments of 1905–15 laid the foundations of the welfare state by introducing social services outside the Poor Law to help those in need. It was a response to the growing sympathy for the poor and a desire for greater social justice. It was only a matter of time before national insurance and old-age pensions, introduced to a limited category of people in the original legislation of 1911, were extended to a wider range of people, and this came in the interwar years.

The First World War accelerated the process. Ordinary men and women, having made great sacrifices during the war, were less prepared to accept their old status and relationships. Furthermore, Lloyd George, the Prime Minister, in an attempt to rekindle flagging national morale, had raised the aspirations of the working class by making promises of a better world after the war with 'homes fit for heroes'. The 1918 Representation of the People Act gave the vote to all men over 21 and women over 30 and thus increased the political power of the working class and ensured that their raised aspirations would at least have to be partially met.

After the short boom period to 1920, fear of revolutionary violence by large sections of the working class was one of the reasons which led the government to introduce transitional payments outside the insurance scheme – an admission that every worker had the right to be protected from poverty caused by unemployment.

Mistaken views on how to deal with economic depression, including the insistence on a balanced budget and need for economy, shared by both Labour and Conservative governments restricted the development of the social services, and in the crisis year of 1931 the introduction of household means-tested transitional payments created great bitterness.

In the interwar years the Labour party replaced the Liberal party as the chief opponent of the Conservatives. Although in office for only two short spells, the fact that it was waiting in the wings to take over government perhaps made the Conservative governments more sensitive to the need for social reform.

The Second World War again stimulated interest in social reform, but this time it was not only the war but also the wish not to go back to the bad old days of the 1930s. That was one of the reasons why there was so much interest in the Beveridge Report. Inspired by this, the next major advance was made by the Labour governments from 1945 to 1951. National insurance, to guard against loss of earning power, was made compulsory for everyone, even the self-employed. In the meantime, just prior to the Labour Party coming to power, the coalition government had introduced family allowances (now called child benefit).

At the same time the administration of national insurance was centralised in a new government department – the Ministry of National Insurance. The system of approved societies was abandoned and the new department supervised the contributions and the benefits. The free medical service provided by the original insurance scheme, which did not, however, cover dependants, was superseded by a comprehensive and virtually free National Health Service. The Poor Law was replaced by a more humane system of national assistance (later to be called supplementary benefit and now income support) intended as a safety-net for those not adequately covered by national insurance. But as the insurance benefits were insufficient (and still are insufficient) to live on, without any other source of income based on the prevailing poverty line, far more people had to claim assistance than originally intended.

ASSIGNMENTS

1. By making use of the reference books in the library, write short bio-graphical accounts of the following people: Charles Booth, Seebohm Rowntree, William Beveridge.

2 Go to the reference library and ask to see a copy of the Beveridge

Report (*Report on Social Insurance and Allied Services*, HMSO, 1942). Read pages 2 to 20 of the Report and answer the following questions:
   (a) What was the third of the three guiding principles of the Report's recommendations?
   (b) What was 'the main feature of the Plan for Social Security' in the Report? What were its six fundamental principles?
   (c) Why did the report stress the insurance principle (i.e. 'benefit in return for contributions rather than free allowances from the State')?
   (d) Why did only the Chairman of the Committee (Beveridge) sign the Report?
   (e) Who was the Minister who set up the Committee?
   (f) Who was the Secretary of the Committee?
   (g) To which Minister was the Report submitted, and the date?
3. Using the cost-of-living index in *Whitaker's Almanack*, make an estimate of the value of the retirement pension in 1914 at present-day values.
4. What is meant by 'the awakening of the social conscience in later Victorian times'? [INTERMEDIATE DMA, 1959]

READING

Paul Addison, *The Road to 1945* (Quartet Books, 1977).
Paul Barker (ed.), *Founders of the Welfare State* (Heinemann, 1984).
Corelli Barnett, *The Audit of War – the Illusion and Reality of Britain as a Great Nation* (Macmillan, 1987), chs 1 and 2.
Beveridge Report, *Report on Social Insurance and Allied Services*, Cmd 6404 (HMSO, 1942).
Maurice Bruce, *The Coming of the Welfare State* (Batsford, 1971).
Maurice Bruce (ed.), *The Rise of the Welfare State: English Social Policy 1601–1971* (Weidenfeld & Nicolson, 1973).
Charles Carter and Thomas Wilson, *Discussing the Welfare State* (Policy Studies Institute, 1980).
D. V. Donnison and Valerie Chapman, *Social Policy and Administration* (Allen & Unwin, 1965), ch. 2.
Derek Fraser, *Evolution of the Welfare State*, 2nd edn (Macmillan, 1984).
S. Gand and E. O. A. Checkland (eds), *The Poor Law Report of 1843* (Penguin, 1974).
Bentley B. Gilbert, *British Social Policy 1914–1939* (Batsford, 1973).
Bentley B. Gilbert, *Evolution of National Insurance in Great Britain* (Michael Joseph, 1966).

Brian Inglis, *Poverty and the Industrial Revolution* (Hodder & Stoughton, 1971).

Norman Longmate, *The Workhouse* (Temple Smith, 1974).

David C. Marsh (ed.), *An Introduction to the Study of Social Administration* (Routledge & Kegan Paul, 1965), ch. 2 by Joan L. M. Eyden.

T. H. Marshall, *Social Policy*, 5th edn (Hutchinson, 1985).

Robert Pinker, *Social Theory and Social Policy* (Heinemann, 1971).

Robert Roberts, *The Classic Slum*, 3rd impression (Manchester University Press, 1978).

Michael E. Rose, *The Relief of Poverty, 1834–1914*, 2nd edn (Macmillan, 1986).

Pat Thane, *The Foundations of the Welfare State* (Longman, 1982).

4 Social Security Today

Social security is concerned with ensuring, for all citizens above school-leaving age, a basic income when they cannot earn enough money to maintain themselves and their dependants.

The main social security services are:

1. National insurance.
2. Income support (formerly called supplementary benefit)
3. Child benefit (formerly family allowance)
4. Family credit (formerly family income supplement)
5. Miscellaneous benefits including Housing benefit
6. Redundancy payments

NATIONAL INSURANCE

Like any other form of insurance, people in the national insurance scheme contribute to a fund out of which payments are made to those who suffer loss providing the contribution conditions are satisfied. In the case of national insurance, loss is 'loss of income by interruption of earnings'. The 'risks' which can cause loss of earnings and which are covered by national insurance are as follows:

(a) sickness during working life, including chronic sickness
(b) unemployment
(c) disablement
(d) old age (a 'desirable risk')
(e) maternity
(f) widowhood

All workers, even the self-employed, have to be in the national insurance scheme. Before 1961 all categories (i.e. under 18s, employed, self-employed) paid the same flat-rate contribution and all received the same flat-rate benefit. But the National Insurance Act 1959 introduced a pension scheme with earnings-related contributions and benefits which came into operation in April 1961. The 1975 Social Security (Pensions)

26

Act introduced a new pension scheme and made all national insurance contributions and benefits earnings-related except those of the self-employed.

In January 1982 the earnings-related supplement for the following short-term benefits – sickness, unemployment and widows' allowance – was abolished. For these, new claimants only received the flat-rate benefit. But the earnings-related addition was retained for retirement pensions, widows' pensions and invalidity benefit. Since 1975, the main insurance benefits have been index-linked. Unemployment benefit and supplementary benefit paid to registered unemployed became taxable from 5 July 1982.

National insurance is paid for by:

(a)   contributions from employees
(b)   contributions from employers as they pay part of the employee's contribution
(c)   an Exchequer contribution paid for out of taxation which in recent years has been greatly reduced
(d)   interest on investments of the Insurance Fund.

Benefits under the national insurance scheme are paid as of right – there is no means test.

National insurance is administered by the Department of Social Security (DSS) and the minister in charge is the Secretary of State for Social Security. However, by April 1991, much of the Department's work had been delegated to executive agencies but with the minister still responsible for overall policy. One such agency is the Social Security Benefits Agency. The minister is advised by the civil servants in his department and by a Social Security Advisory Committee (SSAC). But, apart from advising the minister, the SSAC can initiate its own investigations and reports. The SSAC replaced, in November 1980, the former Supplementary Benefits Commission and the National Insurance Advisory Committee. There is a separate Industrial Injuries Advisory Council which advises the minister on matters relating to industrial injuries. There are also medical appeal tribunals which hear appeals against the decisions of medical boards in relation to assessment of disablement.

If insured persons are dissatisfied with the benefits received or are denied benefit, they can appeal to a local social security appeal tribunal. The tribunals are independent of the government. The procedure is informal and it costs the claimant nothing. Three people usually sit on the tribunal – the chairman, who normally has legal qualifications, one person from the management side of industry, and one from the trade-union side. The social security commissioner hears appeals on points of law arising from decisions of social security appeal tribunals and medical appeal tribunals.

Sickness Benefit

Sickness benefit, for the first 28 weeks of sickness, is paid by the employer. This is called statutory sick pay. Until April 1991, the employer received back from the Government the full amount he paid out in sick pay, but since then the Government has been liable for only 80 per cent of sick pay costs – the other 20 per cent being the employer's responsibility.

If an employee is still sick after 28 weeks, he goes on to what is called invalidity pension. Those employees who, for a number of reasons, are not entitled to statutory sick pay, may claim the State national insurance sickness benefit and, after 28 weeks, if still sick, obtain a non-contributory invalidity pension. For those seriously disabled who cannot work and who have not paid enough national insurance contributions, there is a severe disablement allowance. For the above benefits there are additions for wife and children. An invalidity allowance may be paid with the invalidity pension to a person who becomes sick more than five years before minimum retirement age.

Sickness benefit may be denied to people up to a period of six weeks if their sickness is considered to be due to their own negligence.

It was from April 1986, under the 1985 Social Security Act, that national insurance sickness benefit was replaced for most people by statutory sick pay when the employers' liability to pay statutory sick pay went up from 8 weeks to 28 weeks, thus virtually privatising sickness benefit.

Unemployment Benefit

Unemployment benefit is paid for up to one year and then, if still unemployed a person can claim income support. But to draw benefit an unemployed person must be available for work and, since October 1989, give proof, if need be, that he or she is 'actively seeking work'. A person who loses his or her job because of misconduct or voluntarily leaves it without reasonable cause may be denied unemployment benefit for a period of up to 26 weeks. Part-time workers, under certain conditions, can receive unemployment benefit.

Before the 1986 Social Security Act came into force, after one year of unemployment benefit, the unemployed person, if still unemployed, went on to supplementary benefit (now called income support) but he or she could not claim the long-term supplementary benefit rate (unless over 60 years of age) which other supplementary benefit claimants went on to after 12 months. Thus the First Report of the Social Security Advisory

Committee stated in 1981: 'the growing band of long-term unemployed has to exist on a basic level of personal benefit which is little more than two-thirds of the minimum the Government has established for others in similar circumstances.' The rule was made when there was comparatively little unemployment and it was felt that most of the unemployed would get a job within twelve months. Long and short-term rates have been abolished under income support.

On 1 August 1989, Mr Fowler, the then Secretary of State for Employ-ment, reported that up to 10 per cent of those claiming unemployment ben-efit did so without justification as they already had jobs. (The unemployed are only allowed to earn up to £5 a week without it affecting their benefit.) The Secretary of State's figure was based on the proportion of those claimants who, when requested to call for another interview, withdraw their claim. Whilst not condoning dishonesty, critics state (Molly Meacher, *Guardian*, 3 August 1989) that for many young families unemployment benefit is no longer sufficient to cover basic expenses and 'many of the so-called unjustified claimants are in fact innocent people wrongly denied their benefit'. Furthermore, underpayment on unemployment benefit, as reported by the National Audit Office, is another factor to be taken into consideration.

Two rulings which adversely affected unemployment benefit were the abolition of the earnings-related supplement for unemployment benefit and the taxing of unemployment benefit, which came into effect as from 5 July 1982. There are also fears that the 'actively seeking work' regu-lation (see above) will enable certain employers to employ people at a cheap rate.

The abolition of the earnings related supplement for unemployment benefit was considered by many to be indefensible. This was because the assumption had always been that benefits based on a claimant's contributions, under the earnings-related schemes, were yours as of right. Thus when Lord Montgomery, seen queuing up at the Post Office to receive his State pension, was asked why he wanted the pension he replied: 'Because I've paid for it.' A more recent example of this kind of moral lapse is a rule, introduced in January 1989, whereby workers between the age of 55 and 60 who are made redundant and, because of their age, are entitled to an occupational pension, cannot draw their full entitlement to unemployment benefit if their pension is over £35 a week. For every 10p above £35 they lose 10p unemployment benefit. This means some will receive no unemployment benefit at all. The Government defend this by pointing to the rule that to draw unemployment benefit claimants must be genuinely seeking work, which is unlikely to be the case with such redundant workers, and in fact many of them choose to retire early. Those under the age of 55 are not affected by this rule.

Benefits for Disablement

Under the National Insurance scheme disablement benefits are paid arising from accidents at work or disablement caused by particular types of illness resulting from work. There is a qualifying period of 15 weeks but, in the meantime, statutory sick pay or sickness benefit may be payable. For those who do not qualify for the National Insurance invalidity pension there is a severe disablement allowance. There is a non-contributory attendance allowance, which is not means-tested, payable to severely disabled people – the amount depending on the care and attention needed. And the carers, if between the age of 16 and pension age, may obtain an invalid care allowance (non-contributory) to give them some compensation for their not being able to go out to work. Thanks to the ruling of the European Court of Justice, the allowance was extended to married women previously excluded. For people who cannot do their regular job because of disablement and have to take a less well-paid job, there is a reduced earnings allowance. When these people reach an age when they can retire they may be entitled to a retirement allowance. For those people who are unable or virtually unable to walk there is a tax-free mobility allowance (non-contributory) providing that when one claims, one is age 5 or over and under 66. For disabled people on income support, there is a disability premium and a severe disablement premium (see under income support).

For all types of disablement the amount and type of benefit depends, to a great extent, on the degree of disablement and how long it is expected to last and all this is assessed by a medical committee.

The review of social security commissioned by the Government, which eventually resulted in the 1986 Social Security Act, did not embrace benefits for the disabled. Instead a separate review of the position of the disabled was to be carried out from the Office of Population Censuses and Surveys (OPCS). Its second report in 1988 stated that two-thirds of Britain's 6.2 million disabled adults say they were either 'getting into difficulties' with money or 'just getting by' (see the *Guardian*, 16 November 1988). The average income, the report calculates, for a non-pensioner disabled adult plus family was £98.30 compared with the average income of the population as a whole of £136.50. The final report, the sixth, was expected in 1989.

Retirement

Under the national insurance scheme, women employees receive a pension at 60, men at 65. Even so, although receiving a pension at 60, the 1986 Sex Discrimination Act makes it illegal for an employer to compulsorily retire men and women at different ages so that, in effect, where men are not retired until the age of 65, women, although receiving the State pension, are able to continue working, if they so wish, until the age of 65.

The State pension comprises a basic pension plus an earnings related addition. Since 1 October 1989, pensioners can earn any amount in retirement without affecting their State pension. Those staying on at work after the pension age of 65 (60 for women) earn an increased pension when they retire but when they reach 70 the retirement pension is paid to them even if still working. There is a small weekly addition to the pension for people over 80. Those over 80 who have not qualified for a State pension can receive, subject to certain residential qualifications, a non-contributory pension. Those whose pension is not enough to live on can claim income support. About one million out of a total of nine and three-quarter million pensioners do so and from 9 October 1989 they received a higher amount of income support. Furthermore, the amount of housing benefit was increased for poorer pensioners not on income support, the amount of the increase depending on their income.

Mothers who do not go out to work or those people who give up work to look after a severely disabled relative retain their rights to the basic pension.

The present plan for pensions, introduced by the 1986 Social Security Act, replaced the scheme popularly known as SERPS (State Earnings-Related Pension Scheme) introduced by the 1975 Social Security Act which, unlike the 1986 Act, had the support of both Labour and Conservative parties. (Previous attempts at reform of pensions had failed to get all-party agreement.) The 1975 Act, operative from April 1978, aimed to progressively reduce the number of pensioners who had to claim a supplementary pension.

The Thatcher government considered that SERPS was based on too rosy a picture of the economy and hence too costly. Its 1986 Act introduced a simpler basic pension relying on the employee to augment the basic State pension by contributing to an occupational pension scheme provided by his employer or taking out a personal pension. (One advantage of a personal pension is that it is 'portable from job to job' whereas it is not always possible to transfer pension rights in an occupational scheme.)

Thus the present pension scheme provides a smaller basic State pension than SERPS would have done for it is based on average lifetime earnings whereas SERPS was based on the best twenty years of earnings, and the pension rate is reduced to 20 per cent of earnings from 25 per cent under SERPS. Widows under SERPS inherited the whole of their husband's pension rights (up to a ceiling) but, under the 1986 Act, they inherit only half of them. The main advantage of the Act from the Government point of view is that future generations are relieved of a financial burden. It sees an advantage in all employees having a private pension as well as a State pension which normally only applies to the better off. Furthermore, money saved under the new scheme could provide more money for the basic pension and insurance funds from private schemes will provide capital for investment. Although the present pension scheme, like SERPS, is inflation-proof there is no hint that the basic pension will allow for higher living standards for pensioners. For example, from 1975 the main insurance benefits were index-linked but pensions were not only linked to prices, like other benefits, but also to wages, increasing in line with whichever showed the larger percentage increase during the year. In this way, pensioners were intended to share in the increased wealth of the country but, in 1981, the Thatcher government linked pensions to prices only so that the State pension ceased to increase in real terms. The fact that the basic State pension will give less than the previous scheme in retirement is fair enough if the private pension schemes make up the difference and everyone is covered by a sound private scheme. But much criticism of the new scheme relates to how far one can trust all employers to provide an adequate pension plan. It is claimed that few private pension schemes have succeeded in maintaining pensions in line with inflation.

One of the conditions of contracting out of the State scheme is that an occupational scheme must guarantee a minimum pension. Under the 1990 Social Security Act an Ombudsman is to be appointed to deal with complaints against occupational pension schemes. But personal pensions depend on the investment yields and administrative costs of the scheme. However, there is a 2 per cent special incentive paid by the DSS into personal pension schemes on behalf of most personal pension holders which will continue until 5 April 1993. Furthermore the schemes are subject to tax relief.

There is special provision for those not earning enough to build up full pension rights – those who take time off work to bring up children, disabled people and those not earning because they are looking after the disabled. Even so, these groups will still need a minimum of 20 years earnings to get full pension rights under the State's basic scheme. On the other hand, those not in the above categories – the unemployed, for example – will have their State pension based on their lifetime earnings and hence unemployment and low wages will reduce their eventual pension. For occupational pension schemes the Government requires a minimum contribution of 4 per cent of salary of which at least 2 per cent falls on the employer. The changes do not affect anyone retiring before the year 2000 and there is a transition period until the year 2010 but, eventually, there will be a system, the Government hopes, in which everybody will be able to contribute either to an occupational scheme or to a personal pension as well as the State basic pension. The advertising campaign by personal pension providers plus the Government's financial inducements, which some cynics call bribery, have resulted in more people applying for a personal pension than the Government expected. These people, plus those in occupational schemes who have also contracted out of SERPS, have resulted in the National Insurance Fund having to be subsidised from general taxation because of the Fund's reduced income.

Maternity
Under the authority of the 1986 Social Security Act a new maternity pay scheme was introduced, operative from April 1987. Women who leave work to have a baby receive maternity pay from their employer providing they have been working continuously for the same employer for at least 26 weeks immediately prior to receiving the benefit. Furthermore, their average weekly earnings must not be lower than the lower earnings limit for national insurance contributions. Maternity pay normally lasts for 18 weeks. There are two rates of pay depending on the length of time with the same employer. Thus, if it is over two years, 90 per cent of average weekly earnings is paid for the first 6 weeks and a lower rate for the remaining 12 weeks. Between 6 months and 2 years, only the lower rate is paid. A maternity allowance is paid for 18 weeks to women who do not qualify for maternity pay – for example, the self-employed or those who have changed or given up their job – but these women must have paid the standard rate National Insurance contribution for at least 26 weeks of the pregnancy. If the income from either maternity pay or maternity allowance is considered insufficient to live on, income support may be claimed or, if the husband or partner is working more than 24 hours a week and there is already one child in the family, then family credit may be claimed but, in this case, such a family would also be receiving child benefit. Further, if the pregnancy lasts for at least 28 weeks a family on income support or family credit can claim a grant of £100 from the social fund. (See later pages for income support, including the social fund, family credit and child benefit.)

Widowhood

Since April 1988, under the 1986 Social Security Act, a widow who qualifies for benefit (i.e. her late husband satisfied the National Insurance contribution conditions) receives a tax free lump sum, called widow's payment, of £1000. But if the widow is over 60 years of age she only receives the payment if her husband was not getting a retirement pension when he died. This is because a widow whose husband dies when both are over pensionable age inherits her husband's pension rights, as does the husband if his wife dies and both are over pensionable age. The following benefits paid to widows also depend on the late husband having satisfied the National Insurance contribution conditions. A widowed mother, in addition to the payment, receives a widowed mother's allowance with an addition for each dependant child. A widow's pension is paid if a widow is over 45 when her husband died or over 45 when her entitlement to widowed mother's allowance ended. Thus no woman can draw both a widow's allowance and a widow's pension. Benefits cease on re-marriage. Widow's pension ceases on receiving a retirement pension which will be the same amount as the widow's pension. The above benefits are based on the assumption that the husband is the breadwinner and hence are compensation for the loss of a husband's income but there is no limit on the amount a widow may earn when receiving widow's benefits.

The 1986 Social Security Act worsened the position for widows in their forties. It was reported in *The Guardian* (11 February 1989) that a widow whose husband died the day before her 45th birthday was refused a widow's pension. Before the 1986 Act a widow qualified for a pension at the age of 40. The Government reason for changing the rules was given by Mr Nicholas Scott, then Minister for Social Security to the House of Commons, 6 February 1989. 'Ninety per cent of widows aged between 40 and 44 re-marry,' he said. But what seemed unjust is that this particular widow's husband died six months before 11 April 1988, when the new age rule became operative – the new age rule being applied retrospectively. However, the Government gave way following a Commissioner's decision and under the 1989 Social Security Act those who were widowed before 11 April 1988 and were refused a pension because they were under 45 were to be given a pension and paid arrears of benefit.

Income Support

In spite of the national insurance scheme and the universal state child benefit (see below), there are still people without what is considered an adequate income and hence there is a need for a safety net. Today that safety net is provided by income support introduced in 1988 by the 1986 Social Security Act. Previous safety nets were supplementary benefit which income support replaced and before that national assistance which replaced the Poor Law, the earliest safety net of them all. All these safety nets varied in the degree of 'safety' they provided. Income support, like previous safety nets is means-tested. Everyone over 18 and not in full-time work and whose partner (if any) is not in full-time work can claim income support providing their total income is below a certain minimum considered necessary for a person's requirements and their capital does not exceed £8000. The actual benefit is the difference between income and assessed requirements. The full benefit is paid to a person whose capital does not exceed £3000. Between £3000 and £8000 the benefit gets progressively smaller. A person is considered to be in full-time work if he or she works 24 hours a week or more. One of the conditions for obtaining benefit (although there are exceptions) is that, if under 60, one must be available for full-time work. Before September 1988, 16- to 17-year-olds could claim income support. Now they can only do so under special circumstances.

Income support includes a personal allowance which varies according to a person's age and whether he or she is part of a twofold household or a single parent or single person. In addition to the personal allowance there are extra payments called premiums which relate to certain categories of claimants and reflect their particular needs.

Thus pensioners 60 or over receive a premium with a higher premium for those over 74 and a higher premium still if 80 or over. Where there is a couple living together and one of them is over 60, he or she will receive more money than a single pensioner.

Families with children receive a family premium for each dependant child. Couples with no children receive only the personal allowance.

For single parents there is a lone parent premium.

Disabled people, including the long-term sick receive a disability premium and a disablement premium for each disabled child. Severely disabled people receive an additional premium.

Families on income support can obtain free school meals, free milk and vitamins for children under five years old (i.e. school age), free prescriptions, free dental treatment, free spectacles and free travel to hospital for any necessary treatment plus housing benefit to help towards the cost of rent and the community charge and, if an owner occupier, help with the mortgage. However, 20 per cent of the community charge must be paid by those on income support and they must pay the water and sewage charges in full. At the time of the introduction of the community charge (popularly known as poll tax) the Government said adjustments would be made to income support to cover the 20 per cent of the charge claimants would have to pay.

If claimants do not get the amount of income support they think they are entitled to, they can ask for their claim to be reviewed again by the DSS office and, if still dissatisfied, they can appeal to a local social security appeal tribunal. A final appeal is to a social security commissioner but this can only be on a point of law. There is a separate appeals procedure for the social fund (see below).

As a general rule, where there is an appeals tribunal procedure, ministerial responsibility does not apply. This is to ensure that only judicial considerations and not political ones are taken into account when an appeal is being considered. There is a Council on Tribunals which has the job of keeping an eye on how these administrative tribunals are functioning, particularly in regard to fairness. It makes recommendations, where necessary, for their improvement to the Lord Chancellor who is responsible for them.

Social Fund

The other part of income support is the social fund out of which payments are made to meet special needs not covered by income support, the following categories of need are covered by the fund which began operating in April 1987.

1. Grants under the fund are provided to meet maternity and funeral costs.
2. Community care grants can be made to help, for example, handicapped people to re-establish themselves in the community and thus avoid institutional care or a grant can be made to ease the pressure on the family with a handicapped person or an elderly person in need of attention – the grant helping to pay for domiciliary services.
3. A cold weather payment is also provided under the fund if there is a period of seven consecutive days when the average mean temperature is below freezing, although, in February 1991, this seven-day rule was relaxed and the system of cold weather payments is to be reviewed.

    But to qualify for the above grants in full, a person must not have more than £500 in savings. For every pound over that amount one pound is deducted from the full benefit.
4. Interest-free crisis loans are provided to meet expenses from some disaster – a robbery, a flood, a fire etc or even to help if one is

stranded away from home. But crisis loans are only given to people who have resources to eventually draw upon and are recovered when circumstances allow and the maximum loan is £1000.

5. Budgeting loans are given to help meet special household expenses such as items of furniture or a cooker etc. But such loans are only given if the claimant has less than £500 savings after meeting the cost of the item required.

Income support and the provision of grants for maternity and funeral expenses and cold weather payments under the social fund are governed by regulations, and hence appeals against decisions relating to them are heard by a social security appeals tribunal. But other special needs payments, under the social fund, comprising loans and grants, are discretionary and, if help is refused, appeals are not heard by an independent tribunal but by a social fund inspectorate. Under the previous system of supplementary benefit, all special needs payments were based on a regulatory framework. Explaining the reasons for the change from regulation to discretion within the social fund, the Government argued that having a regulatory framework for special needs makes the system very complicated and often it provides 'only a broad approximation of need'. Furthermore, a regulatory system encourages claimants 'to define their needs in terms of what the regulations provide rather than simply explaining their needs as they see them'. In other words, the Government is hinting that, in its view, claims for special needs have been made, irrespective of whether the claimant has such needs but simply because in the regulations it states that such special needs can be claimed for. Thus the Government has emphasised that under the regulatory system there was a big increase in the number of single payments. However, one reason for the upsurge in claims for special needs (i.e. single payments) could have been the campaigns of certain local authorities and voluntary bodies which, for the first time, made many people aware of their entitlement rights. Furthermore, the right of appeal to the social security tribunals resulted in many appeals being upheld. This gave further publicity to special needs (single) payments.

Income support came into effect from 24 November 1980. Until then Income support was called supplementary benefit and it was the Supplementary Benefits Commission (now replaced by the Social Security Advisory Committee) which recommended a regulatory framework as against a largely discretionary system which was then in use. It argued that discretionary payments sometimes lead to payments being made on moral judgements; to claimants being uncertain of their rights, and sometimes to conflict between claimants and officers. Furthermore, discretionary decisions make the scheme more complex and more difficult to administer fairly. They can lead to different decisions being made by different officers from a similar set of circumstances. On the other hand, benefits based on a legal framework give more publicity to the benefits and make it easier for Parliament to scrutinise the working of the system. But the Commission did admit that in reducing the amount of discretion, there was a danger that the system could become too rigid and certain cases which justified help would not receive it. Hence, even with a regulatory framework the Commission wanted discretion retained 'for really exceptional cases'. A discretionary system is, of course, a more flexible system. On the other hand it puts a lot of worrying responsibility on DSS staff who administer it.

Concern has been expressed that appeals against the discretionary decisions relating to the social fund are not dealt with as impartially as they should be because the officer dealing with the appeal is an officer of the DSS. However, there is a Social Fund Commissioner, independent of the DSS, who appoints the inspectors who in turn monitor the quality of social fund decisions. Hence the inspectors state that they are independent of the DSS. They have to decide not just whether the social fund officers acted legally but whether their decisions were merited. Annual reports by the Secretary of State for Social Security on the social fund (the first was for the financial year 1988–9) reveal that a fair proportion of appeals were upheld, which suggests fair adjudicating by the Inspectorate.

Another concern is that each local DSS office has, except for maternity and funeral payments, a fixed budget for making payments from the social fund. What happens when the money runs out and there are still needs to be met? The Government promised a contingency fund 'to meet unexpected demands which put pressure on the allocation of individual offices'. (Commons *Hansard*, 28 January 1986). But there is also a fixed amount for the contingency fund. Whilst during the first year, 1988–9, the social fund was underspent it was heading for an overspend in the financial year 1989–90, with an increase in refusals. For the financial year 1990–1 the fund was increased but the increase was well behind the rate of inflation. In spite of that the DSS said the fund was adequate to meet 'greatest need'. (*Guardian*, 15 November 1989). The adjective 'greatest' might suggest that the Government has tightened up on its definition of 'need'. Loans are expected to be repaid within 18 weeks and only 'very exceptionally' extended for a further 26 weeks.

Rich people can employ accountants to help them manage their financial affairs. Originally the Government would have liked social workers to do the same for poor people, especially those among them who are refused a loan because of their inability to repay it. But social workers were reluctant to be involved because there was the danger that it could have led them into advising the DSS as to who should get a loan which might, in some cases, seem to clash with the social worker's aim of doing his or her best for the client. The DSS itself now gives advice on money matters. However, social workers and those people involved in the relevant voluntary organisations accept the importance of claimants for loans seeking advice before putting in a claim on the social fund as experience has shown that their chance of obtaining it is thereby enhanced.

Two serious criticisms have been made of the social fund. The Chairman of the Social Security Advisory Committee stated in 1991 that it is underfunded and needs increasing in real terms by 'a substantial amount.' And another critic has pointed out that although it is true, as the government states, that it is meeting real need there is much real need it does not meet. Thus there is no evidence that many of those who are refused help are better off than those who are given help.

Child Benefit

Child benefit is a universal (i.e. not means-tested) benefit, paid for out of taxation to the mother for each child under 16 or under 19 if in full-time education. For one-parent families, there is an extra benefit called one-parent benefit. Child benefit replaced family allowances and child tax allowances in 1977. The idea of a family allowance was pioneered by Eleanor Rathbone in the 1920s and 1930s. As a person's wage is related to his job and not his needs, an unskilled worker with a wife and family may not find his wages sufficient to keep his family above the poverty line. (Income support is not paid to a worker in a full-time job). The Beveridge Report included a proposal for family allowances and they were introduced in 1945 but were only paid to a family with two children or more.

The Conservative government frowns upon universal benefits, stressing the need to pin-point help on the really needy. It argues that the money saved on not giving to those who do not need it means there is more money for those who do. Thus at the July 1986 interim uprating of benefits, child benefit ceased to be linked with the inflation rate with the result that its value in real terms declined. Apart from targeting the really needy, the Government argues that many low income families do not, in any case, benefit from an increase in child benefit because income support is reduced by the amount of any increase in child benefit. The Government also said (House of Commons, 27 August 1988) that those on family credit would be no better off for the same reason, but child benefit is, in fact, ignored in assessing the amount of family credit and is therefore of great benefit to low-wage families. In addition, being a universal benefit, child benefit has virtually a 100 per cent take-up and is particularly helpful to poorer people whose take-up of means-tested benefits is very much less. Hence the freezing of the benefit so that, in real terms, it is worth less than in 1979, can hit poor families who, because of ignorance or apathy do not claim all the benefits to which they are entitled – for example, housing benefit, income support or family credit. Furthermore, the freezing of child benefit results in more families having to claim means-tested benefits. And, as the Child Poverty Action Group (CPAG) pointed out, not all of the money saved on freezing child benefit has gone on increasing means-tested benefits (*Poverty*, Winter 1989–90).

On a wider canvas the CPAG has argued that child benefit represents 'society's recognition to all families of the additional costs of bringing up children by redistributing income between those who do not have children and those who do'. However, child benefit was unfrozen in April 1991 when an extra £1 was given for the first child and an extra 25p for each other child. And from April 1992 it is to be once again indexed in line with inflation. This reversal of policy was enacted under the newly installed government of John Major, but one-parent benefit remained frozen.

If there is reluctance on the Government's part to give child benefit to those families who do not need the money, why not tax it? Family allowances used to be taxed but, in those days, there were child tax allowances. Because child benefit was made tax-free, child tax allowances were abolished. In the 1968 Budget the entire extra payment of an increase in family allowances was recovered from all who paid tax at the standard rate. However, because of the low tax threshold the extra amount of family allowance was clawed back from families who needed it. This was one of the reasons for inhibiting the Conservative government (1970–74) from substantially increasing family allowances as promised. But if the tax system could be adjusted so that those on an income low enough to be subsidised from public funds did not pay income tax, then taxing child benefit might be the best way of substantially increasing it without making too big an increase in public expenditure. It would certainly go to those who needed it, being a universal benefit, and taken back from those who did not.

Low-wage Families

Those in full-time work cannot claim income support yet, due to their low rate of pay, their income might not be sufficient for their families to live on. Hence, in 1970, was passed the Family Income Supplement Act, operative from 1971, to give financial help to such families providing they had one child or more. Under the 1986 Social Security Act the principle of subsidising low-wage families who had children was continued but the benefit was renamed Family Credit (operative from 11 April 1988). Apart from cash support those on family credit, like those on FIS previously, are entitled to free prescriptions, free dental treatment, vouchers for spectacles but not, as with income support, free school meals and free school milk and vitamins, although the credit is supposed to include an amount to cover these items. To obtain the full amount of family credit the family income must be below a certain income, and this amount varies with the size of the family and the age of the children. For each pound over that amount deductions are made. Deductions are also made for capital over £3000 and, if the capital is over £8000, family credit cannot be claimed.

Because of strong opposition, even from many of its own supporters, the Government withdrew its proposal for family credit to be paid by employers which, in the vast majority of cases, would have meant it would go to the father and not, as with FIS, to the mother. But the Government saw the paying of family credit by employers as a small step towards integration of the tax and social security systems – a long-term goal. The Government White Paper (Cmn 9691) gave the assurance that family credit would be set at a level 'which will almost always prove more generous than the FIS which the same family would receive . . . ' The benefit is, in fact, higher in real terms than FIS was. Furthermore, many more families are entitled to family credit because under FIS the breadwinner had to work 30 hours a week unless a single parent whereas with family credit the minimum working week is 24 hours. On the other hand, many low-wage families are now no longer entitled to claim because their capital is more than £8000, whereas with FIS a claimant's capital was not taken into consideration.

Does family credit bring poor families up to income support level of income? It is difficult to say because the benefits under family credit are the same for all families with a similar number of children and with similar net incomes irrespective of their normal outgoings (for example, it does not take into account mortgage repayments), whereas the amount of income support varies according to the outgoings as well as the income of the family.

The Government's aim of targeting resources on the poorest made it hope that family credit would have a high take-up, thus making universal child benefit less significant in combating poverty. But the take-up of family credit was so disappointing that the Government had to embark on a TV advertising campaign to persuade all those who were entitled to family credit to claim it. Arising from this some people queried whether the job of the DSS was to get people to claim benefits to which they were entitled or simply to make known what the benefits were.

The Speenhamland system introduced in 1795 in Berkshire subsidised farm workers' wages and was criticised, among other things, for encouraging low wages. Nobody seems to make the same criticism today of family credit. In fact, low wages are considered by some economists as an economic asset.

Minimum Wage

Instead of family credit why not a minimum wage made legally binding by Act of Parliament? Although this would help all low-wage earners whose wages were below the proposed minimum, it would not raise every low-paid worker and worker's family above the poverty line, as there would still be low-wage families with exceptional expenditure – perhaps because of many children in the family. But the main objection to a minimum wage is that it would send up labour costs and increase unemployment – but not everyone agrees with this argument (see Ruth Kelly, 'The time may have to come to bring in a minimum wage', *Guardian*, 7 January 1991).

About 3 million workers have a legally binding minimum wage fixed by wages councils (successors to trade boards). These are workers who are in trades or industries with inadequate wage-negotiating machinery. About 80 per cent are female workers. Inspectors from the Department of Employment make occasional checks to ensure that employers are not paying below the legal minimum rate. However, many employers continue to pay below the statutory minimum. The Government sympathise with the view put forward by certain economists that minimum wage legislation increases unemployment, especially among young people. It considered the wages' councils minimum wages for them were too high, so that employers were reluctant to employ young people but would do so if their wages were lower. Hence, under the 1986 Wages Act, wages councils no longer fix minimum wage rates for young people under 21.

Housing Benefit and Community Charge Benefit

Housing benefit and Community Charge benefit are means-tested benefits financed by Central Government but administered by local authorities. They provide financial help with rent and the community charge (popularly known as the poll tax). Those on low incomes but whose capital exceeds £16000 are not entitled to housing benefit. Capital of under £3000 is ignored for benefit purposes but over £3000 capital the benefit gets less the nearer a person's capital approaches £16000. Those on income support or low income pay only 20 per cent of the community charge and can receive the maximum rent rebate of 100 per cent.

Help with rates goes back to the 1966 Rating Act which introduced rate rebates for low-income households. As rates were a tax on property and not related to the income of the household, they could cause hardship, especially to pensioners. The 1972 Housing Finance Act introduced rent rebates for council house tenants on low incomes and rent allowance for low-income families in private accommodation.

The housing benefit scheme came into operation under the 1982 Social Security and Housing Benefits Act. Before that time there were two schemes providing help for rent and rates – the Department of Health and Social Security (DHSS) gave help for rent and rates in supplementary benefit (now called income support) and the local authorities administered rent and rate rebates and rent allowances. But the method of working out how much a claimant should receive was not the same for each scheme and claimants could be better off under one scheme than the other. It seemed logical, therefore, to merge the schemes and it was left to local authorities to administer the unified scheme under the name of housing benefit. At the time the change came into operation in 1983, it was estimated that there would be a saving of 2400 staff at the DHSS. But critics argued that because it would put an excessive burden on local authority staffs it would necessitate local authorities recruiting more staff and overall there would be no saving in manpower. In fact, some cynics said the only reason for the exercise was to cut civil service staff.

In Scotland the community charge replaced rates in 1989, followed by its implementation in England and Wales in 1990. It was the 1986 Social Security Act which made even the poorest pay 20 per cent of their community charge but this was supposed to be taken into consideration when deciding the level of income support. One reason for this was perhaps the concern of the Government that all households should be aware of the financial consequences on family budgets of what the Government considered to be unnecessarily high local government expenditure. Although the rent of those on income support is paid in full, they receive no help for water and sewerage charges.

The 1986 Social Security Act resulted in cuts in housing benefit for thousands of people. The Government view was that people too high up the income scale were receiving benefit. Many people were denied housing benefit altogether. One reason for this was the introduction in the 1986 Act of the capital limit of £6000, later raised to £8000 for benefit. The Major government raised it to £16 000. Under the previous housing benefit scheme there was no capital limit, only income was taken into consideration.

Redundancy Payments

Redundancy payments are lump-sum payments made by employers to employees who are made redundant through no fault of their own – victims, in many cases of technological progress. The amount paid is related to age and years of service. Although strictly compensation payments, they have been included under social security because they often help a worker to keep going until a job is found.

Under the 1965 Redundancy Payments Act, which introduced the scheme, employers pay a surcharge on their weekly national insurance contributions for each of their employees, and this goes to the Central Redundancy Fund. An employer can claim a rebate from the Fund to cover part of the redundancy payment. In this way the costs of the redundancy payments are evenly shared by employers as a whole.

The scheme is administered by the employers themselves, except that the Secretary of State for Employment is responsible for the Central Redundancy Fund and he authorises payments from it.

The following are taxable – unemployment benefit, income support paid to registered unemployed, sick pay, maternity pay, widow's benefits, invalid care allowance, retirement pension. Other benefits are tax free.

SUMMARY

The main social security service is national insurance augmented by income support and child benefit. Low-wage families who cannot claim income support can claim family credit.

ASSIGNMENTS

1. Obtain from your DSS office the latest copy of *Which Benefit?* (FB2). From reading the pamphlet list the benefits that can be obtained by people on income support. Against each benefit give, where available, the number of the leaflet which explains the benefit in more detail.
2. Find out the following benefit rates:
    (a) The standard rate basic retirement pension (leaflet N146)

(b) The amount of sickness benefit for a man under 65 and a woman under 60 who are not receiving statutory sick pay (SSP) (leaflet NI 16).

(c) The amount of mobility allowance (NI 211).

(A very useful leaflet is NI 196 because it gives a comprehensive list of benefit rates.)

3. Why, in spite of comprehensive national insurance scheme, is there such a large number of people on income support? Why has their number increased over the years?

READING

CPAG, *National Welfare Benefits Handbook* (published annually).
CPAG, *Rights Guide to Non-Means-Tested Benefits* (published annually).
David Donnison, 'Against Discretion', *New Society*, 15 September 1977.
Family Welfare Association, *Guide to the Social Services* (Longmans, published annually).
Bill Jordan, 'Against Donnison', *New Society*, 13 October 1977.
Leaflets prepared by the DSS and the COI.

5 Problems of Social Security

WHO ARE THE POOR?

One definition is that the poor are all those people who are dependent on income support plus those living below the income support level. If we accept this definition, then the number of poor people has considerably increased, particularly in recent years. Thus the number of people receiving income support in Great Britain has quadrupled since 1948 from just over one million to just under four and a half million in 1989 (*Social Trends*, 1991). And if we take into consideration their dependants and those living below income support level (approximately two and a half million) the number of poor can be put at around nine million. One reason for the increase in the number of people dependent on income support is the increase over the years in its real value, so that more people find their income below the income support level and can thus claim income support. As a nation becomes richer, people's expectations become higher. Other reasons include the increase in the number of one-parent families arising both from more married couples separating and more children being born to unmarried mothers; an increasing proportion of retired people in the population, many of whom receive only the state pension and, in more recent times, the great increase in the number of unemployed families who have overtaken pensioners as the largest group on income support. By the end of 1991 there were approximately two and a half million registered unemployed, well over half of whom are on income support. But a person on income support today is better off than was a person on national assistance in 1948. Hence, as many people have pointed out, to maintain that all people on an income below income support level are in poverty means that poverty is actually increased the more you increase in real terms the value of income support, which is ludicrous. Hence the Government has rejected the concept of a poverty line and the 'Low Income Family Statistics', which used the income support level as a measure of poverty, has been replaced by 'Households Below Average Income', which makes it difficult to see how many individuals fall below income support level. But defenders of the new statistics say people in households share their incomes which makes the new households survey a truer indication of the extent of poverty. If, however, poverty is defined in relative terms – not having what the vast majority of people take for granted – then even though the

46

poor have been more than protected against inflation, they are no better off than in 1948 because income support has progressively become less as a percentage of average net earnings. Thus income support level can be described as a relative poverty line. But the degree to which the real incomes of those on income support and the low paid have progressed is a subject of controversy. Mr John Moore, when Secretary of State for Social Security, stated in his booklet, *The End of the Line for Poverty*: 'It is clear that people at all income levels now have substantially more money to spend in real terms than they did in the 1970s.' He writes of 'a 26 per cent increase in overall average household income for all households and, for families on income support, a 28 per cent increase above prices.' From the Government point of view the main reason for this greater spending power for even the poorest would be what is called the 'trickle down effect', which means as the rich get richer, there are more crumbs for the poor. In contrast, Frank Field, Chairman of the Commons Social Services Select Committee has argued (*Guardian*, 1 August 1988) that the poorest did better between 1970–79 when economic growth was more modest.

If the incomes of families on income support have increased in real terms, it must be because the benefit rates have improved – it cannot be because of other sources of income because support would be reduced in proportion to those other sources. Family credit has also increased in real terms but unemployment benefit, according to the Child Poverty Action Group has 'risen less than prices since 1978–79'. However, when judging the living standards of the poorer sections of the community, we must accept the fact that not all income related benefits are claimed, leaving many households below the income support level (see Commons *Hansard*, 27 July 1989, column 877). Family credit has only (or had before the advertising campaign) about a 60 per cent take-up. And those people living just above income support level have seen cuts in housing benefit, the increased cost of school meals and a very big rise in prescription charges and dental charges; and because of high interest rates, those buying their own homes have experienced big rises in mortgage repayments. Even those on income support have now to pay 20 per cent of their community charge which, for many, has not been compensated for in their income support, and all on income support have to pay the water and sewerage charges, charges which have considerably increased in recent years and which, before 1988, were paid for by the DHSS. The actual cash benefit of income support may be better in real terms but with all the other added expenses referred to above and cuts in certain other benefits over the years there are those who think that certain categories of poor people – individuals and childless couples, for example – have actually had a cut in their living standards. According to Frank Field, the poorest 20 per cent suffered such a cut between 1979–87 (*Guardian* 27 June 1990). In any case, income support barely provides, if at all, an adequate life style. And though the gap between the poorer and richer members of society is ever widening, the Government sees no cause for concern in this growing inequality in our society. Inequality, it believes, is essential for economic growth.

POLICIES TO REDUCE POVERTY

Is the Beveridge goal of security against want without a means-test still possible? If by want is meant anything below the income support level of living then, to avoid means-testing, the main national insurance benefits would have to be considerably increased to bring them up to the level of income support plus housing benefit. This would necessitate a large increase in contributions and higher taxation to cover a possible increase in the contribution of the Exchequer, although all benefits could be considered as income for tax purposes so that the Exchequer would get some of the money back. In the present political and economic climate it is doubtful if the main political parties would think such an increase possible. But, even if it were possible, there are many people, including members of the Conservative government, who would argue that all benefits should be means-tested. Why give money to better-off people who do not need it? – they can afford to pay for their own welfare. And by not giving money to richer people, more money can be given to poorer people who really need it. Furthermore, means-testing (or selectivity as it is often called) allows public expenditure to be reduced, providing more resources for the private sector on which the country's wealth mainly depends. It lessens the burden of national insurance contributions and taxation, thus giving an incentive to people to work harder thereby increasing the country's wealth. The main argument against means-tested benefits is that they are not claimed by many poor people entitled to them. This is sometimes due to pride but more often it is due to ignorance of the benefit system. (There are over 40 means-tested benefits.) Hence universal benefits are a much better way of targeting the poor.

Furthermore, means testing creates what is known as the poverty trap. This refers to families whose income is just low enough to qualify them for welfare benefits and as their income rises, welfare benefits are withdrawn. If the breadwinner is unemployed, it might not pay him or her to take a job because he or she could be just as well off, or perhaps better off, on unemployment benefit or unemployment benefit plus income

support because, when working, there would be extra tax to pay, plus
the payment of national insurance contributions, perhaps travelling costs
and, if on income support, loss of free prescriptions and other benefits.
Low-paid workers on family credit might not be better off with a pay rise
because their family credit would be reduced accordingly. However, in this
connection, some blame for the poverty trap must lie with the low wages
many employers pay and also the low tax threshold.

Means-testing is administratively much more costly than a system of
universal benefits would be. But, more important, means-testing is socially
divisive when the aim of social policy should be conducive to making
the nation more united. Thus there is a case for retaining some universal
benefits. For example, the late Professor Titmuss gave as an example the
national insurance pension for the retired. This is a universal benefit but
the supplementary pension paid under income support is means-tested and
paid at the post office in the same book as the basic pension. Thus nobody
knows whether a person drawing a pension at the post office is drawing the
basic pension or the supplementary as well. Without the universal benefit,
those going to the post office to draw their pension would be labelled
poor. Hence as Professor Titmuss stated, providing means-tested benefits
for certain categories of people can operate within a universal system, they
need not be socially divisive. Peter Kellner, writing in *The Independent*
(21 November 1988) under the title 'What makes a rich society civilised'
argues the case for universal benefits and, after analysing the tax consequences of child benefit, shows that it 'is misleading to imply that the
rich reap great rewards from universal benefits . . . what matters is not just
the distribution of benefits, but the distribution of taxes to pay for them.'
And what of 'universal benefits' that 'broadly rise with income', sometimes
referred to as the 'hidden welfare state' – tax allowances such as 'mortgage
tax relief and pension tax relief'? Like Professor Titmuss, Peter Kellner
sees universal benefits as 'a vital part of any strategy that holds that we
should strive to be one nation . . . a principle not questioned – in theory at
least – in the provision of public goods: defence, police, street-lighting and
so on.' Peter Kellner concludes: 'universal benefits, like universal public
services, are part of what makes a wealthy society civilised.'

Alan Walker (*New Statesman and Society*, 10 November 1989) argues
that we can abolish poverty. Research indicates that the true poverty
line (based on the concept of relative poverty) is 150 per cent of the
income support levels. Below this level relative poverty begins. To raise
income support to this level, based on November 1989 figures, would
cost £14.6 billion a year. But since 1979 '90 billion has been cut from
income tax with about £50 billion going to the richest 10 per cent'.

Is there an automatic correlation between taxation and enterprise? There is no hard evidence that there is. Whilst it is obvious that a very high rate of taxation might discourage enterprise because the return after tax was so small, there is a wide range of tax options within which the entrepreneurial spirit could remain the same. People are motivated by other factors apart from money. Does increased public expenditure mean fewer resources for the private sector? This was argued over in the 1920s and 1930s when, as today, there was much unemployment. There is an influential body of opinion which takes the view like the majority of economists in the inter-war years, that during a period when there are many unemployed resources, an increase in public expenditure does not mean fewer resources for the private sector. It may well be that it is upon the private sector that the country mainly depends for its prosperity but there is a whole range of public services without which the private sector could not function adequately, if at all.

For many years now there has been, from time to time, discussion on the introduction of a tax-credit scheme – sometimes called a scheme of negative income tax – which would put an end, once and for all, to the controversy over universal as against means-tested benefits. It is a scheme for bringing together personal taxation and social security. Under the scheme a single tax form would be used from which the right to benefit or the liability to tax would be worked out. The tax form would be used, as now, to assess the amount of tax to be paid by people above the taxpaying level, but it would also be a means of giving cash benefits (negative income tax) to those below the tax level.

The Labour government, when it took office in 1964, hoped to bring in this reform under the name of an income guarantee scheme which would deal with the problem of poverty in a comprehensive way. It would replace all the means-tested and universal benefits and guarantee a minimum income at subsistence level for everyone, including an average allowance for housing. But the tax form is normally only submitted once a year, and therefore information about a person's income and expenditure held by the Inland Revenue might be up to a year out of date and as, at any time within that twelve months, a person's circumstances might have changed. Hence the government dropped the scheme because it was not sufficiently flexible to adjust benefit quickly enough to meet changing circumstances. The scheme proposed by the Conservative government (1970–4), called a *tax-credit scheme*, avoided this because it was more modest. It would have replaced the main income-tax personal allowances and family allowances (now child benefit) and, except for a few outside the scheme, family income supplement (now called family credit). But national insurance and supplementary benefit (now called income support) would have continued, but on a reduced scale. Hence a person receiving a tax credit would also have been able to claim supplementary benefit if their circumstances worsened, until such time as the Inland Revenue adjusted his or her code in accordance with the worsened circumstances. The scheme would not have covered about 10 per cent of the population and this included the self-employed and those on very low income.

The then estimated cost of the scheme was £1300 million, yet the late Professor Kaldor of Cambridge University estimated that only £150 million would go to those earning less than £1000 a year. Hence some people argued that there would have been a greater reduction in the number of people having to claim means-tested benefits if the £1300 million were spent on increasing the normal social security benefits – pensions, family allowances, and so on. But other tax-credit schemes have been put forward which purport to avoid this criticism, notably one by the Young Conservatives (*A Credit to Us All*, 1976). For a number of years little was heard of the tax-credit scheme due to administrative problems of a technical nature which have to be overcome before an effective scheme can be seriously considered. However, in more recent years there has been a growing awareness in all political parties that some move towards integration of the tax and benefit system is necessary and fresh schemes have been put forward (see Hermione Parker, *Instead of Dole*).

Much criticism has been levelled at the DSS for the poor service many of its local offices provide for claimants. Indeed the Department itself admits the service provided needs to be improved not only to give better service to the public but to make life less stressful for the staff, and it is hoped that the computerisation programme underway since 1982 will go a long way to doing this. There will be a large saving in staff but it is hoped it can all be attained without any compulsory redundancies.

Because of the complexity of the benefit system, it is very difficult for most claimants to fully understand their entitlement and check it and they feel at a disadvantage and vulnerable. In fact, the Commons' Public Accounts Committee, in its Report (3 June 1989) reported an underpayment of unemployment benefit between £34 million and £89 million. Hence the importance of openness in explaining to clients just how their benefit is worked out. The microcomputers now in each office should be of great benefit in providing such information.

When the computerisation programme is fully completed, information on any claimant will be obtained from a central source so that it will not be necessary to process claims in the local office.

SUMMARY

If we take poverty to mean an income below a minimum considered
necessary to meet requirements (requirements increasing as the country
grows richer) then, in spite of the recession, we should be able to abolish
poverty as we have the resources to bring everyone up to this basic
minimum. What prevents us doing it? Some people might argue the lack
of political will; others might answer the existing economic system makes
change difficult – that for capitalism to thrive, poverty for a section of
the population must prevail. Others would argue that by retaining some
universal benefits too big a proportion of the money spent on welfare goes
to people who do not need it. But at a more practical level it is often due
to not knowing who are in need and, even if we know who the needy are,
ignorance of all the circumstances which give rise to their need. Ignorance
of those in need can be reduced by government publicity to encourage those
who are entitled to claim benefit to do so. Similar work can be done by local
authorities and, in recent years, there has been much publicity on these
lines. Some local authorities have appointed welfare rights officers who,
like the accountants who help the better off not to pay too much tax to the
Inland Revenue, help the poor to get all the money they are entitled to from
the DSS. What blunts the effectiveness of this work is that much poverty
is among those who are the most unaware of their rights and are, therefore,
least likely to be affected by publicity. Furthermore, we are so concerned
not to give money to those who are not entitled to it that we have developed
a complex system of checks on claimants' incomes which is off-putting to
many people who need help. The large bureaucracy necessitated by this
complex system is a further off-putting factor especially when, as under
a government anxious to contain public expenditure, attempts to reduce
that bureaucracy results in overworked staff in the DSS and the danger
that some claimants perhaps do not get the attention they deserve, or that
a claimant is inadvertently given less money than he or she is entitled to.

A system of universal benefits would make the system much simpler and
ensure all receive benefits, reducing means testing to a minimum but it does
seem rather absurd to give benefits to everyone in order to ensure that the
minority who really need them actually receive them. Even so, for the sake
of social unity it may still be better to retain some universal benefits even
if all the benefits involving cash payments can not be universal because of
the huge government expenditure this would involve or, where insurance
contributions formed the basis of entitlement, the contributions would
have to be set at an unacceptably high rate. There is a point, however,
that if all income were taxed, much of this huge government expenditure

would be recouped by the Government. Proposals have been made for everyone to receive a basic tax free income but all income above this would be taxed. There would still have to be additions to meet exceptional circumstances with claimants having to justify exceptional circumstances. The Government does, however, consider its proposed personal allowance, within the proposed income support scheme, as sufficient basic income in itself for most households.

Various negative income tax schemes, called tax credit schemes, have been put forward, where everyone completes a form giving details of their income as they do now for the Inland Revenue and would receive a credit if below a basic minimum considered necessary for their needs but taxed if above this basic minimum. Such schemes would substantially reduce the amount of means-testing except for the form all would have to complete. All so far, like the original one put forward under the 1970–74 Conservative Government, have been found to have weaknesses. In any case, all these schemes, like the basic income scheme, need an integration of the tax and social security systems that we seem a long way from attaining. But the Government claims that sick pay, now being paid by the employer, and its proposals for maternity benefit to be paid by the employer are small steps towards the integration of the two systems.

The microcomputers now in each local DSS office should help to bring that integration nearer. The computers should also help claimants by relieving some of the pressure on the officers.

The problem of ensuring that poor people get the best possible help (simply giving money may not abolish the poverty of the claimant) calls for co-operation between income support officers in the DSS and social workers in the local authorities. There is some official contact between them. But how far should staff play a welfare role in helping claimants with their problems? The pressures on them would seem to suggest that they will have all their time taken up in simply ensuring claimants get the money to which they are entitled and no more. The White Paper (Cmnd 9691) did suggest that officers who administered the proposed social fund should have some liaison with social workers and others, and the computerisation of the local offices plus the proposed simpler system of social security by relieving some of that pressure on the staff, may make it possible to increase those contacts, hopefully for the benefit of claimants.

Under the Thatcher government the social security system was greatly modified. The Government admitted that its reforms would mean some people would be worse off but many people, it stated, would be better off and, as an example, claimed that the change from FIS to family credit would mean 400000 working families on low incomes would be better off (Commons *Hansard*, 28 January 1986). Critics can point to losers – widows, many of next century's pensioners, especially those in insecure employment, many people with modest savings and young people under 25. Hostile critics have argued that the Government's reforms are not really about meeting needs adequately but about cutting expenditure, an accusation strongly denied by the Government. But the original review teams were told that no extra cash was available – hence if some people benefited, others would be worse off. The Government would argue that we can only do what we can afford. As one of its former ministers said: 'The future of the welfare state and the future of industry are two sides of the same coin' (Patrick Jenkin). But what the Government thinks we can afford falls short of what its critics think we can and should afford.

The undermining of the basic principle of the welfare state continues – the principle that adequate cash benefits would be given as of right under a system of national insurance with means-testing kept to a minimum. But if the tax and benefit system could be effectively merged cash benefits could be given as of right. The form giving details of income would not be considered a means test in the generally accepted sense. But we have waited so long to hear news of the development of such a system that one wonders if it will ever come into operation. In the meantime, child benefit and insurance benefits (with the possible exception of the retirement pension) buy less than they did in 1979, with a resulting increase in the number of claimants for income support. In addition, taxation, except for the rich, has increased, with the poorer sections of the community now paying a greater proportion of their income in taxation.

ASSIGNMENTS

1. Discuss how far means-testing should be a necessary part of the social security system.
2. How has our concept of poverty changed since the days of Charles Booth?
3. Give the Government's five reasons for the need to reform the system of social security by referring to its White Paper, 'Reform of Social Security' (Cmnd 9691, December 1985). Discuss any one of these reasons in relation to the 1986 Social Security Act. (Literature critical of the Government's proposals can be obtained

from the Child Poverty Action Group, 1 Macklin Street, London WC2B 5NH.)

4. 'A welfare state makes provision for everyone. It fulfils different support functions at different stages throughout life. It recognises a legitimate redistributive role and provides collectively for the common need. The alternative, state welfare, is a system of provision established to cater for the poor. A system which caters only for the poor very quickly degenerates into a poor system' (Archy Kirkwood MP). How far do you think we have travelled the road, if at all, from a welfare state to state welfare since 1945? Give reasons for your answer.

5. Poverty is a social problem, not an individual problem. Discuss.

6. Poverty is an economic problem, not a moral problem. Discuss.

READING

K. Andrews and John Jacobs, *Punishing the Poor* (Macmillan, 1990).

John Baker, 'The Paradox of rising incomes and increasing hardship', *Policy and Politics*, January 1991.

Michael Beenstock 'Poverty, Taxation and the Welfare State', *National Westminster Bank Review*, August 1980.

Fran Bennett, 'Windows of Opportunity: Public Policy and the Poor' (CPAG, 1991).

David Blake and Paul Ormerod (eds), *The Economics of Prosperity* (Grant McIntyre, 1980).

Jonathan Bradshaw and Hilary Holmes, *Living on the Edge – a study of the living standards of families on benefit in Tyne and Wear* (Tyneside CPAG, 1989).

Muriel Brown and Sarah Payne, *Introduction to Social Administration*, 7th edn (Unwin Hyman, 1990).

Stephen Davies, *Beveridge Revisited* (Centre for Policy Studies, 1986).

Frank Field, *Losing out* (Basil Blackwell, 1989).

Frank Field, *Poverty and Politics* (Heinemann, 1982), chs 1–6.

Howard Glennerster, 'In Praise of Public Expenditure', *New Statesman*, 27 February 1976.

David Heathfield, 'Poverty and Income Distribution in the UK', *The Economic Review* (Southampton University, May 1989).

HMSO, *Better Pensions*, Cmnd 5713 (HMSO, September 1974).

HMSO, *Housing Benefit Review*, Cmnd 9520 (HMSO, June 1985).

HMSO, *Proposals for a Tax-Credit System*, Cmnd 5116 (HMSO, October 1972).

HMSO, *Reform of Social Security. Programme for Action*, Cmnd 9691 (HMSO, December 1985).

HMSO, *Reform of Social Security*, Volume 1, Cmnd 9517 (HMSO, June 1985).

House of Commons, 'Debate on Family Hardship', *Hansard*, vol. 187, No. 75, 13 March 1991.

House of Commons Select Committee on Tax-Credit, Session 1972–3, *Report*, vol. 1 (HMSO, 1973).

House of Commons, Social Security Bill, 2nd Reading, *Hansard*, vol. 90, no. 45, 28 January 1986.

Rudolph Klein, 'Privatisation and the Welfare State', *Lloyds Bank Review*, January 1984.

Steward Lansley, 'What Hope for the Poor?' *Lloyds Bank Review*, April 1979.

John Micklewright, 'Fiction versus Fact: Unemployment Benefits in Britain', *National Westminster Bank Review*, May 1985.

John Moore, *The End of the Line for Poverty* (Conservative Political Centre, May 1989).

Hermione Parker, *Instead of Dole – an enquiry into the integration of the tax and benefit systems* (Routledge, 1989).

Social Security Consortium, *Of Little Benefit: a critical guide to the social Security Act 1986* (Child Poverty Action Group, 1986).

SSAC, *First Report of the Social Security Advisory Committee, 1981* (HMSO, 1982).

Peter Townsend, 'An Alternative Anti-Poverty Programme', *New Society*, 7 October 1982.

Peter Townsend, *Poverty in the United Kingdom* (Penguin, 1979).

Peter Townsend, 'Slipping through the net', *Guardian*, 29 November 1989.

6 Health

DEVELOPMENT OF THE HEALTH SERVICES

General

In the nineteenth century the biggest threat to health was contagious diseases. The enormous growth of towns due to rapid population increase and, in the case of the industrial towns in the north, an influx of people seeking work in the developing industries, led in many instances to overcrowded houses, inadequate sanitation and impure water supply, with which the traditional forms of local government could not cope. In spite of the efforts, in certain areas, of *ad hoc* statutory bodies to deal with the problems in the first half of the nineteenth century, deaths from disease continued to rise. Influential reports from doctors and others warned of the dangers of uncollected sewage and contaminated water, but it was not until 1848 that the government acted, and then only after a cholera epidemic in the London area killed over 60 000 people.

The 1848 Public Health Act – the first of its kind – made compulsory the setting up of local boards of health in areas where the death rate was above the national average. In other areas it was left to the local people to decide whether or not to set up a local board. The result was that there was progress in some areas but none in others. The Board of Health, set up under the Act to give central direction and frame general policy, was unpopular and was dissolved in 1854. *The Times* of 1 August 1854 wrote: 'We prefer to take our chance of cholera and the rest than be bullied into health.' Compulsion at last came with the 1866 Sanitary Act, which ordered local authorities to appoint sanitary inspectors with power to take action about water, sewerage and 'nuisances'. The Report of a Royal Commission on Public Health set up in 1869 led to the 1875 Public Health Act, which made compulsory in every area local health authorities under the control of a medical officer of health. In the meantime central direction was restored by making health the responsibility of the Local Government Board, a new government department created in 1871 to be responsible for health and the Poor Law. From this date progress was rapid, so that by the end of the nineteenth century infectious diseases had been greatly reduced. Incidentally, this helped the finances of the Poor Law, as ill health and poverty are closely related. In the nineteenth century it was the sanitary inspector rather than the doctor who did most to save life. By today's standards medical science was backward. For example, it was not until 1858 that the French chemist Louis Pasteur demonstrated the connection between dirt and disease by discovering the presence of bacteria in the surrounding atmosphere. The discovery led to an emphasis on cleanliness to kill the organisms, or at least to stop them from spreading. Lister pioneered the way by his discovery of antiseptics – he used carbolic acid as a steriliser soon after Pasteur's discovery.

The biggest saver of life in the twentieth century has been the great advances in medical science. While public health is still important, it is the personal health services which are now the biggest factor in keeping people fit. Public health has, however, had to meet fresh problems – atmospheric pollution from motor-cars, pesticides, dumping of toxic wastes, and now a threat to the Earth's environment itself. Hence we now tend to speak of environmental health rather than public health.

Hospitals

Until Lister's day hospitals were dangerous places because of the risk of infection, especially for surgical cases. Surgeons often wore old and dirty coats, nurses were often drunk. It was easy to see that hospitals were for the poor, while the rich were treated in their own homes. Thanks mainly to Florence Nightingale, a middle-class woman who devoted her life to hospital nursing, nursing standards greatly improved from the time of the Crimean War in 1854.

In the nineteenth century there were three types of hospital. First, there were the voluntary hospitals, the most famous of them, like St Thomas's and St Bartholomew's, being founded in the Middle Ages. Many smaller ones were founded in the eighteenth and nineteenth centuries by voluntary subscription. Then, as the century progressed, there evolved workhouse hospitals, called infirmaries, out of workhouse sick bays. (See 1876 Metropolitan Poor Act and 1869 Poor Law Amendment Act.) Third, there were a few isolation hospitals or fever hospitals run by the local authorities. Free vaccination against cholera was introduced in 1840 and the Poor Law medical officers who worked for the Poor Law Guardians, were responsible for its provision to all categories of people who demanded it – not just paupers.

In 1929 the Poor Law was taken over by local authorities, and they thus took over all the workhouse hospitals as well as retaining the fever hospitals. They could also build new hospitals if they wished. More money was spent by local government on the newly acquired hospitals to eliminate, as far as possible, the atmosphere of the workhouse, and gradually the local authority hospitals began to rival the voluntary hospitals.

The 1946 National Health Service Act nationalised the hospitals and, except for some teaching hospitals, put them under the administration of regional hospital boards.

Doctors

Doctors who worked in voluntary hospitals used to give their services free but obtained their income from treating private patients either in their surgery or in the patient's home.

Working-class people, including the poor, could go to the out-patients' department of a voluntary hospital and, by the end of the century, it was quite respectable for the working class to use the Poor Law hospital. Apart from this there was the local dispensary, public or private, run by a local committee where working-class men, women and children, by the payment of 1*d* to 2*d* a week, could obtain free medical treatment and medicine providing they were not obtaining relief from the Poor Law. Better-off working-class people, and even quite rich people, insured themselves against sickness by joining a friendly society, and receiving medical treatment in return. The very poor had the Poor Law doctor. For those people not covered by these schemes a charge would be made for each visit. In the poor areas the doctor might engage a collector to collect so much from each patient each week, and this would cover visit, treatment and medicine. But in working-class areas most doctors had unpaid bills – a good doctor could not very well cease to treat someone simply because that person had no money. The biggest stimulus to the development of a comprehensive health service came with the 1911 National Insurance Act, Part 1 of which provided compulsory health insurance for all workers earning £160 a year or less. It covered sickness benefit, disability benefit, maternity benefit, a doctor's services and prescriptions, and free sanatorium treatment for TB. The benefits were administered by friendly societies, insurance companies and trade unions, known collectively as *approved societies*. Doctors and patients still retained their freedom of choice – doctors to choose their patients and patients their doctors – and doctors were represented on all the committees concerned with administration.

Thus there was a doctor on the local insurance committees that supervised the scheme in the local areas and one of the insurance commissioners responsible for the overall management of the scheme was a doctor. Doctors were paid a fixed sum for each insured patient on their 'panel', and this gave them much greater financial security. An extra source of income was private treatment of richer people and others excluded from the insurance scheme.

By 1939 the maximum income for compulsory health insurance had been raised to £420 a year, and this covered virtually all workers. The weakness of the scheme, as the Royal Commission on Health Insurance of 1924–6 pointed out, was that it did not cover the insured person's dependants – wife, children and old parents. Thus about half the population still had to pay fees as private patients or join a sick club where a doctor's services could be obtained by the payment of a regular contribution each week. Furthermore, health insurance did not cover hospital treatment, and a person lucky enough to be in one of the wealthier approved societies received extra benefits from the society.

The Royal Commission anticipated the modern National Health Service by recommending its separation from the insurance scheme, and, instead, its financing from 'the general public funds'.

The Setting-up of the Ministry of Health

In 1919 the Local Government Board was abolished and its work given to the newly created Ministry of Health, which also took over the work of the insurance commissioners. It was felt that the Local Government Board had been too preoccupied with the Poor Law, and the fear of national physical deterioration arising from the Boer War recruitment shock gave support to those who wanted a special department of health to promote actively the nation's health. The new Ministry thus became responsible for public health, national health insurance, local authority housing, health promotion and the Poor Law.

The National Health Service

The 1946 National Health Service Act introduced a virtually free health service operative from July 1948, including free specialist treatment in hospitals. Local insurance committees, which previously supervised the doctors, were replaced by executive councils (now called Family Health Services Authorities – FHSAs) which supervised all the personal practitioners – doctors, dentists, opticians and pharmacists. Doctors still retained their clinical freedom and continued to receive, among other payments, so much money for each patient on their list.

The 1946 National Insurance Act (operative from July 1948) abolished the approved societies and sickness benefit was paid by the newly created

Ministry of National Insurance, now part of the Department of Social Security.

Local Authority Services

The local authority health services evolved in the latter part of the nineteenth century largely out of concern for children. Between 1850 and 1900, in spite of the big fall in the death rate, the infant mortality rate remained high. As late as 1900 the figure was 156 per 1000 live births – roughly the same as in 1850 (today, it is less than 20). This meant that out of every 1000 babies born alive, 156 died before their first birthday. The main reason for this was ignorance and poverty.

Compulsory education, introduced in 1880, had put all the nation's children on view and the large number suffering from poverty and malnutrition was disturbing.

The fear of national physical deterioration at the beginning of the century was another factor emphasising the importance of the nation's children.

Voluntary action preceded state action. As early as 1859, William Rathbone had started a system of district nursing in Liverpool which provided skilled medical attention in people's homes. Dr Drew Harris, a medical officer, established at St Helens the first infant milk depot, and another medical officer of health, Dr James Kerr, pioneered medical inspection of schoolchildren at Bradford.

The 1902 Midwives Act was aimed at ensuring that midwives were properly qualified. It set up a Central Midwives Board to lay down rules for the training of midwives and to supervise them. The 1936 Midwives Act set up a full-time salaried midwifery service and made local authorities responsible for ensuring there was an adequate number of midwives in their area and that they were competent.

Registration of births had been made compulsory in 1836 but it was only for statistical purposes. The 1907 Notification of Births Act, where adopted by a local authority, required that the local medical officer of health should be notified of any birth within thirty-six hours, to enable him, if necessary, to check on the progress of mother and baby. In 1915 notification was made compulsory in all local authority areas and, at the same time, permission was given to local authorities to look after mother and child. The 1918 Maternity and Child Welfare Act extended this help to children up to the age of 5. Financial assistance was given from the central government to enable this service to be developed. Today the three aspects of child care are (a) notification; (b) a health visitor who is a registered general nurse (RGN) with additional special qualifications;

and (c) somewhere the mother can take the baby – a clinic or the family doctor.

In the meantime Education Acts in 1906 and 1907 had brought school meals and school medical inspection.

Other health functions taken on by local authorities were the care of mental defectives in 1913, care and after-care of TB patients in 1914, and treatment of venereal disease in 1917.

The scope of the local health service was considerably extended by the National Health Service Act of 1946.

Under a reorganisation of the NHS in 1974 the local authority health services and the school health services were put under the control of the NHS authorities.

Factors Leading to the 1946 National Health Service Act

A comprehensive National Health Service, which started operating in July 1948, was an almost inevitable development after the passing of the 1911 National Insurance Act. There was no logical reason why free medical treatment should be limited to a particular insured group of the population. But more immediate reasons for it were:

1. Rapid scientific developments in medicine were making the health services increasingly expensive, especially hospital treatment, and it seemed that only the state would have the resources to develop a health service to meet the needs of all the people.
2. The Emergency Hospital Service set up during the Second World War to meet the anticipated thousands of air-raid casualties highlighted the need to share medical resources more evenly throughout the country, and only some form of central organisation could do this. Thus before 1948 the best specialists worked in voluntary hospitals but drew their income from private fees. Hence they were concentrated in the wealthier areas. By introducing a salaried service for hospital doctors the 1946 National Health Service Act facilitated their more even distribution throughout the country.
3. It was felt that local authority hospitals could not be given back to local government after the war, as they needed, for efficient management, much larger units of administration than the existing areas of local authorities.
4. A National Health Service was seen not only as a means of improving the nation's health but also as part of a campaign to abolish want. (The Beveridge Report in 1942 on social security – see

Chapter 3 – had stressed the need for a National Health Service and family allowance to supplement the national insurance scheme.)

The Basic Principles of the National Health Service

1. Free access to medical care for all who want it.
2. Freedom for the patient to choose his or her doctor.
3. Professional freedom for the doctor to choose his or her patient and to engage in private practice.
4. The retention of the traditional doctor-patient relationship, with the family doctor as a link between hospital and local services.

Doctors' attitudes to the development of a state medical service have been very much influenced by the fear that it would mean coming under the control of some government department. These fears were the underlying reason for the British Medical Association's wrangle with Lloyd George in the years 1911–13 over the introduction of national health insurance (which came into operation in 1913), and with Aneurin Bevan after the Second World War, when negotiations for the setting up of a National Health Service took place. Permitting private practice was a concession Bevan had to make because he knew many doctors would not accept a full-time salaried service. Hospital consultants were given the option of a full-time or part-time contract. There are charges for prescriptions, spectacles and dental treatment. At the beginning of the NHS there were no charges and, until recently, they were considered modest so that the basic principles still stood.

However, under the Thatcher government, the prescription charge greatly increased and dental charges increased sharply. There is still, however, financial help with charges for the less well-off and provision for the better off who wish to pay for treatment outside the NHS.

SUMMARY

In the nineteenth century the developments in public health were the biggest single factor in keeping people fit; in the twentieth century advances in medical science have been more important. By the end of the nineteenth century it was realised that the health of individuals was not simply their concern but was also the concern of the nation. National greatness and perhaps even national survival, depended on the nation's health. Furthermore, it had become increasingly realised that poverty was to a great extent caused by ill health.

The first developments were services to protect the health of young mothers and children. The health insurance scheme which became operative in 1913 was perhaps the biggest step towards a health service for everyone. On a limited scale to begin with, its extension to virtually all workers in the interwar years made inevitable the introduction of a National Health Service available to all. But for the bad economic situation in the interwar years, it might have come earlier.

ASSIGNMENTS

1.   What factors have led to increasing demands being made on the National Health Service since its inception in 1948?
2.   How far has the National Health Service fulfilled its fundamental aims?
3.   What were the main deficiencies in the health service between 1918 and 1939.
4.   Write a brief biographical account of Edwin Chadwick and explain the importance of his work in improving the nation's health.

READING

B. Abel-Smith, *A History of the Nursing Profession* (Heinemann, 1960).
Brian Abel-Smith, *NHS – The First Thirty Years* (HMSO, 1978).
W. J. Braithwaite, *Lloyd George's Ambulance Wagon* (Cedric Chivers, 1970).
Asa Briggs, 'The Achievements, Failures and Aspirations of the NHS', *New Society*, 23 November 1978.
H. Eckstein, *The English Health Service: Its Origins, Structure and Achievements* (Oxford University Press, 1959).
Ministry of Health, *A National Health Service*, Cmd 6502 (HMSO, 1944).
Brian Watkin, *The National Health Service: The First Phase* (Allen & Unwin, 1978), ch. 1.
Charles Webster, *The Health Service since the War: Volume 1: The NHS before 1957* (HMSO, 1988).

7   The National Health Service Today

The Secretary of State for Health in England and the Secretaries of State for Scotland, Wales and Northern Ireland are responsible in their respective countries for the NHS which they administer in line with the policy for health laid down by the Central Government. (The former Department of Health and Social Security was split into two separate departments in July 1988 – the Department of Health and the Department of Social Security.) Under the National Health Service Act 1946 (as amended by subsequent acts) the Secretary has the duty of promoting 'the establishment in England and Wales [there are separate acts for Scotland and Northern Ireland] of a comprehensive health service designed to secure improvement in the physical and mental health of the people of England and Wales and the prevention, diagnosis and treatment of illness'.

A Royal Commission on the NHS was appointed in 1976 and reported in 1979. Its terms of reference were 'to consider, in the interest of both patients and those who work on the NHS, the best use and management of financial and man power resources'. It recommended important changes in the structure of the NHS, many of which became operative from April 1982.

The National Health Service has three main divisions:

1. The family (personal) practitioner services (doctors, dentists, opticians, chemists who are independent practitioners but who work with community nurses and midwives to provide what is called primary health care).
2. Hospitals for specialist treatment.
3. Community health services (previously known as personal health services and now coming under the general title of primary health care services).

Supervising all three divisions is an NHS Management Executive headed by a chief executive, responsible for day-to-day administration and responsible to a Policy Board, chaired by the Secretary of State for Health, which determines broad policy influenced by how much money is obtained from the Treasury. The Minister is also advised on health matters by standing advisory committees and also by *ad hoc* advisory committees dealing with special subjects which he appoints after consultation with interested bodies.

THE PERSONAL PRACTITIONER SERVICES

Family Practitioner Committees (FPCs), now called Family Practitioner Service Authorities (FPSAs) are responsible for the management of the personal practitioner services. This includes entering into contracts of service with the practitioners, preparing lists of them, paying them and investigating complaints against a practitioner. The purpose of the complaints procedure is simply 'to settle disputes about whether or not practitioners have fulfilled the terms of their contract' and not necessarily to remedy a patient's grievance. Since 1 April 1985, when they gained independence from the district health authorities, they have expanded their role to include, among other things, monitoring standards of service provided by practitioners. At the time of gaining independence, there were no cash limits on general practitioners (doctors) and FPCs, as they were called, were encouraged to give greater attentions to general practitioners' expenditure. Now, under the recent reform of the NHS (see below) cash restrictions have, for the first time, been imposed on general practitioners and FPSAs have the duty of setting up 'a small unit of doctors and other staff . . . to monitor the medical audit procedures'.

Before the recent reform of the NHS, representatives of the practitioners, normally fifteen of them, comprised half the membership of a FPSA; the other half was made up of representatives of the District Health Authority (DHA), local authorities and some independent members nominated by local lay people. Now their total membership has been reduced to eleven, including the chairman appointed by the Secretary of State and with the regional health authority appointing four professional and five lay members. A chief executive is appointed by the chairman. FPSAs have now been made accountable to RHAs (in England) bringing, so the Government says 'responsibility for primary health care and hospital services together at a strategic level'.

FPSAs liaise with other sections of the NHS on matters of joint concern, particularly with regard to community services – services in which local authorities are also involved. The administrative areas of FPSAs used to follow that of the county councils and metropolitan district councils. Since the 1982 reorganisation each FPSA includes part of a number of local authorities and one or more district health authorities.

Doctors, dentists, opticians and pharmacists each have their own local professional committees which are consulted by the FPSA. Doctors and dentists working in the NHS can have private patients.

Doctors

The General Medical Council lays down the minimum qualifications a doctor must have and keeps a register of those entitled to practice. The more serious charges against a doctor can be referred to the General Medical Council, and if the charge is proved the doctor can be struck off the register.

There is a Medical Practices Committee charged with the duty among other things, of trying to ensure an even distribution of doctors throughout the country. It is appointed by the minister and normally consists of seven doctors (five of whom must be in active practice) and two lay people. When a doctor wishes to start a new practice or apply for a vacant practice, he or she must submit an application to the local FPSA, which consults the local medical committee and then sends the application with its recommendations to the Medical Practices Committee. If the doctor's application is refused, he or she has the right to appeal to the minister.

This control over the distribution of doctors is only a negative control – the Medical Practices Committee cannot compel a doctor to practice in a certain area, but there are financial inducements to encourage doctors to practice in unpopular areas. However, the 1990 NHS and Community Care Act gives the Secretary of State more say on the distribution of doctors.

From April 1990 GPs (often referred to as family doctors) have had to accept a new employment contract from the Government. Previously they were paid according to the number of patients they had, the age of patients and the level of services provided, services such as immunisation of children, the cervical cancer smear, doing minor surgery and thus relieving pressure on the hospitals and health promotion. In order to be paid for the smear and immunisation, a minimum percentage of patients have to be dealt with, otherwise no payment is made at all. The Government must feel that some doctors are not pulling their weight and the new percentage rule is to encourage them to do so.

Doctors are now expected to give a health check to all new patients and a health check every three years, which patients over seventy-five can have in their own homes.

The former basic practice allowance has been reduced and completely abolished for doctors with fewer than 500 patients but there is extra money for taking on more patients and for doctors who work in rural areas and in deprived areas like inner cities.

Perhaps, to many doctors, the most onerous aspect of the new contract is the requirement that doctors must be available to patients 26 hours a week over five days and 42 weeks a year. This face-to-face contact with patients does seem excessive when one considers all the other work doctors must do – the extra administrative work arising from the NHS reforms, week-end calls, correspondence, reports – including the annual report – and information leaflets about the practice now obligatory under the contract, case discussion with colleagues and the abolition of the deputy service for night calls as demanded in the contract. At the same time doctors are being encouraged to take on more patients with the inducement of more money, which might result in some patients receiving a poorer quality of care because their doctors are overworked. The Government might argue that there are now more doctors resulting, on average, in less patients per doctor than there used to be. However, in 1991, talks on the contract began between the representatives of the GPs and the minister. The government would like to see the development of patient groups to discuss problems relating to the GP's practice which affect patients. When the group was in consultation with the doctor it might help the doctor to see where the practice could be improved. Some such patient groups were founded in the 1970s and some included in their activities organising voluntary help where needed to patients within the practice.

About four-fifths of doctors work in partnership or in a group practice. A group practice might comprise a primary health-care team headed by the doctors, with community nurses, midwives and sometimes a social worker plus administrative staff. A group practice may operate from a purpose built health centre.

Dentists

Dentists may practice in any area. Their governing body is the General Dental Council. Under a new contract, introduced in October 1990, a patient registers with a dentist as with a GP. The government pays the dentist so much for each patient registered and pays 25 per cent of the cost of treatment. But as the NHS patient pays 75 per cent of the cost of the treatment it is no wonder that about half the population no longer visit a dentist on a regular basis. However, as with doctors' prescriptions, certain categories of people are exempt from charges. The dentists state that Government payments to them are inadequate. Hence since the new contract was introduced (which 62 per cent of dentists opposed) approximately 10 per cent of dentists have opted out of the NHS and only accept private patients. This has caused distress to those patients who cannot afford private treatment and are unable to find in their area a dentist who accepts NHS patients.

Chemists (Pharmacists)
There is a charge for each prescription, but about two-thirds are supplied free to various categories – the poor, the young, the chronically sick, women over 60 and men over 65.

Ophthalmic Services
Ophthalmic services are one of the specialist services provided by hospitals, but there is also a general ophthalmic service under the FPSAs. The supply of spectacles has been privatised but certain categories of people can receive a voucher which they can take to the optician and obtain certain spectacles free. There is now a charge for eye-testing but, again, certain categories of people are exempt from payment.

THE HOSPITALS AND COMMUNITY HEALTH

District health authorities (DHAs) are responsible for the hospitals and the community health services. Each district has a district general hospital and a number of other hospitals, some of which may be part of the district general hospital. But a district is not supposed to be so large that members of the authority are 'remote from the service for which they are responsible'. As far as possible the boundaries of the new district authorities follow the boundaries of the old districts, which operated previously under the guidance of the now defunct area health authorities (AHAs). The total membership of a DHA was normally about seventeen including the chairman. Members appointed by the regional health authority (RHA) were a hospital consultant, a general practitioner, one nurse, midwife or health visitor. There was and still is a nominee from a university with a medical school, four members were appointed by local authorities, plus other members known as 'generalists', one of whom was recommended by the trade-union movement. The chairman was and still is appointed by the Secretary of State. Arising from recent Government reforms membership has been reduced. A DHA now comprises five non-executive members, appointed by the RHA because of the abilities they can bring to the authority; up to five executive members including the general manager and the finance officer. The general manager is appointed by the non-executive members and they also appoint the executive members acting with the general manager. The chairman is appointed by the Secretary of State. According to the Government, the weakness of the previous representation was that many councillors and professional people saw themselves as representatives for specific interests rather than as members of a management team. The DHA is advised by a district management team (DMT) led by a general manager who, himself, is a member of the authority, supported by professional staff. The composition and type of organisational structure of the DMT varies as between one DHA and another. The professional chief officers have normally direct access to the DHA on matters relating to their professional speciality but, in matters of administration (now called management), they are responsible to the district general manager. Below the DMT there are 'units of management', each led by a unit general manager and responsible for a particular aspect of the service – for example, a large hospital, or group of smaller hospitals, the community services of the district or the maternity services or mental health and so on. These unit managers are also involved in district-level management and report direct to the district general manager. In most hospitals there are some private beds which can be used by part-time consultants to treat private fee-paying patients. These private patients pay the full cost of the hospital accommodation and services as well as the consultant's fee.

Many hospitals have small wards or single rooms for those requiring privacy, which NHS patients may use for a daily charge. Treatment is still free.

The DHAs must work with the local authorities on matters of joint concern and hence there are joint consultative committees, as under the previous structure, and which were given statutory authority under the 1973 National Health Reorganisation Act. Local authority social workers are the main people closely involved in working with the health services, some are based in hospitals. Problems which are the concern of the social worker can often cause ill health or, putting it the other way round, ill health in a family can create problems necessitating the help of the social worker. The DHAs are responsible for the School Health Service, so this involves them with the education departments of local authorities. There are also links with the local authority housing department. Not only can bad housing cause ill health but often medical advice is needed by the local authority to help it decide on the housing needs of elderly people living on their own. There are also strong links between the DHAs and local government because of the responsibility of local authorities for environmental health and community care, including the welfare of the disabled.

Not only are there joint consultative committees linking the NHS and local government but, since 1976, there has been a system of joint financing. This allows NHS funds to be used on projects of common interest which have in mind the better care of patients. Voluntary bodies also involved in community care can be helped financially from this system of joint financing. Under the recent reform of the NHS and community care, the Government wishes to see in operation, not just joint plans for particular issues but also planning agreements between health authorities and local authorities covering broader long-term issues and principles.

Health-care planning teams operate at district level and are permanent or *ad hoc*, with the job of reviewing specific health needs. There can be one for the physically handicapped, one for the mentally handicapped, one for the elderly, and so on. The teams comprise representatives of medical, administrative, nursing and social disciplines, as well as representatives from the social services department of the local authority, since health and welfare are closely linked. The DMT uses the reports of the health care planning teams, as necessary, to prepare plans for consideration by the DHA.

The community health physician is a member of the DMT and replaces the old medical officer of health who was formerly employed in local government. Apart from working with other members of the DMT in meeting health needs, this official advises the local authority on environmental health, still the responsibility of the local authorities and previously known as public health.

Regional Health Authorities (RHAs)

These are in England only; in Wales and Scotland there are none. The regional health authorities appointed by the Secretary of State act as agents, being responsible for the long-term planning of hospital building, regional services and the allocation of resources between the district health authorities. Their chairmen report direct to the Secretary of State. They are also responsible for the design and construction of new buildings and they will undertake the more important building projects. They also provide services some district authorities cannot provide – a blood transfusion service for example. RHAs are advised by professional officers led by a general manager. The Government has reduced the membership of an RHA so that its size and composition is similar to that of a DHA – five non-executive and up to five executive members plus a non-executive chairman. The Secretary of State appoints the chairmen of the RHAs and their non-executive members. Again, as with DHAs, the executive members will include the general manager, appointed by non-executive members, plus the finance officer.

Community Health Councils (CHCs)
These represent the views of the consumer and there is one for each of the districts. They are funded by the RHAs. Half their members are appointed by local government, one-third by voluntary organisations and the remainder by the regional health authority. They comprise from around eighteen to thirty members. The councils have the right to be consulted, the power to secure information, to visit hospitals and other institutions. They have access to the district health authority and to the senior officers administering the district services. They have the duty of issuing an annual report. In general they can look at the adequacy of the health service provided for the community and comment on plans for future development. They can assess how local provision compares with the national picture. In fact, the community health councils can have influence on the development of the health service, but the degree of influence depends on the abilities and enthusiasm of their members. However, they have now lost their right to be represented at private meetings of the DHA where, as a rule, the more important decisions are taken – which some people see as reducing the DHAs accountability to patients. Individual DHAs can still choose to admit a CHC representative to a private meeting as an observer.

Community Health Services

One of the main jobs in the field of community health is care and after-care of patients in their own homes in co-operation with the patient's doctor and local authority services. This is in line with the growing practice of helping people as far as possible in their own home and surroundings (see *Care in the Community*, DHSS, 1981). Thus a patient should go to a hospital for treatment and nursing care if the hospital is the only place where these can be provided.

Home nursing
District nurses provide nursing in the patient's home. In some areas the nurses work as a team assisted by ancillaries and in close touch with the doctor and the hospital. The majority of patients are the elderly and chronically sick, but in certain cases home nursing is provided for children. Their work includes applying dressings, giving injections and medicine and generally looking after bed-ridden patients.

Health visiting
Like district nurses, health visitors are registered general nurses (formerly called State registered nurses) who have taken post-registered training. They visit mothers in their own homes (especially mothers who have left hospital after having a baby) and give advice on the care of the young child. They also advise expectant mothers. Their visits are not just to help the mothers but to see that the baby is being properly looked after. Health visitors also give advice on the prevention of illness and give support to vulnerable families and to the elderly.

Other community nurses are school nurses, community psychiatric and mental-handicap nurses and midwives. They come under the DHAs although some GPs employ nursing staff.

Nursing homes
These are provided by the NHS for people requiring continual care. These are mainly the elderly. But in many health authorities private nursing homes provide more beds than are provided by the NHS. The private sector in this field is growing.

Maternity and child-health centres
These centres give advice on the care of children under 5. (At this age they come under the care of the School Health Service.) The health visitors work closely with the centres. However, some pregnant women, and mothers with young children, prefer to get all their help and advice from the family doctor rather than go to the child health centre.

Family planning
This is now part of the National Health Service and includes vasectomy and free contraceptives.

Midwifery service
Midwives attend mothers confined at home and co-operate with the family doctor. They may also visit mothers at home who have had their babies in hospital, until such time as the health visitor takes over.

Ambulance service
Ambulances are provided to convey the sick to and from hospital when they are unable to travel by ordinary transport. They also take those injured in accidents to hospital. In certain areas voluntary organisations organise a hospital car service where owner-drivers take suitable cases to and from hospital. This is an addition to the ambulance service.

Care and after-care

Care and after-care cover persons suffering from tuberculosis and other illnesses and those suffering from mental disorder. (Care and after-care of the mentally disordered is the responsibility of the social services department of local government.) It also covers chiropody, especially for the old, and loan of nursing equipment. After-care is important for those leaving hospital.

Prevention of illness

This includes vaccination and immunisation against diphtheria, measles, polio, smallpox, tetanus and whooping cough at clinics or by family doctors. It also includes giving advice on health matters. (The School Health Service also provides vaccination against tuberculosis, diphtheria, polio, etc.)

The environmental health services run by local government help to prevent illness by, hopefully, keeping the environment clean. These services include controlling atmospheric pollution, ensuring pure water supply – although the water authorities now have the main responsibility for this – checking on cleanliness in restaurants and food warehouses, and so on.

Health Centres

These were originally built and maintained by local authorities, then built and maintained by the area health authorities and now by the new district health authorities. Some of the services provided in them are general medical, dental, ophthalmic and pharmaceutical services and also specialist services for hospital out-patients. The community health services also operate from health centres. Home nurses, health visitors and midwives in these centres work for a particular group of doctors and only serve the patients of that group. In this way they get to know the patients much better.

When the National Health Service started it was hoped that most doctors would soon be operating from health centres, but for many years very few were built. But since 1965 the building of health centres has accelerated. About one quarter of all doctors operate from health centres.

General practitioners pay a certain amount for the use of the health centre, but payment is made via the family practitioner service authorities.

Paying for the National Health Service

About 84 per cent of the cost is paid out of taxation, about 11 per cent out of part of National Insurance contributions and 5 per cent out of charges.

Local Authority Social Services Department Services (linked with Health)

Home helps
Home helps can be provided where a sick person or expectant mother or disabled person cannot be adequately looked after or where help is needed with the housework. Home helps are now mainly involved with the elderly. There is a charge for the service usually based on the person's income, though a few local authorities have made the service free – or more recently flat rate – because of the administrative costs involved in assessing charges.

Care and after-care of the mentally handicapped.
Mental illness is an acquired condition; mental subnormality (i.e. incomplete development of mind) exists from birth. The local authorities employ psychiatric social workers to visit such people in their own homes. Local authorities also provide for them training centres, clubs and residential accommodation.

Residential accommodation
Local authorities provide residential accommodation for persons who require care and attention which is not otherwise available to them. Apart from residential accommodation for certain categories of mentally ill and mentally subnormal people, local authorities provide residential accommodation for the elderly either in homes run by the local authority or private homes or homes run by voluntary organisations. Homes are also provided for the blind and physically handicapped to suit their special needs.

Other services for the elderly
Apart from residential homes and home helps, local authorities can also provide, either themselves or through the agency of voluntary organisations, meals in the homes of the elderly, social clubs, outings and holidays and a laundry service. A charge may be made for these services.

Services for the physically handicapped
These services include practical assistance in the home, recreational facilities outside the home, home adaptations, help in travelling, provisions of meals in the home, reasonable access to public buildings, and finding out who the physically handicapped are and making them aware of the services available to them.

Some handicapped persons are helped by a specialist social worker.

Environmental health

Before the community health services were taken over by the DHAs (April 1974), local authorities employed a medical officer of health to advise on environmental health. Advice is now given by doctors who specialise in community health and who are employed by the DHAs.

Environmental health officers, previously known as public health inspectors, are employed by local authorities to keep the environment, as far as possible, free from health hazards. This includes such hazards to health as impure air, impure drinking water, bad sanitation, overcrowded housing, contaminated food, excessive noise.

Other services provided by local authorities

Social services departments can arrange for bed linen or clothing to be washed and laundered and can arrange recuperative holidays. For certain of these services a charge may be made. All social workers attached to the NHS are employed by the social services departments of the local authority.

SUMMARY

The National Health Service is under the control of the government. The minister in charge is the Secretary of State for Health who is the political head of the Department of Health.

The National Health Service has three branches – personal practitioners, hospitals and community health services – which between them provide a comprehensive range of health services available to everyone. It does allow for private fee-paying patients.

The NHS has close links with the local authority welfare services.

ASSIGNMENTS

1.   Construct an organisational chart for England of the National Health Service. At the top start with the Secretary of State, the Department of Health and then a pyramid of the management structure.
2.   Obtain a copy of the annual report of your community health council. Take what you consider to be three of the most important issues discussed and explain why you consider them important and give the decisions or conclusions arrived at by the council.

3. Find the address of your district health authority. On a map draw the boundaries its administration covers. List the local authorities which come within these boundaries.

READING

Department of Health, *Health and personal social services statistics for England* (HMSO, published annually) .

8 Problems in the Health Service

REORGANISATIONS OF THE NATIONAL HEALTH SERVICE

Before April 1974, the community health services as well as the School Health Service were administered by local government. In 1974 the community health services were brought under the same administrative umbrella as the hospital services run in those days by area health authorities. The main reason for this change was to ensure better liaison between the hospitals and the community services for when a patient was discharged from hospital but still needed after-care. There were then in England regional health authorities and area health authorities. The RHAs allocated resources to the AHAs. Most AHAs were divided into districts with each district having its own management team of professional officers appointed by the AHA to do the day-to-day running of the hospital or hospitals and liaise with local authorities.

The Report of the Royal Commission on the National Health Service (18 July 1979) criticised the 1974 structure as follows: 'too many tiers, too many administrators in all disciplines, failure to make quick decisions, money wasted.' This is best illustrated by looking at the relationship between the area health authority and the district management team. The district management team of professional officers did the day-to-day work and reported to the area health authority. It was not responsible to the area team of professional officers. The area officers recommended to the area health authority the acceptance, the rejection or the amendment of the district management team's decision. 'It seems a complete anomaly to have more highly paid and presumably more experienced officers hiding behind their area committee, merely recommending instead of making these decisions' (Coyne, 1976). It was felt by many that area officers had no proper job of work to do. Hence a further reorganisation took place in 1982 and in line with the Royal Commission, area health authorities with their team of professional officers, were abolished. The district health authorities now became responsible for the hospital services which meant that each administrative area run by a DHA was smaller than the previous AHA area so that officers were closer to the people they served. Furthermore, as there were no intermediate teams of officers between DHAs and RHAs, the district management teams of professional officers had the chance to be more creative.

Management

Under the new structure of 1982 there was still consensus management. Each of the chief officers who formed the district team of officers – administrator, treasurer, medical officer and nursing officer, plus a general practitioner and hospital consultant – had to reach decisions, as among equals, by agreement. Each had the power of veto. Often the chairmanship of meetings was taken in rotation. The unfortunate results of consensus management were that it could happen that a decision was made at a meeting but there was nobody to take responsibility for ensuring the decision was implemented as there would have been with a chief executive able to give leadership and keep an eye on how the administrative machine was ticking over. This criticism also applied to the regional health authorities.

Acting on the recommendations of the Griffiths NHS Management Inquiry Report, published in 1983, consensus management was abolished. General managers were introduced at regional, district and unit level and a Supervisory Board, chaired by the Secretary of State, decided broad policy. The Board included the Permanent Secretary of the then DHSS, the Chief Medical Officer and about three other members. The planning of the effective implementation of the Supervisory Board's policy was the job of a Management Board comprising civil servants, business men and members of the Health Service. The Minister of Health was made chairman of the Management Board in October 1986 and, as he could make political decisions, this ensured better liaison with the Supervisory Board. Previously when there was a non-political chairman of the Management Board there had been misunderstandings over the interpretation of the Supervisory Board's policy objectives.

Under the reform of the NHS, recently introduced, the Supervisory Board is now called the NHS Policy Board responsible for finance and broad policy but still chaired by the Secretary of State. The former Management Board has become the NHS Management Executive chaired by a Chief Executive responsible for operational matters but answerable to the Policy Board. No minister sits on the Management Executive as with the Management Board so rapport is envisaged between the Policy Board and the Executive. But the change does emphasise the Government's intention to keep aloof from the day-to-day running of the NHS and to distance itself, as far as possible, from industrial unrest. The Management

Executive is now not only responsible for hospitals and community health services but also the family practitioner services. This was recommended by the Griffiths Report but not previously implemented. Thus the whole of the NHS is now under a single authority. Some critics see no need for the Policy Board as responsibility for broad policy lies with the Cabinet.

It was interesting to note that when management posts were first introduced and open to anyone inside and outside the NHS, irrespective of the particular profession of the applicant, the number of appointments from the private sector was comparatively small. Out of a total number of 676 managers at all levels – regional, district and unit – only 81 were made from the private sector. More than 100 managers were doctors and 55 were nurses but the vast majority, around 400, were former administrators. Altogether about 85 per cent of the manager posts went to former NHS staff. Some people thought and perhaps still think that the new organisational structure could give rise to friction between management and medical or nursing staff who, in some cases, would be subject to managers who know nothing about medical treatment and cannot therefore assess the competence of doctors and nurses. This sort of criticism is found in most large organisations where there are professional officers carrying out the professional work for which the organisation was set up and, on the other hand, administrators (now called managers in the NHS) keeping an eye on broad policy and efficiency. It was voiced particularly in the Civil Service where top people were and, in the main, still are recruited for their administrative ability rather than for specialised professional expertise.

But of course, managers do not normally make decisions on matters where specialised professional knowledge is necessary without consulting the relevant professional officers. Thus, although nurses are worried that they are no longer, as previously, represented on the district management team, each health authority has been instructed by the minister to designate a senior nurse as its principal nursing adviser with guaranteed access to the health authority. And the manager at unit level must consult with the relevant professional officers, including nurses, and respect their expertise. And 55 former nurses were made unit managers. Thus, although the old-style consensus management has been abolished, managers and professional officers must still work together as a team.

In the reform of the NHS, under the 1990 NHS and Community Care Act, operative from April 1991, competition and decentralisation are seen by the Government as the main means of increasing efficiency and improving the quality of care. To further competition for hospital services, the DHAs which provide the services no longer fund them. Instead hospitals compete with one another to provide services but they are paid for by the clients seeking the services for their patients – for example, DHAs, independent NHS hospitals and GPs with their own budgets (see below) and even private hospitals. Hence the more patients a hospital treats, the more money it receives. Hence, argues the Government, hospitals have the incentive to maintain a high quality of service to attract patients. But the changeover from April 1991 proceeded slowly and the contracts made with hospitals tended to follow the same referral pattern as in previous years. GPs are encouraged to advertise their services so that patients are better able to judge which GP will suit them best and, to facilitate choice, the procedure for changing one's doctor has been simplified. As with hospitals, the more patients a doctor has, the more money he or she will earn and, to further this, a greater proportion of a doctor's income now comes from patient numbers. Again, the theory is doctors will get more patients only if their services are good and hence competition will encourage GPs to maintain a high standard of service because of the greater financial incentive.

To further decentralisation and get the administrative unit for the patients' care as near to the patients as possible, NHS hospitals, subject to Government approval, can now become independent of the DHA although still remaining within the NHS and are known as NHS Hospital Trusts. The DHAs, are expected to delegate as much of their functions as possible to the hospitals remaining under their control. Again in line with decentralisation, doctors with a practice of 11 000 patients or more can have, if they so wish, their own budgets from the RHA and hence, when patients need to be referred to a hospital, these doctors can, on their own account, shop around the various hospitals to get the best buy for their patients. Furthermore, savings on their budgets can be ploughed back into the practice. Those doctors without a budget of their own have their patients needing hospital treatment referred to a hospital by the DHA. The DHA has the duty to buy the best service it can for the doctor's patient, either from its own hospitals, from independent NHS hospitals, from other DHA hospitals or from private hospitals. Decentralisation is again emphasised in that DHAs are expected to take into consideration the hospitals preferred by the doctor or, to use the official phrase, his or her 'referral patterns'.

However, there are accidents and illnesses where immediate attention is necessary and so patients, in these cases, must have a local hospital to go to. Services to cover such eventualities are called 'core' services and hospitals under a DHA receive a special 'management budget' from the DHA to pay for them.

Again in pursuit of efficiency, doctors, for the first time, have cash limits on their prescribing. Under the 1988 Health and Medicines Act all doctors have a drugs budget. Because of the wide variations in prescribing between practices, it is felt that some doctors are over-prescribing. But the Government has stated that no doctor will be denied making a prescription for a patient even if his or her budget is overspent. Where there is consistent overspending a medical audit will be introduced supervised by the FPSAs – the audit being done by a small group of doctors. FPSAs receive an amount of money for drugs from which they set a budget for each practice in their area.

NHS Hospital Trusts

These hospitals are free to manage themselves, including the power to buy and sell assets and borrow money up to a financial limit. Any financial surplus can be used as they think best and, in employing staff, they can fix their own rates of pay. Their income comes from the organisations for which they provide services. These can include DHAs, family doctors with their own budgets, other self-governing hospitals within the NHS, private hospitals and private patients. They have to publish reports of their activities, be subject to investigation by the Audit Commission and have their accounts sent to the Secretary of State who, in the last resort, can issue a directive or initiate an inquiry. They must provide the core services (see above) and apply NHS procedures for complaints and pest control.

They are run by a board of directors with an equal number of non-executive and executive directors and, in addition, a non-executive chairman appointed by the Secretary of State. Two non-executive directors come from the local community, appointed by the RHA and the remaining non-executive directors are appointed by the Secretary of State after consultation with the chairman and after the posts have been advertised. The executive directors comprise the general manager, appointed by the chairman, the medical director, senior nurse manager and director of finance. The Government believes that this smaller management set-up will give better leadership – executives are brought in to manage for the first time and local authorities are no longer represented as of right because the Government feels many councillors come to a committee – e.g. a DHA – with the specific purpose of pursuing a party political line. There is a similar streamlined set-up for the composition of RHAs and DHAs.

Hospitals in general

To gain more resources for the NHS, the Government presses hospitals to continue to let or sell unused property assets. It believes efficiency can be improved and perhaps financial savings made by increased delegation of duties – for example, many jobs done by nurses can be done by professional support staff (nursing auxiliaries) and the go-ahead for this was given in 1990. Some work done by junior doctors could be done by nurses. Some of the work done by other professionals might be suitable for delegation to non-professionals.

Perhaps the most important of all the suggested reforms for improving efficiency is the tighter control over consultants and their being brought closer to the management role in the hospital. As the White Paper Cm 555, 'Working for Patients', pointed out, general managers are accountable for the spending in their hospitals but it is mainly the consultants' decisions which determine how the money allocated to the hospital is used. Hence, the Government argued, consultants must be more involved in the use of resources. What perhaps inhibited (and perhaps still does) general managers in England in their relationship with consultants on matters of financial control is that consultants are appointed by RHAs (except for those in teaching districts). Hence their accountability to the DHA was vague. Under the reforms, introduced in 1991, DHAs now act as agents of the RHAs in discussing with consultants the consultants' duties in each hospital. Consultants now are supposed to have a fuller job description than they had previously to cover 'their responsibility for the quality of their work, their use of resources, the extent of the services they provide for NHS patients and the time they devote to the NHS', and the number of outpatient clinics a consultant is expected to hold. District managers are now directly involved in the appointment procedure of consultants to ensure the appointments committee is made aware that, as well as clinical competence, the applicant has to meet other requirements – the need to fit into the broad managerial plan. This again strengthens the role of the manager *vis-à-vis* the consultants. The next point highlights what this means. Distinction awards which lead to higher pay are now to be based not just on clinical performance but on the consultants' effective use of resources and 'their commitment to management and development of the services'. In brief consultants must be accountable because their decisions commit 'substantial levels of resources'. To underline the above, the Government has urged that the committee which makes the distinction awards should not be solely professional but should be chaired by the chairman and include senior managers as well as clinical members and, to be successful, the candidate should have the support of both.

For the market system now introduced into the NHS, the various services had to be costed to enable prices to be quoted. From November 1986 pilot schemes were introduced. A new post of Chief Research and Development of the NHS has been created all part of what is called the Resource

Management Initiative begun in 1986 to improve management efficiency. The reforms were 'progressively' implemented from April 1991.

From the Government point of view the reforms outlined above were necessary because of the inadequacy of much of the NHS, the long waiting lists for certain surgical operations, the wide variations in performance between hospitals. For the poorest performers, the long waiting lists were not due, so the Government says, to underfunding but to poor management and 'poor output per surgeon'. Thus whilst hospital staffs may have wished to reduce waiting lists, because they were on a fixed budget, there was no financial reward to give them that extra impetus to do so. There were (and probably still are) wide variations in the prescribing of GPs, suggesting that in some cases there was extravagance in prescribing. The introduction of a cash limit on prescribing should help to reduce unnecessary expenditure. Thus it is hoped that the reforms will help to bring the least efficient hospitals and GPs up to the higher performance standards of the remainder.

The old system of funding by the providers of the service penalised efficiency. Thus when a DHA was efficient and dealing with patients quickly – 'increasing its throughput' – it more quickly used up its financial allocation because of the fixed budgets of the old system. Hence it had to cut its activities until it received more money, reaching a stage where GP referrals were not welcome. Under today's reformed system, there are no financial constraints on efficiency because the more patients a hospital deals with, the more money it receives. For example, Withington Hospital in Manchester has a machine called a Lithotripter which removes gall stones without the use of surgery. It cost £1 million. In the first year of its use it was given enough money to treat 400 cases. When these 400 cases had been dealt with its financial allocation had been used up and no more cases could be treated. It, therefore, sent requests for patients to other hospitals charging £500 per patient. Under the new system, operative from April 1991, with such an advanced machine, Withington Hospital would have had a continuing flow of patients arranged for it under the contract system and hence no worry of possible financial constraints limiting the machine's use.

Greater decentralisation as provided by NHS Hospital Trusts running their own show should enhance the relationship between the hospital and the community.

But perhaps, in the long run, the most important change will be the costing of the services within the NHS. Nobody knows approximately how much money is needed to run the NHS adequately. The Thatcher government put more money into it in real terms than ever before yet still it was criticised for not putting in enough. Once the NHS is fully costed the Government will have a much better idea how much money is needed and the Health minister will be better armed when facing the Treasury. Both sides, supporters and opponents of the reform, agree the need for costing the Service.

In the long run, the Government argues, patient care will be much improved with less need for people to use private health care.

Some criticisms of the NHS reforms
In the view of the Government's ideological commitment to hold public expenditure on a tight rein, a cynic might argue that the main purpose of the reforms is to save money. There is little evidence that the Government is intending to increase funding in real terms to any great extent and underfunding has been the main criticism levelled against the Government's policy towards the NHS. For example, the extra £2.4 billion announced for the NHS in November 1989 will, critics argue, barely cover the cost of computerisation to meet the contract system plus rising costs due to higher inflation (see the *Guardian*, 29 November 1989). It would appear, therefore, that the Government hopes that any significant increase in expenditure in real terms will come from savings within the NHS through greater efficiency and extra money from the continuing sale or leasing of premises to private concerns, and a greater reliance on public subscription – a euphemism for charity. Furthermore, the strengthening of the role of the manager *vis-à-vis* the consultants, the introduction of cash limits for general practice can be seen as further means to contain expenditure. These two developments are reasonable if the money saved is put back into the development of the NHS and is not used simply to keep expenditure at a particular level. Many people believe that if those who work in the NHS could be assured the Service would be adequately funded, a great deal of the bitter opposition of the medical profession to the reforms would disappear. Incidentally, the strengthening of the role of the general manager makes it more difficult for consultants to speak publicly about problems in connection with their work in the NHS.

There is also the fear among some critics that, in view of the Government's ideological commitment to private enterprise and the market system, its aim will be eventually to privatise much of the NHS, starting with the NHS Hospital Trusts; many of the ancillary services having already been privatised. Thus some critics see the Trust hospitals selling more and more of their services to the private sector so that they become increasingly dependent on the private sector for a comfortable survival – privatisation through the back door.

As for competition improving efficiency and the quality of care in the NHS, there is no guarantee that competition itself will do this. Much depends on the attitude of the workforce. Whereas before the reforms staffs of the various hospitals were colleagues, now under the market system, they are competitors. This might change for the worse the sense of collective service within the NHS. And as the House of Commons Social Services Committee pointed out (Eighth Report, Session 1988–89) the contract system might result not in price competition but hospitals co-operating to reach agreement among themselves on prices. On the other hand, if competition is strong, 'unfair methods' as the Committee puts it might be employed. Thus, in spite of the Government's intention that the quality of care in hospitals should be monitored as well as costs, financial pressures arising from the need to win contracts might result in a poorer quality of service in order to keep prices competitive.

The Government claimed that the reforms would give patients a greater choice as to which hospital in which to be treated. But do they? Surely the patient has to go to the hospital for which a contract for his particular complaint has been made, either by the GP with a budget or a DHA. In fact, it might be that as far as hospital treatment is concerned patient choice is more limited because, previously, a doctor could refer a patient to any hospital he thought suitable for his patient. In any case, choice presupposes knowledge of the quality of care being offered. How can a patient judge the quality of care? The average patient can only go on hearsay which, in the case of hospital treatment, would not be easy to come by or, at least, of dubious reliability. For the local GP practices it is much easier to learn something about them which could be useful in deciding which doctor to go to.

And what of patient choice on the question of whether a hospital should be an NHS Hospital Trust? There is no consultation with local people. If a hospital decides to opt for self-government, it is the Secretary of State who decides whether to allow it or not.

There are fears that drug budgets for GPs could affect the trust between doctor and patient because, in certain circumstances, the patient might believe the doctor had prescribed a medicament which was second best because it was cheaper. Most probably this would be untrue but even the possibility of such a decision might affect trust in the doctor, which is such a necessary ingredient for patient recovery. This fear can apply to GP practices with their own budgets.

Again, the doctor-patient relationship might be adversely affected in the case of GPs with their own budgets, because they will now have to make out their own waiting lists for hospital treatment – a responsibility they perhaps do not enjoy because now some patients might blame them for what they consider to be an undue delay in getting to hospital.

The Government claims that the new administrative arrangements for DHAs will provide 'better local leadership'. It could well be. But under the new arrangements there are no representatives of local authorities or the professions. The Secretary of State appoints the RHAs which, in turn, appoint the non-executive members of the DHAs who, in turn elect the executive members. This gives a more cohesive system of management but it means, say the critics, that DHAs will simply be boards of management to implement Government policy with inadequate representation of practitioners and consumers to put forward an independent view.

As for efficiency, the cost of running the NHS is low compared with other countries – only 4.5 per cent of total expenditure or 6 per cent of GNP (Gross National Product). The reforms necessitate an increase in accountants and other ancillary staff. In addition, to ensure everything is going satisfactorily, particularly that competition does not reduce quality, a regulatory framework has been introduced. Hence administrative costs will rise and one of the main advantages of the old system will be lost.

And what of the frail and elderly? They might appear a burden on the GPs' finances in spite of the extra weighting in money for treating them. Furthermore, as a larger proportion of the pay doctors receive depends on the number of patients they have, this might encourage some doctors to spend less time with patients. DHAs and own budget GPs could threaten to contract elsewhere unless they get preferential treatment for their patients and hospitals could offer preferential treatment to DHAs and doctors who are willing to pay a premium above the contract rate. In this way, the basic principle of the NHS that, as far as possible, treatment should be based on need, not money, could perhaps be in danger of being undermined.

Finally, there is the criticism that the reforms have been put through without sufficient preliminary research., The late decision (December 1989) to create the post of Chief Research and Development Officer for the NHS might suggest that this was at last realised by the Government.

FINANCE

The real cost of the National Health Service has risen over the years for the following reasons:

1. The development of medical science has made treatment more expensive.

2.   The real wages of its employees have risen.
3.   The proportion of older people in the population who need care has been growing.
4.   There is an increasing use of drugs to treat depression and stress.
5.   There is never enough money for health and thus, as the country grows richer, the real expenditure on the NHS increases.

Problems arising from increasing costs
If about 84 per cent of the NHS is paid for out of taxation, why cannot taxation be raised to meet increasing costs? Even the Labour party admits that to keep on raising taxation to meet rising costs would not be politically feasible even if, which is doubtful, it was economically sound. Alternative sources of income must therefore be found.

About 11 per cent of the cost of the NHS is financed out of part of the National Insurance contribution. Extra income could be found by increasing the contributions.

Charges account for about 5 per cent of the cost of the service. Should they not be increased? Even if charges were considerably increased, the percentage of the income provided would still be comparatively small. And they would defeat one of the main principles of the NHS: that nobody because of lack of money should feel discouraged from making full use of the services available, although many people might feel increases in dental charges have done just that for dental services. Could the cost of drugs supplied to the NHS be reduced by more thoughtful prescribing by doctors? The government has acted on this by limiting the drugs that can be prescribed but it claims that the prescribed drugs are as effective as those that are blacklisted. They are, of course, cheaper and in the first year of the blacklist 1985/86 it has been estimated that there was a £70 million saving on a total drug bill of around £1.5 billion. But some doctors see the blacklist as a 'two-tier health system' as those who can afford and desire a blacklisted drug will obtain a private prescription. The Government has now gone the whole way by introducing, for the first time, cash limits on doctors' prescribing.

Should private medicine, financed by private insurance, be greatly extended? The more people who take out private health insurance, the more money will be coming into the Health Service as a whole, without the need for extra taxation, increased contributions or increased charges. There are two ways of acquiring private medicine: the first is to have a pay bed in an NHS hospital; the other is to be treated by a private hospital. One can also be a private patient of a general practitioner. Private hospitals, which include nursing homes and clinics, must be registered with the health authorities. Tax relief is given to those who take out private health insurance. Supporters of the extension of private insurance for medical treatment say it will develop competition between the public and private sectors of health care services, and will improve overall efficiency. It will, for example, show where the NHS is not meeting demand. It will take some of the heavy load off the NHS and reduce its waiting-lists especially for non-urgent, routine surgery. The Government in its White Paper 'Working for Patients' (Cm 555, January 1989) comments favourably on the already 'growing partnership' between the NHS and the private sector. It gives examples of NHS contracting with private hospitals to treat patients from NHS waiting lists. It cites over 26 000 patients who were treated this way in 1986 at a cost to the NHS of £45m. And supporters of private medicine point out that doctors will still get most of their income from working in the NHS and will therefore still have an interest in making the state system successful. Under the Conservative government, and especially since 1978, there has been a boom in private hospitals, half of which are financed by American business. The opponents of private medicine argue that the use of medical resources should be based on need, not money. Furthermore under any insurance scheme certain people will be excluded (quite apart from those who cannot afford the premiums) because they are not a business proposition. These are the very people who need most health care – the elderly, the chronically sick, the disabled. These will be left for the NHS to look after. Two services would then eventually develop – a better one for those who pay through private insurance and a poorer state service for the residual poor who cannot afford private insurance and for those who are not insurable. But there has been a growth in the number of medical conditions excluded from private insurance quite apart from these categories so that some comparatively rich people are now beginning to have second thoughts about private health insurance. But supporters of private insurance do not see it this way. For example, the then Secretary of State for Social Services, Patrick Jenkin, speaking in Parliament on 3 February 1981 said: 'By relieving the National Health Service of some part of acute in-patient care, that leaves more resources for the National Health Service to spend on those who have no private care, which includes the Cinderella services for the elderly and the handicapped' (*Commons Hansard*, vol. 998, no. 39, 3 February 1981).

Opponents of the extension of private insurance for health care point out that the NHS is controlled by elected ministers and is paid for mainly from taxation, and this leads to a more efficient control over rapidly rising costs than an insurance-based system. This is because taxation is unpopular with the electorate, on which ministers rely for retaining office, while the controllers of private insurance schemes are not elected and can always raise premiums to meet extra costs (see 'The case against extending private insurance', *Guardian*, 3 September 1980). This same article gives examples of resources used wastefully under an insurance scheme – patients receiving hospital treatment because their insurance only covered hospital treatment but they could have been just as well treated as out-patients, or the case of hospital administrators encouraging patients to stay in hospital longer than they need because they are cheaper to care for than new patients. This had arisen where a hospital is paid a flat rate fee per day for each patient.

At least we would expect private patients using NHS facilities to be charged the full cost of these facilities. In many cases this is not so says the House of Commons Select Committee on Public Accounts (see its 46th report, July 1986).

The most painless way to increase the rate of development of the NHS without increasing the burden of taxation is for the country to grow richer more quickly.

Two more immediate ways of improving the finances of the NHS are:

1.   Concentrate more resources on health education and accident preven- tion so that fewer people have to make use of the NHS. This would save money because, in the long run, preventive medicine is cheaper than treatment.
2.   Allocate resources more effectively. In other words, if money is limited, work out better ways of spending the money you have.

This is what the Government claims it has done. Thus the abolition of consensus management in hospital administration and its replacement by general managers was seen by the Government as a means of improving efficiency and keeping costs down, especially if people with managerial ability from private industry with their commercial experience were brought into the NHS. Another important way of saving money, as seen from the Government point of view, was to allow private contractors to ten- der to carry out ancillary hospital services – cleaning, catering and laundry services for example which had previously been done by employees of the NHS. Domestic staff of the NHS have tendered themselves and, in many cases, won the contract. At the end of March 1986, private contractors had won 148 contracts (the more lucrative ones) and organisations representing domestic staff, 522. At the time the Secretary of State said competitive tendering was saving the NHS £52 million a year, providing extra money for the care of patients. On the other hand, a critic might argue that the

Government gave the NHS less money in anticipation of these savings. In general, the financial savings have been at the expense of domestic ancillary staff – less of them employed, hours reduced and less pay. There have been cases where the private contractors have been censured by the health authority for inadequate service. But spokesmen for the private contractors state that they are more efficient because they have to keep strictly to the contract which contains penalty clauses for failure to do so. The same discipline they claim, does not apply to domestic staff. On the other hand, in the United States with its very competitive atmosphere, only about one in six hospitals use outside contractors for cleaning and many hospitals use domestic staff for other services. As one American manager, speaking of outside contractors, said:

> It seems to me that you begin to have a collection of people in the hospital who don't have a fundamental loyalty and identity with the hospital. In Lennox Hill all employees are seen as part of an organization which exists to provide a service to patients and their families even though they may not be direct care givers . . . someone who brings in the patient's tray or is cleaning their room has really got to be part of the team that provides the care and the service. That's very hard to sustain if you have a collection of people, all of whom have different employers, some of whom have short-term gains in mind and are not really here for the long haul. (*Health and Social Service Journal*, 13 February 1986)

The Government would probably now say that the reform of the NHS introduced from April 1991 is its largest single measure in its continuing efforts to use NHS resources more effectively and thus improve efficiency and quality of care.

Allocation of Resources

Geographical allocation
In 1975 a Resource Allocation Working Party (RAWP) was set up and its report in 1976 highlighted the inequalities in respect of resources between areas of the country. Arising from its report, richer regions like Thames and Oxford received a smaller proportion of resources than previously, and other regions like the Northern, North-west and Trent regions received a greater proportion. The richer areas did not like it because, even though they were richer, they still did not have enough resources to do all the things they thought should still be done. The amount of money a region now

receives is based (from April 1990) on its resident population, 'weighted to reflect the health and age of the population, including the numbers of elderly people and the relative cost of providing the services'. Under this formula, the Thames region receives 'a slightly higher level of funding than the rest'. In defending the change, the Government stated in its White Paper, Cm 555 'Working for Patients', that over the years and bearing in mind all the factors, differences between the regions had very much narrowed. Under the RAWP system money is allocated in England to the regional health authorities but there is then still the problem of distributing the money to the districts and then distributing the district allocation to the various sections of the district and the FPSAs.

Social class and resources
A DHSS Working Group chaired by Sir Douglas Black reported in 1980 under the heading *Inequalities in Health*. This pointed out that the health of those in the lower social classes had improved much more slowly than had the health of the more affluent. In some cases it had deteriorated. The lower social classes also use the preventive services – ante-natal care, screening and other GP check-ups – less than the middle and upper classes. In 1991 the findings were still relevant. Why do working-class people on the whole not make use of the NHS as much as middle-class people? Is it because they are not as conversant with the facilities the service offers, are less able to make known their needs than the middle class, or is it because in the poorer working-class areas the facilities are poorer and do not encourage their use as do the services elsewhere? The Black Report did point out that the provision of services was unequal, particularly those concerned with primary care in the inner-city areas.

Priorities in health care
Another aspect of resource allocation is the distribution of resources between the different categories of illness. Medical education quite rightly stresses the curative aspects of medicine, but when resources are limited putting more resources into preventive medicine and less into curative treatment might serve overall health needs better. Governments have been aware of this point and there has been a shift of resources from hospitals to community services, with special emphasis on care of the elderly, the handicapped and mentally ill. There has also been, as part of the development of community health services, a much greater emphasis on health education. However, health education can make some people develop unnecessary worries about their health so that eventually they go to the doctor for treatment to stop worrying!

Again looking at the question of priorities in health needs, would it not be better for more resources to be allocated for the treatment of common illnesses which are not fatal but cause much suffering – arthritis and rheumatism, for example – and less into expensive high-technology treatment for less common illnesses? Perhaps there should be more public discussion of these issues.

THE FAMILY DOCTOR

The average family doctor's financial position has improved under the National Health Service, and he or she has no longer to limit treatment according to the financial standing of patients. Nevertheless, many family doctors feel their status has declined. The reason is that the family doctor has found it increasingly difficult to keep up with the rapid advance in medical science not only in matters of treatment but also diagnosis. Hence doctors have had to refer an increasing proportion of their patients to specialists in hospitals. At the same time, the prestige and rewards of the specialist consultant have increased. (The fact that certain illnesses like pneumonia which previously needed hospital treatment, can now be dealt with by the family doctor, thanks to developments in antibiotics, does not alter the general trend.) However, morale has been restored to some extent due to the new emphasis on primary care and the important role the doctor plays in this, and, since 1966, financial help for improving premises and employing ancillary staff.

Suggested remedies
1.   Family doctors should concentrate on developing more effective treatment for those minor illnesses aggravated by strain and worry. It is this kind of social medicine which the family doctor is in a unique position to develop because, unlike the specialist in the hospital, he or she sees patients as a whole in their social environment, though many doctors would say they do not have the time to study their patients' backgrounds.
     However, because the voluntary and statutory welfare services may be able to assist some of the doctor's patients, it is important that the family doctor is aware of these services. After all, the family doctor is normally the patient's first contact and the link with all the other services.
2.   Doctors should work in a group. In 1982 only about 15 per cent worked on their own. If, as seems preferable, the group practice is

conducted from a health centre, it will have a purpose-built building, specialised equipment and ancillary staff such as nurses, health visitors, social workers and medical secretaries either employed by the district health authority or by the doctors direct. Group practice has the following advantages:

(a) it helps the patient by making it easier for an appointments system to be worked.

(b) it helps the doctor to spend more time with the patient, and this time can be used more effectively because of the background information on the patient provided by ancillary staff.

(c) by working as a team and exchanging ideas, the doctors have a better chance of keeping abreast with developments in medicine.

(d) as a group, the doctors have more resources and cover a much larger number of patients than any one doctor could and therefore it is much more an economic proposition to employ the latest diagnostic aids – they would then have to refer less patients to hospital and this would relieve the junior hospital doctors of some work.

On the other hand, health centres are more impersonal. Most people have to travel much further from their home to see the doctor and are less likely to meet people from their own locality.

All this is not to say that there are not efficient doctors working on their own. After all, what makes a good doctor is not the medical equipment, important as that is, but an interest in and care for the patient.

PRIMARY HEALTH CARE SERVICES

Community health services plus the family practitioners services are now referred to as the primary health care services. They were outlined in the previous chapter. The normal concept of a primary health care team is one led by a general practitioner and including a health visitor, a district nurse, a midwife and could also include a community psychiatric nurse, a mental-handicap nurse and perhaps a local authority social worker who can help with personal or family problems which may have contributed to the illness the doctor is asked to treat. The social worker can also liaise with the other social workers including those concerned with home helps, psychiatric social workers and the housing officers of the local authority all of whose work has a relevance for health. Sick or disabled people often need a home help and bad housing can be a direct cause of ill health. Thus a wide range of people in local government as well as in the Health Service are involved in primary health care. Three administrative structures are involved – the district health authority, the family practitioner service authorities, and the local authority (see next chapter on community care). One of the weaknesses of a GP-led primary health care team is that it only covers the patients on the GP's list. Furthermore, the *Report of the Community Nursing Review* (1986) suggests that some GPs are not aware of the contribution to treatment other disciplines can make. To further improve co-ordination in the provision of primary health care the report recommends the amalgamation of family practitioner service authorities and district health authorities making one administrative body responsible for primary health care. The area covered by this administrative body would be divided into appropriately sized neighbourhood areas each led by a primary health care team led by GPs and nurses in equal partnership. In fact, the government has placed FPSAs under the RHAs. And what of co-ordination with local government? The 1979 Royal Commission on the NHS considered that this liaison between the health authorities and local government had been unsatisfactory and put most of the blame on local government. Since then, while the Government can claim it has increased expenditure on the NHS in real terms, it has reduced financial aid to local government which cannot have improved matters since the Royal Commission reported. There has been criticism of the lack of co-ordination and leadership in primary health care but Government reforms in this field are supposed to help remedy this.

COMPLAINTS

The Secretary of State
The Secretary of State for Social Services has the responsibility for ensuring that the NHS is run in the interests of the people. He and his colleagues in the government have the final word on the shaping of its future.

Community Health Councils
The community health councils make representations to the NHS authorities on behalf of patients in general. However, some community health councils encourage individuals to approach them with their complaints. They are then given advice on what to do. And with many CHCs the secretary will, if requested, represent a person appearing before a FPSA with a complaint against a practitioner.

Family Practitioner Service Authorities

There is a statutory complaints procedure for the personal practitioner services. For each section of the personal practitioner service there is a local service committee – one each for doctors, dentists, opticians and chemists – appointed by the FPSA. A complaint against a practitioner goes to the appropriate committee and the committee's recommendation goes to the FPSA for approval or amendment. If the complaint is found to be justified, part of the personal practitioner's salary may be withheld. An appeal can be made to the minister against the FPSA's decision. In more serious cases the FPSA may recommend that the practitioner be excluded from the NHS. In this case the matter is dealt with by the National Health Service Tribunal.

The complaints procedure against practitioners is not very satisfactory as the local service committees and FPSAs have very strong professional representation and may be over-influenced in the practitioner's favour. The complainant has no professional help and is therefore at a disadvantage to the personal practitioner against whom the complaint is made. Thus the Council on Tribunals in its annual report, published January 1990, stated the procedure was weighted too heavily in favour of doctors. Some improvement has been made since April 1990 – although lawyers are banned from the proceedings other advocates are now allowed. The Government Green Paper (Primary Health Care, April 1986) proposed that for lesser complaints FPSAs should offer an informal conciliation service between patient and practitioner.

Health Service Commissioner

The Health Service Commissioner investigates complaints in connection with hospital treatment and community care where the complainant feels that he or she has suffered injustice or hardship through maladministration or through a failure to provide the necessary treatment and care. The Commissioner only investigates a complaint if it has already been referred to the responsible authorities but has not been resolved to the complainant's satisfaction. He cannot investigate complaints that challenge the clinical judgement of the doctor, though a special complaints procedure has been introduced for this. If the hospital cannot resolve the complaint, the health authority's regional medical officer seeks a second opinion from two independent consultants. But not all consumer groups are happy with the way the procedure has functioned. The Commissioner will not deal with complaints against personal practitioners as there is already the statutory procedure for referring these to the FPSAs previously described. It is in the field of hospital treatment that the lack of an effective complaints procedure has been most felt. This has been particularly true of long-stay mental hospitals where some years ago revelations of cruelty to mental patients came as a great shock.

Hospital Patients' Association
This is a voluntary pressure group which takes up complaints and puts forward its views on the NHS generally to those who run it, including the Secretary of State.

SUMMARY

The National Health Service has ensured that a good standard of medical care is given to everyone irrespective of income. Medical care has therefore greatly expanded. It has enabled medical resources to be more evenly distributed throughout the country, though there is still need for medical resources to be distributed more fairly, always bearing in mind that some areas have greater or less health needs than others. Family doctors have been given financial security and yet, at the same time, have retained their clinical freedom. And because the family doctor does not have to worry about the financial standing of patients when prescribing, he or she can perhaps be more of a family doctor than used to be the case before the days of the NHS providing he or she is not overloaded.

There will never be enough money for the NHS to do all the things one would like it to do, especially as the development of medical science usually makes treatment more expensive. But the financial problems of the NHS are partly due to its success. The development of the service has meant more demands being made upon it. This can be illustrated by the example of major hip surgery, which is now more available with the result that more people demand it. This causes longer waiting-lists but, not only that, a hip operation uses the operating theatre all day, delaying other operations. Furthermore, screening campaigns have revealed hidden illness. The problem of financing the NHS will thus be a permanent one and how it will be dealt with will largely depend on the economic policies in fashion at the time. For example, the Thatcher government, influenced by monetarist theory, attempted to reduce the growth of public expenditure and introduced privatisation of public enterprises (denationalisation). In the NHS privatisation has meant encouraging private medical care and the opening up of domestic and catering services within the hospitals to competitive tendering from outside private contractors, with a view to saving money. The huge increase in the charge for a prescription plus the limited drugs list will also save money and will encourage the buying of medicines outside the NHS. The new organisational structure of general managers is also a means of improving efficiency and hence making financial savings. But the National Health and Community Care Act, which has resulted in the biggest shake up of the NHS since it was introduced in 1948, is seen by the Government, with its faith in the market system for most situations, as a major development in the creation of not just a more effective and hence more efficient NHS but one with a higher quality of service. In spite of that, the reforms seem to have been opposed by the majority of the medical profession and public but nobody really knows what the long-term outcome for the Service will be. One thing at least is required for success and that is that those who work in the NHS should be happy with their pay and conditions which, at the moment, as far as nurses and perhaps junior doctors are concerned, does not seem to be the case. Some 30000 nurses (many under training) leave the NHS each year. But in spite of the Thatcher Government's attitude towards public expenditure it could justly claim that, in real terms, money spent on the NHS was greater than ever before. More patients than ever are being treated and more professional staff employed and new hospitals built. Although the NHS is receiving more money in real terms, it does not seem to be enough. Nine out of ten DHAs had to make cash savings in the winter of 1989 in order to stay within their budgets (see the *Guardian*, 1 November 1989).

Financial demands on the NHS have risen and are still rising. There is the increasing number of elderly, increasing illness due to large-scale unemployment, there is increased drug abuse and increased alcoholism and the high cost of new technology and now the problem of AIDS. In addition, pay increases within the NHS have not been fully met by the Government, leaving health authorities to find the rest of the money; in addition, there are cash limits on Family Practitioner services despite the fact that these services have been increasing at a faster rate than hospital services.

The House of Commons Social Services Committee in its 4th Report (1986), estimated that between 1980/81 and 1985/86 the NHS was under-funded by £1.3 billion. It stated that to keep pace with rising demand real resources should have risen by 2 per cent a year but they only grew by 1 per cent a year. The British Medical Association (BMA) in its report on the Government's White Paper *Working for Patients* states that increased demand is the cause of the NHS financial problems.

The number of people covered by private insurance has doubled over the past ten years to around 5.4 million people of whom 70 per cent are covered by company schemes. The National Audit Office, under the control of the Comptroller and Auditor General, warns that this expansion of private health might result in conflict with the NHS because of the shortage of consultants and nurses. The private sector employs 1750 consultants full-time but depends on another 12000 who work most of their time in the NHS. (The NHS and Independent Hospitals: report of the Comptroller and Auditor General.) But, given the philosophy of the Conservative government, critics might be forgiven for believing (whether true or false) that the Government wants as much private health care as possible within the limits set by our democratic society even if it means two tiers of health care – one for the better off and one – the NHS – for the less well-off. But it must be remembered that health also depends on factors outside the health services, whether private or NHS – for example, living standards, including housing and working conditions and also nutrition and, most important, the way we live.

ASSIGNMENTS

1. Discuss the ways the work of local government and the National Health Service is linked. Find out what liaison exists between your local authority and the NHS. Suggest ways of improving this liaison. For this last part of the question, chance your arm!
2. Discuss the advantages and disadvantages of group practice among general practitioners for doctors and patients. Where possible make use of your own experience of group practice either located in or separate from a health centre.
3. Write to the British United Provident Association (BUPA), which provides private health insurance, and ask for the cost and benefits of private health insurance to the insured. Then, bearing in mind your own reading, give your assessment of the probable consequences to the National Health Service of the extension of private health insurance and its consequence for health care in general.
4. Given that resources are limited, what would be your priorities in health care? Give your reasons.
5. Discuss the family doctor as the leader of a primary health care team.
6. Hospitals no longer get their income from the government via the DHAs but by winning contracts. Doctors with their own budgets and DHAs are supposed to negotiate the best deal with the hospitals for their patients. How do you think these changes will affect the future of the NHS? Chance your arm on this question.

READING

Annual Report of the Health Service in England (HMSO).

Caring Less. The NHS and Community Care Bill – Labour's response (The Labour Party, 150 Walworth Road, London SE17 1JT).

Anne Marie Coyne, 'Stamping Out the Stamp', *Health and Social Service Journal*, 11 December 1976.

'Debate on NHS management', *Hansard*, vol. 93, No. 78, 14 March 1986.

'Debate on the Health Service and Community Care', *Hansard*, vol. 191, No. 107, 14 May 1991.

Leslie Doyal, *The Political Economy of Health* (Pluto Press, 1979).

Eighth Report from the Commons Social Services Committee, Session 1988–89: *Resourcing the National Health Service: The Government's plans for the future of the National Health Service* (HMSO, 19 July 1989).

Christopher Ham, *Health Policy in Britain*, 3rd edn (Macmillan, 1991).

Health Service Journal (published weekly).

Rudolf Klein, *The Politics of the National Health Service* (Longman, 1989).

Jeremy Laurence, 'Are We Getting Value for Money from the Health Service?', *New Society*, 26 August 1982.

Martin Loney, *The Politics of Greed* (Pluto Press, 1986), ch. 5.

T. H. Marshall, *Social Policy*, 5th edn (Hutchinson, 1985).

Alan Maynard, 'Privatizing the National Health Service', *Lloyds Bank Review*, April 1983.

'Minister's Statement on NHS Hospital Trusts', *Hansard*, vol. 190, No. 97, 29 April 1991.

NHS Management Inquiry Report – Griffiths Report (DHSS, 1983).

Report of the Community Nursing Review: Neighbourhood Nursing, A Focus for Care (HMSO, 1986).

Report of the Royal Commission on the National Health Service, Cmnd 7615 (HMSO, 18 July 1979).

Richard Taylor, *Medicine Out of Control* (Macmillan, 1979).

Royal Commission on Medical Education, Report 1965–1968, Cmnd 3569 (HMSO, 1968).

Sharing Resources for Health in England, Report of Resource Allocation Working Party (HMSO, 1976).

Special Report on the Government's White Paper 'Working for Patients' (The Council of the British Medical Association, 1989).

P. Townsend, N. Davidson and M. Whitehead, *Inequalities in Health, the Black Report and the Health Divide* (Penguin, 1988).

Working for Patients, Cm 555 (HMSO, January 1989).

9 Social Needs and Community Care

COMMUNITY CARE

Community care is helping people in need of care as far as possible in their own homes and neighbourhoods rather than in institutions. It provides help for the following groups – the elderly, mothers and young children, after-care of patients leaving hospital, handicapped children, maladjusted children, children in need of care and protection, the physically handicapped and the mentally handicapped.

Statutory responsibility for community care lies with local authorities working in collaboration with the DHAs, voluntary organisations and other interests. The Royal Commission on the Law relating to Mental Illness and Deficiency (1957) began the movement towards community care for, by stressing the need for community care in relation to the mentally handicapped, it created interest in the development of community care for other groups.

The Report of the Inter-departmental Committee on Local Authority and Allied Personal Social Services (Seebohm Report, 1968) was a further landmark in the development of community care. Prior to the implementation of the Seebohm Report, aid to the various categories of people needing help was compartmentalised, with each category having its own specialist social worker and there was little co-ordination between the different specialisms of social work. The Seebohm Report changed all that. It stressed that social need had many causes and therefore different specialist social workers must work together as a team. In other words, social need cannot be divided up so that each part can be successfully dealt with by a specialist social worker in that part, independently of other social workers. In line with this argument, the Report focussed attention on to the family as a unit because stresses within the family can give rise to different types of problems requiring help – for example, delinquency and parents' neglect of children. This was in line with the Ingleby Report (1960) which pointed out that the main reason why children had to be taken into care was the breakdown in family life. Before Seebohm one family could be visited by different specialist social workers, giving rise to overlapping of advice and sometimes confusion for the family. After Seebohm, the emphasis was on social workers of different specialisms looking at the family as a whole. This, it was hoped, would lead to the development of preventive work by anticipating stress within the family and trying to prevent it and so avoiding problems in the future. The new generic approach put forward by the Seebohm Report resulted in the social workers with different specialisms being brought together in one newly-created department of the local authorities called the Social Services Department. This was brought about by the 1970 Local Authorities Social Services Act. The new department became responsible for the care of children previously done by the local authority's Children's Department, the varied work done by the local authority Welfare Department and some services previously done by the local authority Health Department (see chapter 7).

To begin with, the implementation of the Report caused misgivings among social workers. Some interpreted it to mean that a social worker must be able to deal with all categories of need within the family; others interpreted the Report, as the Report intended, to mean that social workers still specialised but consulted among themselves on problem cases and families. The Social Services Department, being a very large department within the local authority, was better able to attract more resources for welfare than the previously smaller, segregated departments. It was also more accessible and there was a flood of claimants for help, necessitating a large increase in the number of social workers and other services (e.g. home helps, meals on wheels and so on). Enormous progress was made in the provision of help to those in need which probably would not have happened when it did without the Seebohm Report.

Another influential report was the Barclay Report published in 1982. It was well known that most caring of those in need of care was done, not by professionals, but by relatives, friends and neighbours. The Barclay Report emphasised the need for social workers to liaise with these unofficial helpers and with voluntary organisations. The social workers would still have a counselling role but also a managerial role in organising the unofficial carers – organising what Barclay called the 'social network'. Professor Pinker, a member of the committee, whilst agreeing that social workers must, where possible, seek the aid of relatives and friends and voluntary organisations, argued that there were not enough resources for social workers to organise a social network and, in any case, it was not advisable because it could lead to social workers getting involved in community action of a political nature in order to change the conditions which gave rise to or aggravated a client's problems. Social workers should concentrate on personal problems and leave campaigning to other organisations. However, if many of the problems which affect families and with which social workers have to deal arise from low incomes and a bad social environment, some social workers would argue that unless they campaigned for social reforms, they were simply acting as 'social tranquillisers' by persuading their clients 'to tolerate the intolerable'.

The role of social workers
1.   To help clients to understand better the nature of their problems.
2.   To give support and to advise their clients on how best to deal with their problems which involves:
     (a) putting their clients in touch with statutory and voluntary organisations which can help them;
     (b) if need be, themselves making known their clients' needs to these organisations
     (c) Working with clients without undermining their clients' independence.

There are those who want increased support for the informal carers by means of increased resources to an enlarged voluntary sector. Some people on the political right support this as a means of reducing the role of the State services. Others, usually on the political left, support it as a means of providing a more flexible, less bureaucratic and more democratic service and one likely to be more successful than local government in organising a social network of carers. But the voluntary organisations would still have to be mainly financed by the State and so bureaucracy would still be necessary to ensure taxpayers' money was being spent effectively. And is there any evidence to suggest that the voluntary organisations would be any more democratic in the sense of being accountable to the public than the State services which are responsible to elected representatives of the people at large? While the general consensus supports an increasing role for the voluntary sector there is no consensus for it being done at the expense of the State sector. The voluntary sector complements the State sector and can best develop by filling the gaps in the State services run by central and local government. But since April 1990 there is perhaps going to be an increasing role for the private sector (see below). The White Paper, published in 1989, outlining the Government's plans for community care (Cm 849), whilst acknowledging that most care is done by unofficial carers – relatives and friends – made no mention of a social network on the Barclay lines but it did accept, as recommended in the Griffiths report *Community Care: Agenda for Action* (1988), that local authorities should continue to have the main responsibility for community care. The proposals in the White

Paper began to be phased in as from April 1991 under the 1990 National Health and Community Care Act, but they will not be fully implemented until April 1993. In line with its proposals for the NHS, the Government plans to ensure that the private sector has a very much greater role in welfare provision, not just in the sphere of residential homes and nursing homes, as now, but also in home (domiciliary) and day care, so that one will speak of a 'mixed economy care'. The responsibilities of the health authorities and especially of the local authorities in relation to community care are now more clearly defined, making it easier, among other things, for the Government to keep a check on the extent and, in particular, the quality of care being provided. Thus local authorities now have to produce and publish plans for the development of community care services, bearing in mind, of course, the views of the health authorities and other organisations involved. The Secretary of State can ask to see the plans and issue guide-lines. Furthermore the plans have to be open to public inspection. In the monitoring of residential homes – private, voluntary and local authority homes – the local authorities have their own inspectorate, independent of the managers of the services in the Social Service departments. This is to ensure that monitoring is just as rigorous for local authority homes as for private and voluntary homes.

Unlike the plans for the NHS, where a market system ensures that the providers of a service do not fund it, a market system is only partially realised in the case of care as local authorities still provide most of the services and pay for them. However, under the new system local authorities are expected to give greater choice to clients and buy services, where appropriate, from the private sector by means of 'competitive tendering' . . . 'with no nationally set limits to the level of fees.' Buying of services from the private sector relates mainly to private residential homes and private nursing homes but the Government hopes that the private sector will eventually be brought into other spheres of care.

Local authorities make the initial assessment of the needs of a person needing care in conjunction with, where appropriate, the primary health care team of the Health Service and any other relevant organisations. After the assessment, the local authority has the duty of 'designing the care arrangements and secure their delivery within available resources.' Some people could be found to need hospital care. Local authorities can charge for services such as home help, home care, provision of meals and other day-care services but they take into consideration the financial circumstances of the person needing a particular service and for some of the above services, some local authorities make no charge.

The Elderly

The development of services for the elderly

In the last quarter of the nineteenth century there was a growing public awareness that old age was one important cause of poverty and, therefore, as part of the growing concern with poverty, there grew a demand for old-age pensions. The 1908 Old Age Pensions Act was the first major help to the aged poor outside the Poor Law. It provided means-tested pensions at 70, paid for out of taxation. A contributory pension scheme was introduced with the 1925 Widows, Orphans and Old Age Contributory Pensions Act. The main community services for the elderly were developed after the Second World War.

Today's services for the elderly (apart from the NHS)

1. There are state pensions for women at 60 and men at 65. The pension is not enough to live on by itself and those pensioners without other sufficient income can claim income support.

2. Residential accommodation is provided by local authorities for the elderly in need of care. This became a statutory duty under the 1948 National Assistance Act. But there are large variations in the availability of homes as between one local authority and another. The 1990 Act, referred to above, may help to remedy this. Not every elderly person requiring a place in a local authority home can get one. In many cases they find a place in a private home. Over a third of them received financial assistance from the DSS and, as over the years, more and more elderly went into private homes the cost to the DSS escalated considerably, especially after the passing of the 1984 Registered Homes Act which introduced registration and inspection by the local authorities of private residential homes. This led to an improved quality of service as many homes had been badly run with untrained staff. The DSS eventually fixed a maximum amount they would contribute which caused hardship to some residents as the maximum did not cover the cost of their care. Under the 1990 National Health and Community Act local authorities will now have this responsibility for payment. The Government envisages an improvement in the community services so that more people needing care can continue to live at home.

3. Domestic help and nursing attention are other statutory services which must be provided under the 1948 National Assistance Act. But they apply to all categories of people and not just the elderly.

4.   Meals can be provided in their homes to those elderly people who are housebound or who have difficulty in shopping. This 'meals-on-wheels' service is provided either by local authorities or by voluntary organisations.

Local authorities or voluntary organisations, or both, also provide the following services for the elderly.

5.   Day centres with recreational facilities.
6.   Social clubs.
7.   Friendly visits.
8.   Social workers' visits to the elderly to give advice and help.
9.   Independently of the work done by local authorities and voluntary organisations, some doctors make regular visits to their elderly patients.
10. Local authorities provide financial assistance for home adaptations considered necessary for the well-being of elderly people. Some of these adaptations are provided by the NHS. The powers and duties given to local authorities under 1948 National Assistance Act were extended under the 1968 Health Services and Public Health Act.

Three categories of old people

1.   Those who are able to live on their own or with relatives.
2.   Those needing residential accommodation but not medical care.
3.   Those requiring medical care.

Among those requiring medical care are those who can be helped in their own home by relatives or friends aided by home care services, those who are frail or dependent in residential homes, and those who must remain in hospital because they need long-term nursing care.

Factors which have aggravated the problem of the elderly

1.   Normally a society can look after its aged without much trouble because they only constitute a small proportion of the population. But in Britain the proportion of old people in the population has been increasing since the last quarter of the nineteenth century. The proportion of men over 65 and women over 60 in Great Britain today is approximately 16 per cent, whereas in 1911 it was 6.8 per cent. The reason for this increasing proportion of old people in the population is the decline in the birth rate from around

1870 and the increasing expectancy of life during the twentieth century.

2. Since 1945 a greater proportion of young people seek work away from their home area and live well away from their parents when they get married, leading to a greater isolation of the parents.
3. Smaller families result in there being fewer children to share the job of looking after ageing parents.
4. Rapid technological change has undermined tradition so that the opinions of older workers are less respected as their experiences relate to different sets of conditions.
5. Greater affluence since 1945 has increased the gap between living standards of those in work and those in retirement.
6. The increase in crime and the disorderly conduct of some young people, which, for the elderly, has created an atmosphere of menace.

What more should be done for the elderly?
We could make them feel more wanted. Should people be allowed to stay on at work longer if they wish to and are still useful? Many people are forced to retire when they are still capable of doing their work effectively, and going out to work gives them an interest among friends and helps to keep them fit. But some people, often trade unionists, object to a later retirement age, even if optional, because they say it would hold up promotions among younger people and would aggravate the unemployment problem.

Sheltered housing
Sheltered housing which local authorities, housing associations and some private builders provide for elderly people is now often the small bungalow type. This allows the elderly to continue to be part of the local community. A group of bungalows is normally under the supervision of a warden, who can be reached by the elderly by simply pressing a bell. Apart from this 'sheltered housing' there are residential homes for the elderly but many of them though not all, are of the institutional type, cut off from the local community, and perhaps progress should be made by constructing more non-institutional-type housing.

One interesting development in just a few local authorities is the setting-up of foster homes for the elderly.

Some local authority services for the elderly are optional and there are wide variations between one local authority and another in the provision of services for the elderly. Perhaps more should be done by central government to spur on the laggards. The 1990 Act may encourage this.

We must remember, however, that many of the elderly are leading happier and healthier lives than were possible in other eras.

Mothers and Young Children

At the end of the nineteenth century there were, apart from growing sympathy for the poor, three main factors which furthered the introduction of state services to protect the health of mothers and young children (see also Chapter 6):

1. There was concern at the continuing high infant mortality rate.
2. The Boer War recruitment shock led to talk of the physical deterioration of the nation.
3. The introduction of compulsory education in 1880 put all children on show to the authorities for the first time and very many children were seen to be in poor health.

The 1902 Midwives Act ensured that midwives were properly trained, and in 1936 local authorities were made responsible for ensuring an adequate number of them in their areas.

By 1915 local authorities had powers to supervise the progress of a mother and her newly born baby. The 1918 Maternity and Child Welfare Act permitted local authorities, with financial assistance from the central government, to provide services for expectant mothers and their children up to the age of 5. Under the 1946 National Health Service Act it was made obligatory for local authorities to provide this service.

Under the 1946 Act part of the service for mothers and young children was the provision of welfare foods like orange juice, vitamin tablets, cod-liver oil, but in the interwar years those local authorities which ran the service provided milk only.

Today's services for mothers and young children

1. The district health authorities are now responsible for the clinics which provide ante- and post-natal medical and dental care for mothers and for the regular examination of their children. The clinics have the services of doctors, nurses and health visitors, and many have dentists. In quite a number of areas now the clinics are part of a health centre where many more services are found. The clinics give a great deal of advice to the mother. They also provide welfare foods.
2. Health visitors visit mother and child in the home. They see that the baby is being looked after properly, give advice to the mother and, if they see any strains within the family relationship, they may ask a social worker to call round.

3. A mother with her young child need not necessarily go to the clinic; she could get all the advice and help she requires from her family doctor.

Young mothers who go out to work

Day nurseries are provided by some local authorities and private organisations where a mother can leave her young child under expert guidance while she goes out to work. Places are occasionally offered for children of ill or disabled mothers, but, as places are scarce, priority is usually given to single parents or others in special need. There are also childminders who in their own homes look after a group of children. Under the Nurseries and Child Minders Regulation Act 1948, private nurseries and child-minding establishments must be registered with the local authority, which has powers of inspection but these private childminders receive support and advice from the local authority. In recent years fears have been expressed that some children are being left with unregistered childminders where conditions may be unsatisfactory. But fears have also been voiced at the inadequacy of much child-minding, whether registered or not. To some people the answer is more local authority nurseries. They see day nurseries not only as a means of helping mothers to go out to work but also a means of giving the child a fuller and richer life, of special value to those children who live in urban areas where there are few open spaces. It is claimed that day nurseries will compensate these children to some extent for their poor home background, which puts them at an educational disadvantage when they start school.

Day nurseries expanded during the Second World War when there was a need to employ as many women as possible in war work, although many were shut down after the war. There are those now who consider day nurseries an unnecessary luxury because they say they are used by women who simply want to maintain a reasonable level of income by going out to work at the ratepayers' and their children's expense. This criticism does not, of course, apply to one-parent families. The Conservative government view is that it is not its job to provide a free or heavily subsidised day nursery service to enable parents to go out to work. Parents themselves have the main responsibility to see that their young children receive proper care. But the government does provide some financial help to voluntary organisations concerned with the under-5s. It is also encouraging employers to provide nursery carers.

There has been no real proof offered that children whose parents are at work all day suffer in any way even if they have to roam the streets awaiting one of their parent's return. On the other hand, there is no proof that they do not suffer. Some working mothers might argue that the money they earn enables them to provide little extras for the children and some could argue that it keeps the family out of poverty.

Single Parents

Arising from the increasing number of couples – married or unmarried – who separate, there has been a big rise in the number of single parents, ten per cent of whom are fathers. Unmarried mothers account for about a third of the total and about two-thirds arise from the break-up of marriage, although there is a smaller number comprising widows and widowers. Seventy per cent of single parents rely on income support and the increasing number has meant increased Government expenditure which has led the Government to query why there has been a big decline in the maintenance payments to the mother left to look after the children. Thus about four out of five single mothers receive no maintenance support. However, if maintenance was paid to these mothers, the majority would be no better off as the amount of maintenance would be deducted from their income support. Government policy is now to trace husbands who are not paying maintenance and to bring them to court. But so much separation and divorce give rise to the possibility of more emotionally disturbed children.

The unmarried mother

Because unmarried mothers have tended to be looked on with disapproval, local authority services for them have been slow in developing. Voluntary organisations have been the main providers of help, especially the religious organisations.

Today the unmarried mother makes use of the community health and welfare services and the services of her doctor in the same way as any other mother, but local authorities are encouraged by the government to provide the following extra services for unmarried mothers, though there is no statutory obligation for them to do so:

1. Local authority social workers try to help them.
2. Local authorities co-operate with voluntary organisations in the provision of hostels and homes for pregnant women or unmarried mothers who need residential care. Again, it is the religious organisations who do most in this field.
3. Where an unmarried mother is unable to look after her child, it may be taken into care of the local authority, or the mother can have it adopted. Adoption is governed by the 1958 Adoption Act and the 1975 Children Act.

Arising from the high mortality rate among illegitimate children, there was set up in 1918 the National Council for the Unmarried Mother and Her Child. It is now called the National Council for One-Parent Families. The body co-ordinates the main organisations concerned with illegitimacy. It is a kind of pressure group to protect the interests of children and their parents. Thus it helps not only unmarried mothers and their families but also the growing number of one-parent families, including single parent fathers, arising from divorce and desertion. It is in regular touch with social workers throughout the country and it can refer any woman needing help to the appropriate social worker. There are other voluntary organisations which exist to help one-parent families – for example, a self-help group called Gingerbread.

Schoolchildren

School meals and school milk

The first state services for schoolchildren were school meals for needy elementary schoolchildren under the 1906 Education (Provision of Meals) Act and medical inspection of elementary schoolchildren under the 1907 Education (Administrative Provisions) Act. They were introduced because of the fear that the nation was deteriorating physically after so many volunteers for the Boer War had been found unfit. Previously some school meals for poor children had been provided by charitable organisations, but their role declined after the 1906 Act. School meals were not obligatory; local authorities could please themselves whether they provided them, and until 1914 their entire cost was borne from the rates. But in 1914 the government gave a 50 per cent grant towards them. This was of particular help to the poorer voluntary schools. During the interwar years school meals were provided in local authority secondary schools and an increasing proportion of children obtained school meals, the local authorities receiving payment from parents who could afford to pay.

In 1921 free milk was provided to needy elementary schoolchildren. The 1934 Milk Act enabled elementary schoolchildren to obtain one third of a pint of milk a day for a halfpenny. The milk was subsidised by the Milk Marketing Board. School dinners and school milk, even if not universally applied, did a great deal to improve the health of children.

The Second World War necessitated married women going out to work to help the war effort. Mid-day meals for schoolchildren and day nurseries became a patriotic necessity. The 1944 Education Act made it obligatory for local authorities to provide school meals and milk for all children who wanted them. The intention was that both school meals and school milk should be free, but, although the milk was free, school meals were free only to the needy but subsidised for everyone else.

Greater affluence has led to greater selectivity in the social services, and in 1971 free school milk in secondary education was abolished, as well as for the 7 to 11 age group in junior schools. To those who said free milk for everyone undermined parental responsibility, supporters of free milk replied that we must protect children from irresponsible parents. Local authorities now have discretion as to what milk, meals and other refreshments to provide and what charges to make. Meals have no longer to meet 'minimal nutritional standards'. Some local authorities have abolished school meals in primary schools and one has abolished them for both primary and secondary schools. At present those on income support receive free school meals. Presumably in those schools where school meals have been abolished children whose parents fall in the above categories will receive a packed lunch. Under the 1986 Social Security Act the discretionary power of a local authority to provide free school meals to low income families was withdrawn from April 1988. People on Family Credit used to get free school meals but this ceased from April 1988 but families receive a higher cash benefit instead.

Originally school meals were to ensure that children received one good meal a day. Fears are now expressed that this will no longer be the case for many children. In fact, there has been a big drop in the number of children taking school meals. Many do not receive a satisfactory diet at home and many buy junk food with the money their parents give them for meals. Again as with the earlier issue of school milk, there are those who say it is up to parents to ensure their children are properly fed and not the State. Ideally yes, but circumstances result in many families not doing just that so why should the children suffer? Under the 1944 Education Act part of the object of school meals was to train children in good food habits and table manners, but since the teachers revolted against the supervising of school meals, the social training part has been neglected.

School meals are very useful where the mother goes out to work or the child has a long way to travel to school, but should they be subsidised for everyone, even for those children whose parents can afford to pay for them? This brings us back to the problem of selectivity discussed earlier.

The School Health Service

In spite of the progress made in the health of schoolchildren due to school meals, the School Health Service and improvements in the general standard of health, progress was slowed down because of general malnutrition. Before the introduction of subsidised milk in 1934, about one quarter to one third of elementary schoolchildren were undernourished. Evacuation of schoolchildren during the Second World War brought home to the better-off the extent of this under-nourishment – they had not realised just how widespread it was. After 1945, with the introduction of the National Health Service, the School Health Service expanded, but the local education authority was still responsible for its administration, though the principal school medical officer was usually the medical officer of health. Today it is administered by the district health authorities. There is now a feeling in some quarters that it is no longer necessary to inspect all schoolchildren and that school nurses should concentrate on children with special needs.

Handicapped Children

The first legislation giving help to handicapped children was the 1893 Elementary Education (Blind and Deaf Children) Act which empowered local authorities to pay for the education and maintenance of blind and deaf children. The 1899 Education (Defective and Epileptic) Act helped mentally defective children. But comprehensive legislation to provide for the needs of handicapped children had to await the 1944 Education Act.

How handicapped children of school age are helped today
The local authority must assess the special educational needs of the handicapped child. It first arranges a medical examination in co-operation with the district health authority. In deciding what to do after receiving the medical report, the local authority considers the views not only of the doctor but also of the teacher or educational psychologist and the wishes of the child's parents. If the parents are dissatisfied with the decision of the local authority, they can appeal to a local appeals committee and ultimately to the Secretary of State.

If at all possible, the child is sent to an ordinary school on the principle that a handicapped child should lead as normal a life as possible. But if the disability is too severe, the local authority may send the child to a residential school or special day school where treatment will also be provided. The blind and the deaf must normally be treated in a special school.

Children with learning difficulties are the largest group needing special treatment. These are educationally retarded children and this retardation can be due either to innate causes or to the child's environment. Most of the children in the subnormal group go to an ordinary school; most of the remainder of those in the subnormal group go to special schools.

But there are children with very severe abnormalities who cannot be educated even in special schools – but they are still the responsibility of the local education authority, even though many of them are in hospital.

Tuition may be given at home in exceptional circumstances.

Maladjusted Children

Under The National Health Service Act of 1946 prevention and treatment is provided in local authority child guidance clinics or in hospital child guidance clinics. Some child guidance is provided by voluntary organisations. One of the jobs of the clinics is to help parents understand their children better and repair any bad relationships between parent and child. In certain cases the clinics may advise that the child lives away from home for a while in a hostel or special school.

Children in Need of Care and Protection

Historical development

Before 1900 children needing care were looked after by the Poor Law or by voluntary organisations like Dr Barnardo's, the NSPCC, and so on. Mainly because of the influence of voluntary organisations, by the end of the nineteenth century laws had been passed against cruelty to and exploitation of children.

A more general concern for children arose, as mentioned earlier, because of the continuing high infant mortality rate, the state's new responsibility for elementary education and concern for the nation's fitness arising from the Boer war recruitment shock. Other factors were revelations of baby-farming (where parents paid unscrupulous people to look after one or more of their children but in reality were ridding themselves of the children), and the concern over the falling birth rate.

The 1908 Children Act strengthened the law on fostering and the inspection procedures for voluntary homes for children. It abolished imprisonment for children under 16 and introduced juvenile courts to keep children away from criminals and it introduced remand homes to avoid children having to go to prison while awaiting trial. The prison atmosphere was considered likely to further corrupt the child.

The 1933 Children and Young Persons Act gave powers to magistrates of juvenile courts to remove children and young persons 'in need of care and protection' from the custody of their parents or guardians and make alternative arrangements for them, usually in foster homes or in children's homes run by the Poor Law, then administered by the public assistance committees of local authorities.

Later acts have been mainly concerned with improving the procedures for dealing with children and young persons brought before a juvenile court either because they were delinquents or because they were quite law abiding but were not being cared for adequately by parents or guardian or were simply abandoned. And it is the local authorities which are still responsible for taking such children into care, providing they are under 17 years. The latest act is the 1989 Children Act, operative from 14 October 1991. The main aim of the 1989 Act is an old one – how to reconcile the rights of parents with the protection of children. In this connection, the Act 'creates a new balance' in favour of parents. It implies that local authorities must do more than they have in the past to help families at risk so as to minimise the need to take children into care. In co-operation with parents and others who are responsible for children, local authorities must help children in need with training and provide advice, when necessary, to all parents and others caring for such children. And for all children aged five or under needing care, there should be day care and for children of school age needing care, there should be supervised activities outside school hours and in school holidays.

As with all community services for which local government is responsible, local authorities must publish information about day care services and introduce a complaints procedure with an 'independent element'. Local authorities must also keep a register of disabled children.

If, however, children have to be taken away from parents and placed in the care of the local authority, it should be done, as far as possible, with the agreement of parents. When a care order has been made by the court, the local authority might send the child or young person to a residential community home, or have him or her placed with a relative or other suitable person – for example, foster parents who are paid an allowance and who can eventually apply for legal custody of the child. A child might be adopted. Local authorities, under a previous act, have to provide an adoption service which they can run themselves or arrange for voluntary organisations to run. A child must only be put in secure accommodation if he or she is likely to abscond or come to harm. For a local authority to take a child into care against the parents' wishes, a court order is necessary. Administrative measures to force compulsory going into care were abolished under the 1989 Act. Local authorities must continue to look after a child or young person when he or she leaves care until the age of 21.

Apart from care orders, there are other orders a juvenile court can make for safeguarding a child's or young person's interest. In the case of young offenders the court may make a supervision order where an offender remains at home under the supervision of a local authority social worker or probation officer for a specified period up to three years. The offender may receive 'intermediate treatment' to give him or her a new interest and environment which may involve living away from home. It normally involves constructive and remedial activities. The 1982 Criminal Justice Act stressed the importance of the court being involved with the supervisor in laying down what activities the offender should carry out under the supervision order. The assumption must be that supervision in some cases had meant too easy a regime. Unlike a probation order, an offender cannot be brought back to court if he or she breaks the supervision order.

Care and supervision orders can only be made on the application of a local authority or an authorised person, eg. an officer of the NSPCC. The Secretary of State has powers to authorise other persons to apply.

In the 1970s there was concern, in some quarters, over the 1969 Children and Young Persons Act which was intended to give social workers an increasing role in the treatment of juvenile delinquents, with the aim of keeping young people, as far as possible, out of juvenile courts. Thus, under the Act, authorised bodies – the police or the NSPCC – wishing to bring a delinquent had normally to consult the local authority social services department and the delinquent was only to be brought before the court if the police or the NSPCC, after consultation with the local authority social workers, were still convinced that nothing less than a court order would do. This procedure was criticised especially by magistrates, who felt that replacing the statutory prescribed action of the courts by informal action out of court often meant no effective action at all. Defenders of the Act pointed out that at a brief court hearing it is not always possible for the magistrates to know what is best for the offender, even when the offender's background has been described in a report to the magistrates by the social worker or the probation and after-care officer. The local authority, on the other hand, has the help, not only of social workers, but of teachers and psychiatrists. However, that part of the Act requiring initial consultation with social workers was never fully implemented. The police, under certain conditions, were allowed to prosecute young offenders before receiving the comments of a social worker and the degree to which the police did consult first with social workers varied greatly as between one police force and another. What seemed to support the views of those who criticised the 1969 Act was the big increase in juvenile crime after the Act was passed. On the other hand, the British Association of Social Workers stated at the time that 'there is a clear correlation between acute delinquent behaviour and social deprivation. Nearly all types of crime have greatly increased since 1969 and the causes are the social and physical environment'.

Physically Handicapped People

Legislation to help the blind, deaf and epileptic goes back to the nineteenth century, but services of a comprehensive nature for the physically handicapped came with the 1946 National Health Service Act and the 1948 National Assistance Act.

Services today for physically handicapped people
1. The family doctor, who is the key link with the various services for the handicapped.
2. Hospital treatment, which can include physiotherapy, remedial gymnastics, occupational therapy, provision of appliances, the medical social worker's help in resettlement, and so on.
3. Local authority services, most of which are provided under the 1948 National Assistance Act and the 1970 Chronically Sick and Disabled Persons Act. The significance of the latter Act is that it makes mandatory on local authorities much of what had been permissive in earlier legislation. It was hoped that this would bring the bad local authorities up to the standard of the good.

In more detail the main services are:

(a) maintenance of registers of handicapped people in the local authority area, as laid down in the 1948 Act, but emphasised by the 1970 Chronically Sick and Disabled Persons Act, to find out who the disabled are and to let them know what services are available to them
(b) practical assistance in the home
(c) help in getting a radio, television, books or other recreational facilities
(d) provision of recreational facilities outside the home
(e) help in travelling to and from home to take part in the above facilities
(f) adaptation of the handicapped person's home to make it easier to live in or the provision of residential accommodation for the disabled
(g) help in taking a holiday
(h) provision of meals in the home, or elsewhere if needed
(i) help in obtaining a telephone and, if needed, special equipment to use it
(j) under the Disabled Persons (Employment) Act of 1958 local authorities can provide work for the disabled under special conditions. In

some cases disabled people have been sent to day centres where they do work for private companies. This has given rise to criticism of exploitation of the disabled.

The following provisions are special to the 1970 Act. In so far as it is 'practicable and reasonable', buildings open to the public either freely or by payment should have facilities in and outside the building for the disabled, and this includes toilets. Such buildings should have a notice stating that provision has been made for the disabled.

Apart from these special services the handicapped have those services which are provided for all who need them whether handicapped or not – domestic help, health visitor, home nursing, ambulance service, and so on.

Social security
Under the National Insurance scheme there are special benefits for disablement including an attendance allowance for certain categories of badly disabled. The disabled can also get a higher rate of Income Support.

Services for special categories of disabled people
These special categories are the blind, the deaf, epileptics and those suffering from TB. Local authorities or voluntary organisations supported by local authorities provide special workshops for the blind or provide them with work to do at home. Local authorities and voluntary organisations provide recreational facilities for all the special categories. For deaf children local authorities provide special residential schools. In certain cases home tuition is provided (see also Chapter 11). There are local authority after-care officers who specialise in TB cases. For severely disabled people, residential accommodation may be provided by local authorities and voluntary organisations and those living at home who need paid domestic support can in some cases, obtain help from the Independent Living Fund set up in 1988 to run for 5 years. When set up, it was given £5 million by the Government.*

Mentally Disordered People

There are two main types of mentally disordered people. There are those who have a normal intelligence but are mentally ill; there are those who have mental disorder because they are mentally handicapped. Psychopathic

* See Chapter 14 for employment services for disabled people

disorders may or may not include mental handicap but the patient is capable of abnormal aggressive or seriously irresponsible conduct. The lack of knowledge concerning either mental illness or mental handicap led in previous centuries to fear and superstition and hence mentally disordered people were isolated from the rest of the community. By the late half of the nineteenth century, fear of illegal detention led to the 1890 Lunacy Act, which provided for the proper certification, care and control of people with unsound minds. Earlier, under the 1845 Lunatics Act, a permanent lunacy Commission had been set up.

It was the development of psychology in the twentieth century, pioneered by Freud, which led to a more rational attitude to mental disorder. The Royal Commission on Lunacy and Mental Disorder 1924–6 (the Macmillan Commission) stressed the interdependence of mental and physical illness and the need for psychiatric treatment. The 1930 Mental Treatment Act made it possible for mental patients to be treated in mental hospitals without certification, and out-patients clinics for mental illness followed, thus reducing the gap between the general medical services and psychiatric treatment. The 1959 Mental Health Act, based on the Report of the Royal Commission on the Laws relating to Mental Illness and Mental Deficiency of 1957, narrowed the gap even further by stressing the need to integrate mental and physical illness.

The 1959 Act, amended by the 1982 Mental Health (Amendment) Act, consolidated by the 1983 Mental Health Act is the basis of today's services for the mentally disordered and its underlying principle is that mentally disordered people should be treated, as far as possible, in the same way as those who are physically ill. Community care should, wherever possible, take the place of long periods in hospital.

The 1959 Act helped to lessen the stigma attached to mental illness, and thus an increasing number of people have been encouraged to come forward for voluntary treatment. Better methods of treatment have also encouraged this. In the 1960s there developed the policy of treating mentally ill people in psychiatric units of general hospitals rather than sending them to special mental hospitals.

Today's hospital services for the mentally disordered
According to the seriousness of the mental disorder, there are out-patient facilities, and facilities for short-stay, medium-stay and long-stay patients. For the long-stay elderly patient suffering from chronic mental disorder there is little which can be done except to give kindness. Dangerous psychopaths and others severely mentally ill are sent to special hospitals like Broadmoor, Rampton or Moss Side.

Admission to hospital is arranged normally with the family doctor and most go willingly. But there are safeguards for those who have to go compulsorily. An application for compulsory admission must be based on two medical recommendations, one of which must be by a practitioner with approved experience in psychiatry (approved by the district health authority). The other doctor must have personal knowledge of the patient. A representative of the social services department of the local authority must also sign the application. The consent of the patient's nearest relative must also be obtained, though he or she can be overruled, in which case the relative can appeal to a mental health review tribunal. Compulsory admission may be for assessment or for treatment. The patient or someone on his behalf can appeal to the mental health review tribunal against continued detention. There was criticism that compulsory admission should operate within a legal framework so that there would be safeguards at law for the patient. The 1983 Mental Health Act goes a long way to meet this criticism. It provided for the setting up of a Mental Health Commission to keep under review the care and treatment of patients. The Commission has to present a report of its activities to Parliament every two years. It appoints the medical practitioners authorised to give treatment, as well as appointing people to make regular visits to patients and examine their records and listen to their complaints. The Secretary of State has overall responsibility. In appeals to the mental health review tribunal against continued detention, patients are now entitled to be legally represented at the tribunal. They can now sue the responsible authority for wrongful detention. Any medical practitioner authorised by or on behalf of the patient, approved by the Secretary of State, can examine hospital records in connection with an appeal to the tribunal. Hospital and nursing home managers must keep patients informed of their rights, especially their right to appeal to the tribunal. There is now an automatic referral to the tribunal when three years have elapsed since the last referral. There are stronger controls over treatment, especially that involving psycho-surgery. In spite of the above safeguards, there is still criticism that the review tribunal gives much greater credence to the evidence of the hospital doctors than that of the patient and his representative. The balance, it is argued, is unfair, and what is needed are trained judges on the tribunal. Another suggestion is that the government should appoint someone as an advocate for all patients appealing to a tribunal.

The 1983 Act lays down that the district health authorities, the local authorities social services departments and voluntary organisations, should be involved where after-care treatment is necessary. The mental welfare officers of local authorities social services departments had the main responsibility for after care and since 1984 have been known as psychiatric social workers.

In line with the principle referred to above of treating mentally disordered people as far as possible in the same way as physically ill people, the 1983 Act gives voluntary (called informal) patients the vote (previously they were disenfranchised).

A person convicted of a criminal offence can be sent to a hospital if the court is satisfied that, on the evidence of two doctors, he or she is mentally ill and hospital treatment is the most suitable way of dealing with the convicted person.

Community services

Local authorities have psychiatric social workers, community psychiatric nurses and home helps who visit the homes of the mentally disordered. Social workers have special responsibility in connection with sending a person to hospital. They make the initial assessment of the problem and give advice to the relatives.

Local authorities, by themselves or in conjunction with voluntary organisations, provide day centres and social clubs, and for the mentally handicapped who are able to live at home they provide training centres for the development of skills and aptitudes. Often they can earn a little in sheltered conditions. For those who cannot live at home some local authorities provide residential training centres or hostels. Some of these are used as a kind of halfway house for those who have been in hospital but are not yet ready for community life. Health authority services include health visitors and domiciliary nursing.

Some local authorities provide homes for old people who are mentally infirm, though they may be looked after in normal residential homes for the elderly.

Under the 1984 Registered Homes Act, private nursing homes for the mentally handicapped have to be registered with the district health authority.

In spite of the official blessing for community care for the mentally handicapped, there are fears that there are still, in many areas, not enough resources to give adequate support to the mentally handicapped transferred from hospital to the community. Central government provides 70 per cent of the money allocated for this purpose – local authorities are supposed to provide 30 per cent. However, many local authorities have financial problems aggravated by the community charge. This may slow down discharges into the community and the level of support for those already in the community, as with other categories like the elderly, may not be as good as it should be. In fact, there is still uncertainty on how to deal with mentally handicapped people in the community. It is now becoming more accepted that a mixture of residential and community provision is perhaps best.

The community services are especially important in giving support to parents who have mentally handicapped children.

The family doctor
The doctor plays an important role in that he or she is normally the first contact in the case of mental disorder and is the link with all the other services. Some doctors give psychiatric treatment for the less serious forms of mental illness.

SUMMARY

In spite of a 68 per cent increase in real terms in the money spent on community care services between 1980 and 1988, there has been much criticism that institutions are being closed too fast for community care services to cope adequately. What growth there has been in community care is unevenly distributed as between the different categories of care and as between the various local authorities. Some local authorities have been reluctant to use joint finance money to develop community care because of what they consider to be financial pressures imposed on them by the Central Government. The new strategy for community care, phased in from 1991, should help to give more purposeful direction and a more even development of the services throughout the country thanks to the greater central control. And, as between the health authorities, voluntary organisations, private bodies and local authorities which provide community care, it is the local authorities which now have been clearly designated as the bodies responsible for its successful operation, this should encourage local authorities to sharpen their management of the services. However, this does necessitate local authorities having adequate finance. As late as September 1991 there was criticism that some local authorities were still unprepared for the implementing of the 1989 Children Act in the following month. The previous assumption that community care was cheaper than institutional care is now being questioned. As with the National Health Service, there will never be enough money for community care especially as demand for it is likely to increase and so, for some services, a form of rationing will continue to be inevitable.

There is also the problem of ensuring adequate financial support for the informal carers who are the main providers of care, usually members of the family of the person needing care. More women at work outside the home and more divorce has, to some extent, undermined this source of help.

The future will see the private sector and voluntary organisations playing an increasing role in the provision of community care services giving rise to the now fashionable term – 'a mixed economy of services' or 'pluralism'.

ASSIGNMENTS

1. What special problems now face the elderly? What services are available to the elderly? To help answer this question write to Age Concern (National Old People's Welfare Council) and ask for information on the needs of the elderly.
2. 'The 1969 Children and Young Persons Act worked well for the vast majority of young offenders but not the small minority of persistent offenders.' Give your views on this statement and if possible get the views of magistrates and social workers.
3. With the growth of 'women's liberation', there is a greater emphasis today than ever on the needs of mothers and young children. Discuss what you consider to be their main needs and how far they are being provided by the state and voluntary bodies.
4. List the duties imposed upon the local authorities by the 1970 Chronically Sick and Disabled Persons Act for helping the disabled. How far do you think local authorities have carried out these duties in full? To help with this write to the Royal Association for Disability and Rehabilitation and ask how far it thinks local authorities have done their statutory duty in connection with the Act. At the same time find out what services your own local authority provides for the disabled.
5. What is meant by *community care*? Illustrate by reference to any one category of people needing help in your local authority – for example, the mentally disordered, the physically handicapped, the elderly, and so on.
6. 'Most real human welfare still comes from society and not the State' (A. H. Halsey). Discuss.

READING

An Introduction to The Children Act 1989 (HMSO, 1989).
Barclay Report, *Social Workers, Their Role and Tasks* (National Institute of

Social Work, 1982).

Michael Bender, 'Crisis of Closure, Analysis of the Effect of the Move from Mental Health Institutions to Community Care', *The Health Service Journal*, 17 April 1986.

Britain 1992: An Official Handbook (HMSO).

Caring for People: Community Care in the next decade and beyond, Cm 849 (HMSO, 1989).

Curtis Report, *Report of the Inter-departmental Committee on the Care of Children*, Cmnd 6922 (HMSO, 1946).

'Debate on Health Service and Community Care', *Hansard*, vol. 191, no. 107, 14 May 1991.

Fifth Report from Commons Social Services Select Committee, Session 1989–90, *Community Care: carers* (HMSO, 1990).

John Forsyth and Hugh Prysor-Jones, 'Social Workers: Society pays to keep the ugliness hidden', *The Listener*, 6 February 1986.

G. Fulcher, *Disabling Policies* (Falmer Press, 1989).

Sir Roy Griffiths, *Community Care: An Agenda for Action* (HMSO, 1988).

Growing Older: the White Paper on the Elderly, Cmnd 8173 (HMSO, 1981).

Health and Welfare: The Development of Community Care, Cmnd 3022 (HMSO, 1966).

C. Hicks, *Who cares – Looking after People at Home* (Virago, 1988).

Ingleby Report, *Report of the Committee on Children and Young Persons*, Cmnd 1191 (HMSO, 1960).

Norman Jackson, 'The Privatisation of Welfare', *Social Policy and Administration*, May 1989.

Jeremy Laurence, 'The Selection of Foster Parents', *New Society*, 9 May 1986.

Review of the Mental Health Act 1969, Cmnd 7320 (HMSO, 1978).

Second Report from the Commons Social Services Committee, Session 1983–84, *Children in Care*, HC360 (HMSO, 1984).

Second Report from the Commons Social Services Committee, Session 1984–85: *Community Care with Special Reference to Adult Mentally Ill and Mentally Handicapped People*, HC13 (HMSO, 1985).

Seebohm Report, *Report of the Committee on Local Authority and Allied Personal Social Services*, Cmnd 3703 (HMSO, 1968).

Sir Thomas Skyrme, *The Changing Image of the Magistracy*, 2nd edn (Macmillan, 1983), ch. 8, 'The Juvenile Courts'.

A. Tilsley, *NHS hospitals and primary healthcare* (National Association of Health Authorities, 1986).

Alan Walker, 'A Caring Community' in Howard Glennerster (ed.), *The Future of the Welfare State* (Heinemann, 1983).

10 Education

Before 1870 education was left entirely to private enterprise in accordance with the prevailing theory of *laissez-faire*. The state's role was limited:

1. It provided grants to the Nonconformist and Anglican Church schools called voluntary schools. The first grant was given in 1833.
2. It provided a certain amount of teacher-training which was the responsibility of a committee of the Privy Council originally set up in 1839 to supervise the grants. The committee also employed inspectors to spread knowledge on educational matters.
3. Under the 1833 Factory Act children who worked in textile mills, except lace and silk mills, had to be provided by their employers with two hours' education every working day.
4. Some Boards of Guardians gave education to pauper children in workhouse schools.

The Church schools were the main providers of education for the working class, though dame schools, which were usually schools run by ladies in their own homes, also gave education to a fair number of working-class children. The middle and upper classes were educated in endowed grammar schools and public schools and many went on to university. Education for the working class was limited mainly to reading, writing and arithmetic.

The 1870 Education Act
This Act introduced state schools for the first time. It set up locally elected school boards to provide schools, financed out of local rates, in areas where no voluntary schools existed or where voluntary schools were inadequate to ensure a school place for every child. These schools were to provide an elementary education for children from age 5 to 13. In 1880 attendance was made compulsory in all schools until the age of 10. It was raised to 11 in 1893 and 12 in 1899. But under the 'half-time' system, abolished by the 1918 Education Act, children who had reached a certain level of attainment could attend school for part of the day and work the rest. In spite of the 1918 Act, there were still about 70 000 half-timers as late as 1922.

The 1870 Act provided a reasonable compromise between those who wanted denominational schools and those who wanted secular education. The reasons for the Act were economic, political and humanitarian.

1.   Although most children received an elementary education under the voluntary system, it was felt there were still too many gaps in it, especially as more and more literate workers with skills were needed for industry and commerce. In fact, economic necessity was perhaps the main reason for the Act. The growing competition after 1870 from the new industrial powers of Germany and the USA underlined this.

2.   The 1867 Reform Act gave the vote to certain categories of working men in the towns. Hence, it was felt there was the need for the new section of the electorate to be reasonably educated to ensure it voted 'intelligently'. When introducing the Bill, the minister, W. E. Forster, underlined the above two points: 'Our industrial prosperity, the safe working of our constitutional system and our national power depended upon it.'

3.   To a great number of people, it was good in itself to give education to anyone who could benefit from it.

In spite of the above, the Act had its opponents who felt it would make the working class discontented with their lowly position in society and less inclined to be obedient to their 'superiors'. And when compulsory education came, some thought it an infringement of personal liberty.

The 1899 Board of Education Act

Before 1899 three bodies were responsible for education: the Education Committee of the Privy Council was responsible for elementary education; the Science and Art Committee of the Privy Council was responsible for secondary and technical education; and the Charity Commission supervised the endowed schools, which gave a grammar school education. The work of the three bodies needed co-ordinating as there was much overlapping. One of the recommendations of the Royal Commission on Secondary Education of 1895 (the Bryce Report) was that there should be a central authority to stop this overlapping. The Board of Education Act 1899 created the Board of Education to provide this central co-ordinating body. It had a minister at its head responsible to Parliament.

Another recommendation of the Bryce Committee, which was implemented by the 1899 Act, was the setting up of a consultative committee of the Board of Education on which distinguished people could serve and investigate and make reports on different aspects of education. The Bryce Committee felt that education should not be solely the responsibility of the representatives and officials of the central and local government. The consultative committee lasted until 1944, when it was replaced by two central advisory councils – one for England and one for Wales. These too, have now been abolished.

The 1902 Education Act

This Act introduced a state system of secondary education which benefited brighter working-class children. Previously secondary education could only be obtained at public schools and endowed grammar schools, though the top forms of some board schools had given some secondary education until it was ruled illegal in 1899 as going beyond the powers of the 1870 Act. Under the 1902 Act children were to be selected at 11 for the state secondary schools. Some working-class leaders preferred the alternative system of developing the elementary schools so that they provided both elementary and secondary education without selection.

The 1902 Act abolished the school boards, and both elementary and secondary education were put under the control of county councils and county borough councils, created under the 1888 Local Government Act. Boroughs with a population over 10000 and urban districts with a population over 20000 were allowed to administer elementary education under delegation from the county councils.

The most controversial part of the Act was the putting of the Church schools (i.e. the voluntary schools) under the administration of the local authorities subject to their managers retaining certain rights over the appointment of teachers. This enabled the Church schools to receive money from the rate fund, and many people objected to this. But the Church schools needed the money as many had fallen behind the board schools because voluntary subscriptions did not equal the money the board schools received from the rates.

The Act also empowered local authorities to provide technical colleges and adult education.

One of the reasons for the Act was again the need for an efficient labour force. Business firms were growing in size and more technicians and managers were wanted.

There was also the desire to help the Church schools financially to help them continue to play a worthy part in the educational system.

There was the desire for a tidier administrative pattern away from *ad hoc* boards to local councils, and this was also in line with democratic trends.

The sort of secondary education the Bryce Report of 1895 had recommended for the working class was of a practical kind, with craftwork in mind. The fact that the local authority secondary schools imitated the endowed grammar schools in the type of education they provided was due mainly to Robert Morant, who drafted the Bill and became Permanent Secretary of the Board of Education in 1903.

The 1918 Education Act

This Act raised the school-leaving age to 14 with no exemptions and recommended it be raised later to 15. It introduced compulsory day release from industry so that young people under 18 could attend school for an equivalent period of three half-days a week, but economic conditions in the interwar years virtually killed this idea.

The day-release scheme under the Act arose from the concern that the juvenile should not be regarded simply as a wage-earner but as a 'workman and citizen in training'. This was the view expressed by the Departmental Committee on Juvenile Employment, which reported in 1917.

Local authorities were required to provide an appropriate education for older children in elementary schools, and this, in effect, meant giving an education beyond the elementary stage to these children. Since 1911 it has been possible for local authorities to provide separate schools for these older children. They were built in certain areas and became known as central schools but, in most cases, a selection process was applied for entry to these schools. But, even before 1914, some people were suggesting that all children at 11 should go to a separate secondary school.

The 1918 Act provided for more central direction of education. Local authorities now had not only to provide education but report progress to the Board of Education. One reason for more central control was that some local authorities pushed ahead with educational advance but some did not.

Under the Act central government was to bear more of the cost of education – at least not less than 50 per cent.

It abolished fees for elementary schools and extended school medical inspection to secondary schools.

The interwar years

In the interwar years there grew a demand for secondary education for all influenced by a number of factors – the need for greater economic efficiency, the need for a reasonably educated electorate after the 1918 Representation of the People Act extended the vote to all men over 21 and women over 30, and the desire for greater social equality.

The Hadow Report 1926 (Report of the Consultative Committee of the Board of Education on the Education of the Adolescent) recommended secondary education for all, along with the raising of the school-leaving age to 15. It stated: 'Individual and national character would be strengthened through the placing of youth, in the hour of its growth, in a congenial and inspiring environment.' The then existing local authority secondary schools gave a grammar school education and the Report recommended the creation of modern schools to give a secondary education of a more practical nature. It stressed the need for 'parity of esteem' between modern school and grammar school. 'The modern school', it said, 'is not an inferior species and it ought not to be hampered by conditions of accommodation and equipment inferior to those of grammar schools.' Finally, it recommended that secondary education should begin at 11, and thus the separate systems of elementary and secondary education should be replaced by a single education process split into two successive stages.

The Hadow Report had been mainly concerned with children who did not receive a secondary education, but the Report of another Consultative Committee of the Board of Education – the Spens Report of 1938 – was concerned with secondary education with special reference to grammar schools and technical high schools.

The then existing secondary schools, set up by local authorities under the 1902 Education Act, gave a grammar school type of education geared to university entrance. The Spens Report stated that there should also be selective secondary schools for brighter children which would be more vocational, geared to boys and girls 'who desired to enter industry and commerce at 16'. It thus supported three types of secondary education – grammar, technical and the modern (of the Hadow Report). There should be selection at 11, as recommended by Hadow, but with a further review at 13. Both the Hadow and Spens Reports were quite happy with a selective process at 11 because they were much influenced by educational psychologists who believed that children could be reasonably classified by intelligence tests, making the actual selection process reasonably accurate and easy to work. Spens, like Hadow, stressed parity of esteem between all three secondary schools. But the Report recommended the raising of the school-leaving age to 16, as this was the leaving age in grammar schools.

The Hadow and Spens Reports thus pioneered educational advance, but the implementation of their most important recommendations – namely, secondary education for all organised under a tripartite system of grammar, technical and modern with 'parity of esteem' between them plus the raising of the school-leaving age – had to await the 1944 Education Act.

The Private Sector

By the 1930s most endowed grammar schools were open to all children with ability. The main reason for this was that many schools got into financial difficulties and accepted a grant from the Board of Education and, in return, under a 1907 regulation of the Board, they had to provide free places for 25 per cent of their annual entry 'to scholars from public elmementary schools . . . subject to the applicants passing an entrance test'. These became known as direct-grant schools.

The Universities

Until the nineteenth century Oxford and Cambridge were the only universities in England and Wales, though Scotland had four (St Andrews, Glasgow, Aberdeen and Edinburgh). Oxford and Cambridge, but not the Scottish universities, were closed to those who were not members of the Church of England. In the eighteenth century many academies for higher education were formed by outstanding dissenters, and these in many cases gave a better education than Oxford or Cambridge. Thus, if you were not a member of the Church of England and wanted a higher education, you could apply for admission to one of the academies or to a Scottish university.

In England and Wales the first universities after Oxford and Cambridge were London and Durham, both founded in 1836. London University had no religious test for admission. On the other hand, Durham University demanded, like Oxford and Cambridge, that its students should subscribe to the Thirty-Nine Articles of the Church of England. It was not until 1871 that religious tests were abolished for Oxford, Cambridge and Durham.

The technical and social problems created by the Industrial Revolution led to an increasing demand for higher education, especially in the physical and social sciences.

Oxford and Cambridge expanded their system of colleges and curriculum in the latter half of the nineteenth century, but the biggest advance came in the provinces, especially in the industrial areas. In 1884 the federal university of Victoria was formed from colleges at Liverpool and Manchester, and in 1887 it was joined by Leeds. In 1903 the federation was replaced by three separate universities of Manchester, Liverpool and Leeds. Mason College founded in 1880, became Birmingham University in 1900. Sheffield University was founded in 1905 and Bristol University in 1909. Meanwhile, the London School of Economics had been founded in 1895 and became part of the University of London in 1900 to form a new faculty of Economics and Political Science. In 1893 the University of Wales was founded, being based on a federation of colleges at Aberystwyth, Cardiff and Bangor.

It will be seen that many of the provincial universities were first preceded by colleges of higher education which, until they received university status, could not grant degrees. In 1926 Reading University was formed after a similar trial period as a college, and so were many universities founded after 1945 when a big expansion of higher education took place. But as late as 1939 only a small proportion of working-class children went to university.

The 1944 Education Act

1. The Act introduced secondary education for all. The schools that provided it were to be 'sufficient in number, character and equipment to afford for all pupils . . . such variety of instruction and training as may be desirable in view of their different ages, abilities and aptitudes'. This Act, therefore, did not preclude comprehensive schools but, in nearly all areas, it was the tripartite system of grammar, secondary technical and secondary modern which developed.

2. It raised the school-leaving age to 15, but this did not come into force until 1947. It also provided for the raising of the school-leaving age to 16 'as soon as it has become practicable'.

3. Local authorities were also made responsible for the provision of part-time and full-time education for all above school-leaving age. This led to a great expansion of day release, full-time further education and day and evening classes, catering for recreational and cultural leisure activities. Part-time day release was to be compulsory for those under 18 and to be provided in county colleges, but this part of the Act has still not been implemented.

4. The Act thus organised 'public education . . . in three successive stages to be known as primary education, secondary education and further education'. The break from primary to secondary at 11 was accepted.

5. The Board of Education became the Ministry of Education with much greater powers given to the Secretary of State. In the last resort the minister was given the power to direct a local authority or the governors or managers of a school when it was thought that they were acting unreasonably.

6. All secondary schools were to have 'parity of esteem', but this did not work out in practice.

7. The county borough councils and the county councils were made responsible for all stages of education, including nursery schools and special schools for the handicapped, but county councils could, within their areas, delegate educational functions to divisional executives and the larger boroughs and urban districts.

8. Church schools (i.e. the voluntary schools) could choose either to have 'aided' or 'controlled' status. An aided school was to receive grants from the central government to cover teachers' salaries, internal and external repairs, alterations and new construction and maintenance costs. The schools still appointed their own staff and the majority of the governors were appointed by the voluntary body. The governing bodies of controlled schools had to have a majority of local authority representatives, but denominational instruction could continue. The local authority was to be financially responsible for the school.

9. Religious instruction was to be given in all schools.

10. Two central advisory councils on education were set up under the Act – one for England and one for Wales – to advise the minister.

11. All schools, including independent schools, were to be inspected by the Ministry of Education.

12. Fees in state (i.e. maintained) schools were to be abolished.

SUMMARY

Until 1870 education was left to private enterprise. Although under the private enterprise system most people received an elementary education, there were still too many people who remained illiterate – hence the 1870 Education Act was 'to fill the gaps' by providing board schools where no adequate system of voluntary school existed. By 1880 by law all children had to go to school.

In the nineteenth century an elementary education was all that was considered necessary for children of the working class. Only children of middle- and upper-class parents received a secondary education either at endowed grammar schools or public schools. By the end of the First World War there was a growing demand that all children should receive a secondary education. Already the 1902 Education Act had introduced a state system of secondary education administered by local authorities, but the grammar school education it provided was for the brighter working-class children, as there was a selection process at 11. In any case, most working-class parents were apathetic to secondary education. Many felt that it was better for the children to be working at 14 and bringing money into the home than receiving a grammar school education, which, to the parents, seemed irrelevant for the kind of work they expected their children to be taking up. Thus, even as late as 1939, only a comparatively small number of working-class children went to a secondary school. It was not until after the Second World War, as a result of the 1944 Education Act, that the school-leaving age was raised to 15 and all children received a secondary education. It would probably have come earlier but for the economic difficulties of the interwar years.

The ground for the Act had been well prepared in the interwar years with the Hadow and Spens Reports. It is interesting to note that compulsory day release, legislated for under 1918 and 1944 Education Acts, has still not been introduced.

Although there was nothing in the 1944 Act to prevent a local authority giving the three types of secondary education in one comprehensive school, the arguments of the Spens Report against comprehensive schools, plus the emphasis placed on three main student groupings in the Norwood Report of 1943 (Report of the Committee of the Secondary Schools Examination Council on Curriculum and Examinations in Secondary Schools), led to the separate school system being adopted in most areas.

In spite of the development of the state system, the private sector of education, used mainly by the rich, continued to flourish. Not until after 1945 did working-class students start going to the universities in any great numbers.

Two main factors had influenced, and were to continue to influence, the development of education:

(a) the need for more social justice
(b) the need for economic efficiency

ASSIGNMENTS

1. By making use of reference books in your library, write short biographical notes on the following: Robert Raikes, Robert Owen, Thomas Arnold, Sir James Kay-Shuttleworth, W. E. Forster, Miss Emily Davies, R. H. Tawney, R. A. Butler.

2. Write a brief history of your school or college. For what purpose was it founded? What have been the main developments since its foundation?

3. Discuss the statement that economic necessity, political expediency and higher living standards have all contributed to educational advance in the nineteenth and twentieth centuries.

READING

Richard Aldrich, *An Introduction to the History of Education* (Hodder & Stoughton, 1982).

Rodney Barker, *Education and Politics 1900–1951: A Study of the Labour Party* (Oxford University Press, 1972).

H. C. Barnard, *A History of English Education from 1760*, 4th impression (University of London Press, 1966).

G. A. N. Lowndes, *The Silent Revolution* (Oxford University Press, 1969).

J. S. Maclure, *Educational Documents: England and Wales, 1816 to the Present Day*, 6th edn (Methuen, 1986).

Frank Smith, *The Life and Work of Sir James Kay-Shuttleworth* (Cedric Chivers, 1974).

11 The Organisation of Education Today

EDUCATION PROVIDED BY LOCAL AUTHORITIES

1. *Primary education*, which begins at 5 and ends at 11. Some children attend a nursery school, or nursery class which forms part of a primary school, before the age of 5. There are also pre-school playgroups organised by parents and voluntary organisations. Primary education falls into two parts – infant schools for children from 5 to 7 and junior schools for 7 to 11. Both groups are usually housed in the same school building.

2. *Secondary education*, which begins at 11 and is compulsory to 16, but some students voluntarily carry on to 18. There are three main types of secondary school – secondary modern schools, grammar schools, and comprehensive schools. (There are a small number of secondary technical schools, originally intended for a reasonably bright child with a practical bias, but most of them now give a grammar school education.) Some local authorities have established what are called sixth form colleges which provide mainly 'A' level courses. They replace the sixth forms of those secondary schools which had not the number of students in their sixth forms to provide a reasonable range of 'A' level options. Most local authorities have put on a course in their schools called the Technical and Vocational Education Initiative (TVEI) financed by the Training Agency. It is a four-year course of vocational training.

In the primary and secondary sphere each school has a body of school governors who take a general interest in the running of the school and the welfare of the pupils. The governors comprise representatives of the local authority, the parents and teachers. Under the 1986 Education (No 2) Act these school governing bodies have been reformed to give a bigger say to parents. Thus the Act gives parents equal representation with local authority governors. Furthermore, the Act gave governors wider powers making them responsible for the aims of the school, its discipline and giving them a greater say in the appointment and dismissal of staff. Under the 1988 Education Reform Act the governors of primary and secondary

135

schools with more than 200 pupils became responsible under delegation from the local education authority for the major financial decisions relating to their school. Other features of the 1988 Education Reform Act – perhaps the most revolutionary of all education acts this century – are as follows:

(a)   primary and secondary schools with more than 300 pupils are provided with the opportunity to opt out of local authority control. Those that do are financed directly by the Central Government.

(b)   more parents are given their first choice of school for their children

(c)   the idea of catchment areas, where children are placed in a school situated in the district in which the children live, has been abolished. Schools, primary and secondary, now sell themselves in the market place because much of the money they receive depends on the number of pupils they enrol.

(d)   schools are permitted to charge parents for 'extras'.

(e)   all schools must now work to a national curriculum which was introduced September 1989. Its three main (core) subjects are English, Mathematics and Science. Other 'foundation' subjects are History, Geography, Technology, Music, Art. There is an overall framework of study for the various subjects in four stages from primary on into secondary school. These stages are from 5 to 7; 8 to 11; 12 to 14; 15 to the end of compulsory education. Targets are set for students to have attained at the end of each stage and each pupil will be tested at the age of 7, 11, 14 and 16 to see whether he or she has satisfactorily attained that standard set by the target and parents will be notified accordingly. And, in accordance with the spirit of the market place, introduced by the 1988 Act, schools must publicise the results of the testing to give the consumers (i.e. parents) information about the academic standards of the schools so that parents can better exercise choice when deciding to which school to send their children.

There is a National Curriculum Council to supervise and advise on the curriculum.

Further Education

Further education, either full or part-time is provided for students from 16 onwards in technical colleges, colleges of art and commercial colleges – all now usually referred to as further education (FE) colleges. They cover courses from GCSE level and craft level through to 'A' level or intermediate level of professional courses and work related courses. Both in secondary and further education use is made of the College of the Air financed mainly by private enterprise. It became operative from 1 September 1987. As with schools, student numbers are an important factor in determining the amount of funding received. An announcement in the House of Commons on 23 March 1991 stated the Government is to remove FE colleges and the Sixth Form Colleges from local authority control as from April 1993. They will be financed by a new funding council.

OTHER PROVIDERS OF EDUCATION

For primary and secondary education there are:

1. *Independent schools*, which include private and public schools and which receive all their funds from fees and endowments. There were schools known as direct-grant schools because they received a grant direct from the Department of Education and Science provided they allocated 25 per cent of their places in the secondary sphere to pupils from local authority schools but they have been phased out. Some joined the state system; some became completely independent. It was the Labour government which began the phasing out of direct-grant schools because the schools were selective, contrary to the comprehensive principle that government supported. The 1980 Education Act of a Conservative government introduced what is called the 'Assisted Places Scheme' under which local authorities have discretion to give financial help, where considered necessary, to parents whose children are bright enough to qualify for a place at an independent school.
2. *Voluntary schools*, which, normally, are Church schools.
3. *City Technology Colleges* providing secondary education and financed by the Central Government and the private sector (see below). These are privately run colleges providing art, commercial and other courses.

Higher Education

Universities are part of the private sector but all, except Buckingham University College, receive a great deal of money from the government which is now distributed through the Universities Funding Council. The universities are free to use the money as they wish, but their accounts are subject to inspection by the House of Commons Select Committee on Public Accounts. They provide education beyond the secondary sphere (i.e. higher education) with their own degrees and postgraduate courses and extra-mural courses.

Polytechnics and Higher Education Corporations
In order to provide for a concentration of higher education, with a wide range of courses, both full-time and part-time in key parts of the country, certain technical colleges or groupings of colleges were designated polytechnics. Originally administered by local authorities they are now managed by an independent board of governors half of whom are drawn from industry, commerce and the professions. Similarly, higher education colleges run by local authorities have now become independent of local government and have a similar board of management to that of the polytechnics. These higher education establishments are called higher education corporations.

EDUCATION OF HANDICAPPED CHILDREN

This is mainly the responsibility of the local authorities. Where possible the child remains at a normal school and only goes to a special school if absolutely necessary. Local authorities run special schools for different categories of handicapped children. Some children are so handicapped that they cannot even go to a special school, but their education is still the responsibility of the local education department.

FINANCE OF EDUCATION

The cost of the state system of primary, secondary and further education administered by local authorities is shared between the local authorities and central government. Further education and sixth form colleges are to be taken out of local authority control in April 1993. The central government finances just over half of all local government expenditure and about half of each local authority's expenditure goes on education. In the financial year 1989–90 the central government gave extra money to local authorities to help cover the cost of implementing the 1988 Education Reform Act. There are extra grants for local authorities with special social needs, for example, those local authorities with a large immigrant school population.

Primary and secondary education are free; school meals are subsidised by many local authorities although, since 1980, it is no longer obligatory for local authorities to provide them except for children of parents on income support, in which case the meals are free. Poorer parents receive financial help with other expenses.

Nearly 90 per cent of university expenditure and about 55 per cent of university income is financed by the central government via the University Funding Council, which has replaced the University Grants Committee. The central government also gives financial support via the Polytechnics and Colleges Funding Council to polytechnics and other higher education establishments no longer administered by local government. A single funding council for higher education, covering universities, polytechnics and higher education corporations is to be established (see Commons *Hansard*, 20 May 1991). The central government also gives financial assistance to private colleges of education which train teachers. Church schools receive financial help both from central and local government.

Students taking courses at universities and other establishments of higher education receive grants from their local authorities to cover tuition fees and maintenance allowances. But, now, under the 1990 Education (Student Loans) Act the grant system has been partly replaced by a system of student loans. Students can borrow up to a certain amount to supplement their grant, the loan being repayable when they have concluded their course but repayment can be deferred for those on a wage below 85 per cent of national earnings. The grant will cease to be increased with inflation and the eventual aim is for it to cover only half the cost of a student's higher education.

Some advantages of the loan scheme from the Government point of view are that it will eventually reduce the cost of student funding to the Government (i.e. the taxpayer, as the Government prefers to put it) and it will make students more appreciative of the education they receive. Also, it is believed, it will actually increase access to higher education. This is because the means-tested grant system was inadequate and, although parents were supposed to top up the grant to a required amount, 40 per cent did not do so. But even when they did, many students had to take part-time jobs to obtain, what they considered, an adequate income. Now students will be able to supplement their income by means of an interest-free loan which should make higher education affordable for students from poorer homes. But the opponents of the loan system say it will have the opposite effect. The thought of a huge debt at the end of their children's course will deter many parents from encouraging their children to go to university or polytechnic. Furthermore, it is argued, it is wrong on moral grounds to encourage students to get into debt. On the other hand, defenders of the loan scheme argue that young people who receive higher education normally, on its completion, go into higher-earning jobs and, therefore, should make some financial contribution to what the rest of the community has provided for them.

ADMINISTRATION

The Secretary of State's responsibilities
Under the 1944 Education Act the Secretary of State is required to 'secure the effective execution, by local authorities under his control and direction, of the national policy for providing a varied and comprehensive educational service in every area'. The minister can overrule a local authority or the managers or governors of any school in the state system if he or she thinks they have acted, or propose to act, unreasonably, but what is considered 'unreasonable' can be challenged in the courts. In practice the minister rarely uses the power of direction. Persuasion by negotiation is the usual method. Hence there is much consultation between the Department of Education and Science (DES) and the local education authorities. All the chief education officers are known to the DES. Informal contact is therefore very important and, in this connection, note the importance of the minister's inspectors, HMIs, whose task it is to see that the schools and colleges are being run properly and who are available for consultation and advice. In 1991 the government announced that inspection of schools was to be privatised.

The DES is not only responsible for the schools and further education, but it also has links with the universities and other higher education institutions through its links with the funding bodies.

The DES is responsible for promoting civil research via research councils.

Advisory bodies
Under the 1944 Education Act the Minister had to appoint a central advisory council for England and one for Wales. These replaced the consultative committee of the Board of Education set up under the Board of Education Act of 1899. (Note some of the famous reports produced by the central advisory council for England – Crowther, Newsom, Plowden.) But these councils no longer function. There remain specialised advisory committees which, among others, include the funding bodies.

In 1983 the Secondary Examinations Council (SEC) was set up 'to advise the Government on the ways in which the national system of secondary education may best meet the needs of the education service and its clients'. Apart from supervising 'the operations of examinations' in secondary schools, it also covers examinations after the end of the compulsory school period (see Cmnd 9469).

However, the Secretary of State relies mainly on the civil servants in the DES for advice and assistance. These include Her Majesty's Inspectors (HMIs).

The local authorities' responsibilities

The local authorities execute and administer their state education under the DES's control and direction. They employ the teachers and build and maintain the schools and colleges. The local education authorities are the county councils and the metropolitan district councils which must, by law, appoint an education committee to administer education advised by the chief education officer of the local authority. The education committee must have co-opted members, usually one or two teachers and two or three representatives from the churches. It works through a number of sub-committees.

Pressure groups

A number of bodies have access to the Secretary of State for Education and Science and are usually consulted when new matters of policy arise. The local authorities not only act as independent units but act together through their associations which put their views to the government on matters of common interest to all the authorities in their association. They also circulate information to their members.

There are the teachers' unions – the National Union of Teachers, and National Association of Schoolmasters, four associations representing headmasters, headmistresses, assistant masters and assistant mistresses in grammar schools, the National Association of Teachers in Further and Higher Education and the Association of University Teachers, all of which not only protect their members' interests with regard to pay and conditions of work, but, as professional organisations, put forward their views on education. There are also pressure groups representing parents.

Parliament

Parliament obviously influences education policy because the Secretary of State must ultimately seek its approval for the policies pursued.

SUMMARY

There are three main stages in education – primary, secondary and tertiary. Tertiary is sometimes called higher education and is part of further education in that it is undertaken beyond the official school-leaving age.

There is a state system of primary and secondary education administered by local authorities under the supervision of the Department of Education and Science plus state schools financed directly by the Central Government. Large sections of the private sector receive financial assistance from the government; virtually all the universities do. Working closely with the state schools are Church schools, some of which receive financial help from both local government and central government; some are financed entirely by local government. Education, at all stages, has become more orientated to the market place.

ASSIGNMENTS

1.   Explain the relationships between the following: the principal of the college, the academic board, the board of governors, the local authority, the Department of Education and Science, the Secretary of State for Education and Science.
2.   Do you think the education service would be better run if it were taken out of the hands of local government and administered directly by central government? Give reasons for your answer.
3.   In July 1982 Customs and Excise were demanding that VAT (Value-Added Tax) should be paid on adult education courses which are non-vocational, i.e. taken for purely recreational purposes. Vocational courses would not be affected. Discuss how far it is possible to differentiate between the two types of course.

READING

Britain 1992, An Official Handbook (HMSO).

12 Developments in Education since 1945 and Current Problems

HIGHER EDUCATION

1. There has been a great expansion of higher education. (By higher education is meant not only degree courses but professional courses at final level.)

2. The number of universities has increased. In 1945 Britain had seventeen universities. There are now forty-six in Britain and, in addition, the Open University – the 'University of the Air'. In its first academic year, 1970–1, places were available for 25 000 students, which, at that time, was about half the intake of all other universities in England and Wales.

3. Teacher-training colleges, later known as colleges of education, have been reorganised – some merging with polytechnics, some with universities, some continuing as separate colleges but providing other courses apart from teaching courses, while some have closed down. But a small number remain primarily for teacher-training.

4. Universities are no longer the only institutions awarding degrees. In the public sector some colleges and groupings of colleges in certain key areas were, starting in the late 1960s, designated polytechnics (there are now 30 of them) and, along with certain other colleges, were permitted to run their own degree courses outside the university system. The degrees are awarded by the Council for National Academic Awards, which also supervises the courses. This dual system of degree awards is known as the binary system. It will be abolished when the single funding council for higher education is established. Apart from degree courses, polytechnics, as their name indicates, put on a wide variety of high-level courses. In fact, more than half the students in higher education are in polytechnics and other colleges. In May 1991 the Government announced polytechnics are to be called universities.

5. The Ministry of Education was renamed the Department of Education

and Science in 1964 after its merger with the Ministry of Science and divided into two main administrative units – one is concerned with the schools of England and Wales and further education, and the other with the universities and civil science.

6.   The *Report of the Committee of Higher Education* was published in 1963. The Committee was set up in 1961 because the opportunities for higher education did not appear to be expanding fast enough. Chaired by Lord Robbins, it was to report on higher education 'in the light of national needs and resources'.

The Report accepted the need for an expansion of higher education and thought it could be achieved without a lowering of academic standards. There were 'large reservoirs of untapped ability in the population, especially among girls', the Report stated. It estimated that 560 000 places for full-time higher education would be needed in Britain in the academic year 1980–1, i.e. 17 per cent of the age group, compared with 8 per cent at the time of the Report. In the academic year 1988–9 there were 644 000 students in higher education in Britain, including 65 000 overseas students. In 1989 there were 40 000 students following Open University courses at degree level.

It was the Robbins Report which recommended most of the main developments listed above – the creation of new universities, the granting of university status to the colleges of advanced technology, the improved status of teacher-training colleges and the setting up of the Council for National Academic Awards.

The merging of the Ministry of Education with the Ministry of Science in 1964 to form the Department of Education and Science, with one division responsible for higher education and the other for the schools system, was a compromise solution to the proposal of the Robbins Committee that there should be a separate Ministry for Higher Education called the Ministry of Arts and Sciences. The schools did not want a separate ministry; the universities did.

Reasons for the big advance of higher education

1.   The big expansion of secondary education, arising from the 1944 Education Act, meant that the proportion of young people in the secondary field capable of benefiting from higher education increased.

2.   There was a large increase in the number of schoolchildren arising from increased births after the Second World War. In recent years there has been a fall in the number of children starting at primary school.

3.   Economic necessity has been a big factor in the development of higher education. The Robbins Report stated:

> We do not believe that modern societies can achieve their aims of economic growth and higher cultural standards without making the most of the talents of their citizens. This is obviously necessary if we are to compete with the other highly developed countries in an area of rapid technological and social advance.

Almost twenty years earlier two other reports had made the same point. These were the Report of the Social Committee on Higher Technological Education of 1945 (the Percy Report) and the report of a committee appointed by the Lord President of the Council on Scientific Manpower (the Barlow Report), published in 1946. The Barlow Report stated what the Robbins Report later confirmed, that many more young people were capable of taking advantage of a university education. It concluded 'that only about one in five boys and girls, who have intelligence equal to that of the best half of the university students, actually reach universities'.

4.   In line with more egalitarian and democratic trends, accelerated by two world wars and higher living standards, the expansion of higher education was considered right in order that citizens should, as the Robbins Report put it, develop their 'capacity to understand, to contemplate and to create'. Or, to quote Robbins again, 'The good society desires equality of opportunity for its citizens to become not merely good producers but also good men and women'.

5.   Increased financial assistance to students in the post-war years and higher living standards have meant that the more ordinary families can afford to let their children take advantage of higher education.

Current problems in higher education

The Robbins Report reflected the optimism of the Keynsian era of economics when the economy was expanding at a faster rate than at any previous time in our history and there seemed to be plenty of money for education. But, starting in the early 1970s, the world economy moved into recession and economic growth slowed down. In view of the economic difficulties arising from this, the question began to be asked if we could afford to provide a place in higher education for all those who are 'qualified by ability and attainment and who wish to have a place' (the Robbins criteria). In its 1985 Green Paper (Cmnd 9524) the Government admitted a reduction in real terms of about 3.5 per cent in the financial year 1984–5 in the resources provided for higher education compared with 1980–1 while 'student numbers rose substantially.' But in the same Green Paper, in spite of its information about education cuts, it accepted that higher education courses should be available 'to all those who can benefit from them and who wish to do so' – a wider criteria than in the Robbins Report. Furthermore, the then Secretary of State for Education stated in 1989 that the Government's aim was to double the numbers in higher education from the then roughly one million students to two million over the next 25 years. Such an aim was not altruistic as our economic survival depends, in certain fields at any rate, on there being a far greater number of trained graduates. But how was this to come about when there seemed to be less money for education? One way was to rely on the polytechnics and other higher education colleges to take most of the increased numbers of students as the average cost of educating a polytechnic student is roughly £3200 a year whilst for an equivalent student in a university the cost is roughly £5200 a year. One of the reasons for the difference in costs is that the university costs include the money universities receive from the Government for basic research, whilst polytechnics do not receive a grant for research, although individual polytechnics can apply to the Research Council for money to fund research. Thus enrolment on full-time higher education courses at polytechnics rose by 47 per cent between 1979–80 and 1987–8 whilst universities' enrolment increased by only 3 per cent. However, the big increase in polytechnic enrolment has meant a worsening of their student-staff ratio which, to the Government, means an increase in staff productivity. For the universities the cuts have meant not only a slowing down in student intake but the easing of some lecturers into early retirement. Around 40000 young people (the estimate varies) since 1981 have been denied a university education which they would have received if the cuts had not been made. Many of them will have gone to polytechnics or to a higher education college. Hence the Government can rightly claim that, in spite of the cuts, there are more students in higher education than ever before. However the 1990 Education (Student Loans) Act with its gradual replacement of the grant system by repayable loans to students could, in spite of the safeguards the Government claims to have inserted into the Act, result in many working-class parents being put off encouraging their children to go on to higher education because of the eventual financial liability they would face. But as one university vice-chancellor put it, loans confer on students 'the status of paying customers and the customer's right to good services' (*Guardian*, 6 December 1989).

One other reason why there is this seeming paradox of more students in spite of cuts is that both universities and polytechnics and other higher education colleges have sought financial help by doing what the Government intended them to do – develop more links with industry and commerce. Thus many universities and polytechnics receive money from industry for doing research on projects of benefit to industry. About half the income of one university comes in this way from industry. The Government can thus defend the cuts not just on public expenditure grounds, but as an important development towards its aim of (a) a shift of student places to science, technology and vocational subjects and (b) to make higher education, as with all education, more geared to the needs of industry and commerce, necessitating closer co-operation with them. Unfortunately for some universities (and it can apply to polytechnics even though the latter were originally set up to provide an education more related to industry and the business world) not all courses attract private finance and some university departments have had to be closed down.

As with schools, student numbers play an important role in the funding of higher education establishments. Thus both universities, polytechnics and other higher education colleges, like the schools, have to sell themselves in the market place to maintain or increase their income and survive. Universities in particular have made a big push to attract overseas students. They are good customers because they pay the full tuition fee, perhaps aided by their government. The cost of tuition is of course an important factor in selling courses and therefore recruitment. Polytechnics have the advantage here because, as pointed out, their costs are lower as they have not to fund basic research. The search for foreign students who are such a good economic proposition has led to an increasing proportion of them at British universities which is not necessarily a bad thing if it does not mean that fewer places are available for British students. But not every university can increase its intake of foreign students because of the shortage of physical capacity to accommodate them and, ironically, they cannot spend money on increasing the accommodation because of the cuts.

The emphasis the Government places on the role of education serving the enterprise culture of the market place raises the question of the purpose of education, especially university education. As well as the need to have links with industry, education, as the Robbins report put it, is to help people to develop their 'capacity to understand, to contemplate and to create.' Interestingly, at the same time of writing, the CBI seem more in tune with this than the Government. It is looking for graduates not with a specific knowledge of a subject but those who are motivated and can solve problems. Although universities must have links with industry and commerce, they have an important role of developing knowledge for its own sake, which might not give economic and social benefits until decades later and is not, therefore, likely to interest industry.

The Government might reply that higher education has always had a vocational element, providing doctors, lawyers, administrators, engineers, and so on, and all the Government is trying to do is to get a better balance between the humanities and the vocational oriented subjects.

What should be the structure of higher education?
The present binary system of universities with their own degrees, and polytechnics and certain other colleges awarding degrees under the auspices of the Council for National Academic Awards, is to be abolished, should the Government white paper on higher education (Cm 1541) be implemented. Polytechnics, to be called universities, will be able to grant their own degrees, as will the higher education corporations.

Critics see the binary system as acceptance of first- and second-class institutions in higher education similar to grammar and secondary modern schools in secondary education. As in secondary education, the grammar/secondary modern system has been virtually replaced by a comprehensive system, so these critics would like to see a comprehensive system for higher education. Thus there would be 'polyversities' covering work of all higher education institutions. Two main arguments are put forward for the changes. First, all forms of higher education would get their fair share of resources and this would mean that higher education would be better adapted than it is now to meet the needs of the modern technological society. Second, polyversities, like comprehensive schools in secondary education, would further the development of a more homogeneous and egalitarian society.

Those who defend the special position of the existing universities usually believe in the necessity for an educated elite to provide the leadership of the required calibre. Such an elite is best nurtured in the existing type of university, which zealously upholds the liberal tradition of ensuring that a subject is studied in depth from all points of view.

The reorganisation of the colleges of education is in line with the recommendation of the Committee of Inquiry Report 1972 (James Report) on *Teacher Education and Training* that future teachers would benefit from closer association with students in other fields of higher education. Some critics argue that the quality of teacher-training has been adversely affected by being part of one large institution concerned with so many other things. In any case, for many people, experience has shown that most students do not normally mix and interchange ideas with students in other disciplines.

SECONDARY EDUCATION

There was a big expansion of secondary education after 1945 due to the 1944 Education Act and the increased number of school-children, with more students staying on at the different types of schools after school-leaving age. But in spite of great progress in the secondary sphere the Report of the Minister of Education's central advisory council, *Half Our Future*, in 1963 (the Newsom Report), which considered the education of children between the ages of 13 and 16 with average and less than average ability, found that 80 per cent of the schools which these children attended (mainly secondary modern schools) were deficient from the accommodation point of view.

There was a great expansion of all forms of secondary education, not just that provided in secondary schools. Hence there has been a great expansion of the work of further education colleges which provide craft courses and intermediate professional courses including business and technical education courses for those students who have finished compulsory schooling. But in spite of the development of courses at colleges of further education the Report of the Minister of Education's central advisory council in 1959 (the Crowther Report), entitled *15–18*, stated that the majority of young people between 15 and 18 received no full-time or part-time education. Since the mid-1970s a falling birthrate has led to a reduction in the number of schoolchildren.

The great increase in unemployment has resulted in training schemes for unemployed school-leavers under 18 which are a form of vocational education (see Chapter 14). As mentioned in an earlier chapter, a new and very unusual development is a four-year technical and vocational course of training for young people commencing at the age of 14. It is called the Technical and Vocational Education Initiative (TVEI). Pilot schemes began in 1983. The Manpower Services Commission (now the Training Agency) provided the money as well as the overall supervision, and this at a time when cuts had been made in local government funding.

A White Paper (Cmnd 9823) published in 1986 outlined the Government's plans to expand the TVEI scheme by providing new courses. Local authorities have discretion as to whether or not to provide a TVEI course in their schools. The money provided for courses by the Training Agency is a big inducement to participate and the scheme is now a national one. Critics of TVEI say the money should have been put into education as a whole so all students could benefit. They also argue that the course revives the old division between the academic – the bright ones who eventually do 'A' levels – and the not so bright who do practical subjects. However, if in teaching the practical subjects they are related to their social and environmental background, they can be educational in the true sense of the word and not simply vocational. The fact that such a scheme has been introduced could be taken by some people as criticism of our educational system for not providing enough students with sufficient skills for the world of work and the shortsightedness of our commercial and industrial leaders for not sufficiently involving themselves in the education process. A College of the Air has been set up financed mainly by private enterprise, operative from 1 September 1987.

The National Council for Vocational Qualifications (NCVQ) has been created to co-ordinate and rationalise the various vocational courses. It is responsible to the Secretary of State for Employment.

Under the 'Enterprise and Education Initiative' launched in 1988, it is hoped to arrange for all pupils to have had suitable work experience before leaving school. And in its White Paper, 'Education and Training for the 21st C' (May 1991), the Major government outlined plans to improve education and training for young people who leave full-time education at 16 so that, for those among them who can benefit from it, further education and training will become the norm. Business leaders will have much more influence on this post-16 education. (See also Chapter 14.)

City Technology Colleges

A further stage in the by-passing of local authorities in educational provision was the Government's announcement (October 1986) to build twenty City Technology Colleges (CTCs), for 11- to 18-year-olds, some to be located in deprived inner-city areas. The first one opened in Solihull in 1988. There are now seven and fifteen are planned – all in the inner cities. Originally the Government was hoping that industry and commerce would fund all or a substantial amount of the capital cost of building a college. But the response has not been as great as the Government hoped and 80 per cent of the capital cost is borne by the Government and only 20 per cent by the private sector. A CTC trust is in charge of raising money from the private sector and, in February 1991, it had 240 sponsors. The development of City Technology colleges is part of the Government's policy of increasing the role of the private sector in the provision of public services. It is also hoping that CTCs will become centres of excellence pioneering a new type of education and so influence the development of a more work-orientated education in secondary schools. They have close links with their business sponsors. And because of sponsorship and Government money they are better equipped than surrounding schools. In fact, although financed mainly from public funds they are, in essence, independent private schools. Teachers are employed under contract for comparatively short periods at a time and have no security of tenure but enjoy better pay and conditions than teachers in local authority schools. Students have a longer day and shorter holidays. By law they must recruit a broad band of ability – slow learners as well as fast learners. Even so, they are selective, like the old technical schools, in that there are more students wanting to be admitted to them than there are places. At one college as many as four out of five children cannot get a place. Critics say the large amount of money the Government is spending on CTCs should have been spent on better maintenance of existing schools. Links with commerce and industry can and are developed in local authority schools and most have similar courses to those provided by CTCs. In any case, as with higher education, industry and commerce do not necessarily want too vocationally orientated courses. The courses they are mainly interested in are English and Mathematics, which all schools teach. And an education that exposes a child throughout schooling to the culture of business and the market is too narrow an education. Finally, one must consider the depressing effect a CTC with all its affluence must have on the surrounding and more poorly financed schools. 'Where's the justice?' they might say.

The 1964 Industrial Training Act did something to encourage employers to provide day-release facilities for the training of their young employees by setting up industrial training boards each for a particular industry. Each board has the power to make a levy on the employers within the industry (small firms are exempt). But employers receive back a percentage of the levy for each employee they release for training. Hence there is some financial incentive to provide day-release facilities. Much of the teaching is done by teachers in F. E. Colleges, the purely vocational teaching is done by teachers appointed by the appropriate training board. Boards can also provide their own training courses.

The 1981 Employment and Training Act abolished all but seven of the twenty-three boards.

Comprehensive Schools

The most interesting development in education since the 1944 Act has been the swing to comprehensive schools. Just a few local authorities introduced comprehensive schools soon after the 1944 Education Act but the majority kept to the tripartite system. The Labour administrations of 1945–51 did not encourage comprehensive schools and the Conservative administrations of 1951–64 discouraged them except in rural areas. But when the Labour party was returned to power in 1964 its official policy was to abolish the 11-plus examination. In 1965 the DES issued *Circular 10/65*, requesting local authorities to prepare schemes for the reorganisation of secondary education on comprehensive lines.

In 1965, 8 per cent of secondary schoolchildren in England and Wales in state school were in comprehensive schools – and in 1989 86 per cent in England, 99 per cent in Wales and 100 per cent in Scotland. Under Conservative governments local authorities can please themselves whether or not to plan their secondary education on comprehensive lines.

Why has there been a swing towards comprehensive schools?
It was due to a weaknesses in the selection system and the tripartite structure:

1.   The selection process at 11 was not as efficient as originally anticipated. A fair percentage of children (the estimate varies) went to the wrong school, judging by their performances later on.

2.   Although it was possible for a child at 13 to be transferred to another type of school where the selection procedure had obviously been wrong, in practice, because of administrative difficulties, the transfer system did not work satisfactorily in most areas.

3.   The selection procedure works against children from working-class families where the home background is not conducive to study. The proportion of children selected for grammar schools in the middle-class areas was very much higher than the proportion in working-class areas. Hence, a great deal of potential talent was wasted. For evidence of the influence of social class on school performance see the 1954 Report of the Minister of Education's central advisory council, entitled *Early Leaving*.

4.   Selection and the tripartite system is seen by some as a form of educational apartheid conducive to an elitist and authoritarian society. On the other hand, they consider comprehensive schools as conducive to a more homogeneous, democratic and egalitarian society.

5.   In rural areas it is not an economic proposition to have a small grammar school and a small secondary modern school, and thus most people agree that in rural areas comprehensives are what are needed.

What are the arguments against comprehensive schools?
1.   If a grammar and comprehensive school existed in the same area, the grammar school would probably cream off the brighter pupils and the comprehensive school would cease to be comprehensive. Hence

comprehensive schools necessitate the destruction of good grammar schools.

2. The less academic pupil, for his or her own sake, needs a different kind of educational environment than the academic type. In any case, as the Spens Report stated (1938): 'It would be difficult . . . to find Heads who would be competent to control and inspire both developments as to control and inspire one or the other.'

3. The brighter children develop best with other bright children in the more academic atmosphere of a grammar school, and we need to develop brighter children to the utmost to have leaders of industry and commerce and the professions in sufficient numbers and of sufficient calibre.

Some general points on the comprehensive debate

There seems no reason why, given the right sort of school buildings, similar equipment and quality of teachers, as good an education cannot be provided for a bright child in a comprehensive school as in a grammar school. Indeed, some supporters of comprehensives would say they give a better education because a comprehensive school is a better reflection of society than a grammar school.

The main criticism of comprehensive schemes of education arises from a desire to retain the grammar school, or at least it would appear so. But does this go deep enough? Is not our attitude to comprehensive schools in secondary education and polyversities in higher education determined to a great extent by our political faith? The people who support comprehensive schools are usually the same sort of people who support the polyversities, and they tend to be more radical, while more conservative people tend to oppose them. This is because the radical has much more faith than the conservative in the power of the environment to change an individual's way of life: hence his greater faith in blueprints for a better world and a greater willingness to accept change. The radical sees the environment of a comprehensive school, because it embraces children of all abilities and social backgrounds, as being more conducive than the tripartite system to creating the more democratic and homogeneous society which he desires. The conservative, on the other hand, is more inclined than the radical to believe in Original Sin, has less faith in the power of the environment to change individual personality and hence is more distrustful of blueprints and new ideas, tending to see the advantages of the status quo. The grammar schools have served the country well – why destroy them? In any case all this talk of egalitarianism is so much romantic nonsense!

The comprehensive debate, like the polyversities debate, when we get down to it, is a political debate about the kind of society we want.

Comprehensives and the independent sector

While it is possible to abolish the state grammar schools and have a state comprehensive system, what of schools in the private sector? The government might ask them to become comprehensive and integrate into the state system, but it could hardly force them to join in the comprehensive system. Yet the state system will never be truly comprehensive if private schools cream off the brighter children for themselves. Very few are likely to join voluntarily – the majority would argue that to bring in a much wider range of ability into the schools would be to change their nature.

General Certificate of Secondary Education

Approximately 40 per cent of children leave secondary school with inadequate and sometimes no paper qualifications. Some employers have complained that young people come to them hardly literate or numerate. On the other hand, a far larger proportion of students now obtain GCSE level and 'A' level passes than in previous years. In 1985 the Government published a White Paper (Cmnd 9469) outlining its proposals for improving the system of primary and secondary education with its thoughts mainly centred on the 40 per cent of students for whom the normal 'O' level and CSE courses did not appear appropriate. As part of its policy for improving the educational system at secondary level the White Paper outlined the Government's policy for replacing the former GCE 'O' level courses and the CSE by the General Certificate of Secondary Education (GCSE) which became operative from September 1986. The first GCSE examinations were held in 1988. Thus, instead of two separate systems there is one single system. One of the aims is to try and find out what candidates know and hence, although a single system, there are 'differentiated papers or differentiated questions within papers in all subjects'. So all candidates should be able to answer all the required number of questions although some questions require greater skills than others and higher grades are given to those candidates who correctly answer the questions requiring higher skills. Although a single system, most schools divide pupils, after two, three or four years of their school career into different classes according to their supposed abilities. Thus pupils of similar abilities in a particular subject are eventually taught together (see letter from the Deputy Chief Executive, Secondary Examinations Council, *The Listener*, 2 October 1986). This is similar to the streaming which takes place in most comprehensive schools where a pupil can be in a low stream for one subject but a high stream for another subject. The comprehensive school made it possible for the system to be more flexible and it is hoped that the GCSE will increase this flexibility. With the 40 per cent low achievers in mind, the Government in its White Paper emphasises the importance of 'craft and practical skills'. Some schools do provide courses leading to vocational qualifications which the Government wishes to encourage and, apart from these courses, there is the TVEI four-year course.

The GCSE does not affect a GCE 'A' level. That is retained as 'A' level courses 'provide a foundation for degree courses and play an important role in selection for higher education'. The Government is, however, 'taking action to promote greater breadth for those engaged in 'A' level studies, without reducing standards'.

Developments in Secondary Education

Arising from the 1988 Education Reform Act, drastic changes are now in the process of development in the sphere of secondary education. The key changes were outlined in Chapter 11. What are some of the arguments for and against these changes? In the Government's view education had become too dominated by the producers – the teachers and the local authorities creating a cosy conservatism. It argued that more power had to be given to the consumers – the parents and the employers. Whilst not actually blaming teachers and local authorities for the fact that between 40 and 50 per cent of children underachieve, the inference was that if parents and employers had had more say results would have been better. (Education standards are important to employers as well as parents because they affect the efficiency of their labour force.) Hence parents now have increased representation on the boards of school governors and employers are represented as well. And governors have now more power and influence because, under the 1988 Act, under delegation from the local authority, they have become responsible for the major financial decisions of the school providing the school has more than 200 pupils. But, in the Government view, the most important way parent influence can be made effective is through the new way schools are financed. No longer are there catchment areas where children normally go to school in the area in which they live. Instead, as in higher education, schools compete in the market place for pupils as the number of pupils a school has is an important factor in its funding. And because parents decide to which school their children go they have the power to make a school a financial success or failure.

The Government argues that a school will only fail financially if it is known to be a bad school but that this is not likely to happen because when it is not recruiting pupils in sufficient numbers changes will be made to stop the decline, the most effective being a change of headmaster. In this way, thanks to the competition the new financial arrangements have introduced, good schools will remain good and bad schools will become good. For parents to choose schools, they must have information about them. This information is provided by the schools because, to win parental approval, schools must publicise their wares. For a head teacher and senior staff, now more involved with school governors in matters of finance and now having to adopt a 'marketing strategy', there is a great deal of extra work. And all this has come at a time of a teacher shortage, of badly maintained school buildings, and the introduction of a new national curriculum necessitating frequent testing of pupils resulting in much extra paper work.

If experience is anything to go by, the vast majority of parents, although very interested in their children's progress at school, are not interested in the business of helping to run a school and hence are reluctant to volunteer as governors. And those that do, find the work very time consuming and those that continue to carry on are not representative of parents as a whole. The role of parents, critics claim, is to help and support, not to be involved in policy making. Furthermore, the average parent is not in a position to judge the best school for their children. All that parents can do in choosing a school is to go on hearsay and the advertising blurbs schools are producing which, like all advertising, are not likely to tell the whole truth. What further aggravates choice is that some schools have more money than others for advertising and the one that advertises most and impresses most may not be the best school. However, the Government can argue that the National Curriculum, by introducing common attainment standards at different age levels for all schools and the compulsory publishing of their results, does provide for parents a measure not only of their children's progress but also of the standards of the various schools. But is it a fair measurement as so much depends on the family and social background of the children?

As for the power over school budgets which governors have, it is clear that even when an experienced businessman, from parent representation, has been involved in budgeting, funds have been so limited that there has been little room for manoeuvre, which has led to much frustration. Criticisms have thus been made that there is insufficient money to make the budgeting job worthwhile. It is not just insufficient money from the Government but employers have not come forward with money as the Government hoped they would. This, of course, may change. On the other hand, many heads will perhaps echo the words of one primary school head:

'Years of frustration and persuasion on the telephone have rolled away' (*Guardian*, 29 January 1991).

Not all parents are able to send their children to the school of their choice because of the physical limitations on the number of children a school can accommodate. However the Government has encouraged schools to maximise their accommodation where necessary so that an increasing number of parents should get their first choice of school.

The power under the 1988 Act which allows a school, with the consent of the majority of parents and subject to Government approval, to opt out of local authority control and acquire grant-maintained status can adversely affect the remaining schools in the local authority and the educational arrangements within the local authority. This arises if the opting-out school played an important role in the allocation of pupils and courses within the local authority. In March 1989 a legal judgement, arising from a case brought before the court by a local authority, overruled one school's right to opt out because of the adverse effect it would have on other children in the authority.

Most teachers did not oppose the introduction of the national curriculum. They did, however, oppose the speed with which it was introduced. (It became operative from September 1989.)

Now that schools are permitted to charge for extras there is the danger that in some cases parents will be paying for what really is part of their children's basic education, contrary to the spirit of the 1944 Education Act which abolished fees in State-maintained schools. Furthermore, the difference in the facilities between many schools in middle-class areas and those in poorer working-class areas will be made even more startling.

Schools are now supposed to cement links with industry and commerce to include children gaining work experience before they leave school. Judged by the attitude of employers in the past, critics have the right to ask if employers, apart from one or two, will be sufficiently interested to make such links.

PRIMARY EDUCATION

Over the years there has been a revolutionary change in teaching methods. Children now learn by doing rather than being lectured at. There are critics, however, who feel that the large number of school-leavers who cannot do simple arithmetic nor write clearly goes back to the 'new-fangled' teaching methods. They argue that many pupils in secondary schools find it difficult to sit and listen because they never learned the habit in the primary school as the learning by doing necessitated so much moving around. The White Paper, 'Better Schools' (Cmnd 9469) published in 1985 stated that literacy and numeracy would be improved if their teaching was related to the context in which they were needed and that pupils' abilities were often underestimated and that 'they were not given enough responsibility to pursue their own inquiries'.

Many new primary schools have been built but there are still old and inferior buildings being used for primary education; classes are still too big in spite of a greater proportion of the education budget since 1985 having been allotted for primary education. In 1989, 17 per cent of primary classes still had 31 or more pupils (in 1977 it was 34 per cent).

The national curriculum applies to primary schools but only the core subjects of English, Mathematics and Science are assessed in detail.

INDEPENDENT SCHOOLS SINCE 1945

Here we are concerned with possible developments. The main concern has been in the past how to integrate the independent (i.e. private) sector of education into the public sector (about 7 per cent of the school population go to independent schools). The 1944 Report of the Committee on Public Schools (the Fleming Report) expressed concern at 'the unreality of an educational system which segregates so thoroughly the boys of one class from those of another in a world where, much more than in the past, they will meet in later life as equals'. It recommended that a minimum of 25 per cent of places should be reserved at day schools and boarding schools for pupils from local authority schools. Arising from this report, more independent schools (mainly the day schools) opened their doors to pupils from local authority schools. More independent schools accepted financial help from the central government and became direct-grant schools, having to reserve at least 25 per cent of their places free for children from local authority schools. (The local authority paid the direct-grant school for the children's tuition.) In recent years some local authorities with a comprehensive system of education refused to take up places at direct-grant schools for children in local authority schools because the direct-grant schools refused to become comprehensive. Starting in September 1976, direct-grant schools began to be phased out. They had either to join the maintained system (i.e. be financially supported, either wholly or partly, by the local authorities) and become part of the comprehensive system, or they had to become completely independent. In January 1976, 51 had opted to join the maintained sector.

Those direct-grant schools that chose to become independent felt that if they became comprehensive their special qualities would be lost. The phasing out of direct-grant schools was recommended by the Report of the Public Schools Commission of March 1970 (the Donnison Report). It also recommended that independent schools should be integrated into the state system. The 1980 Education Act with its assisted places scheme halted this trend.

EDUCATION FOR LEISURE (ADULT EDUCATION)

There have always been people who take up educational courses in their leisure time simply for the fun of it. Higher living standards since 1945 and, more recently, high unemployment and the growth of active retired people have greatly increased their numbers. Such courses range from pottery to philosophy. Their needs are catered for by the Workers' Educational Association, the extra-mural department of universities, evening classes (including some day classes) in state schools and colleges, radio and television. Because of greater financial stringency on the Government's part all forms of adult education have been adversely affected and in some places severely cut.

Value for Money?

The more we spend on education, the less we can afford other things. Hence it is important that the money is well spent. In other words, the money invested in education should give an adequate return. In business it is possible to express the return on a sum invested as a percentage of that sum of money. This is what is meant by the percentage return on capital and it can be compared with the money return on other investments. It is one way of finding out how to allocate the country's resources between different uses. But how can the return on any given sum spent on education be measured? Education to those who receive it provides a great deal of individual satisfaction, but this cannot be measured in money terms. Education helps economic growth by providing skills but just how much nobody knows, though attempts have been made to measure it. But even if education did not help economic growth, it would still be worthwhile because, by making citizens more knowledgeable, it creates a more understanding society, and therefore a pleasanter society to live in.

Although it might be almost impossible to assess the return on the overall investment in education, perhaps in specific spheres money could be spent more productively. The Government is hoping that one spin-off from its policy of restricting the growth of expenditure on education will be greater efficiency in education, the savings from which will partly compensate for the shortfall in money provided.

Equality of Opportunity

Does our education system provide equality of opportunity? Until recently it did in theory, in that all students using the state or private system of education had the opportunity to get to a university to pursue their studies at the highest level. Thanks to government financial assistance in the form of student grants, no student needed to discontinue his or her education because of lack of money.

But the financial cuts in education and, in addition, the reduction in the real value of student grants (all part of the expenditure cuts of the Thatcher government) have made this no longer true. And the recently introduced loan system (see p. 139) might worsen the situation.

But even if students who are qualified can find a place in higher education, it does not mean there is equal opportunity for all students to pursue their studies to the highest stage commensurate with their abilities. Thus two young people might have equal intelligence, yet one might gain a university degree and the other leave school at 15 without an academic certificate. The following are some of the factors that might be responsible for this and thus stand in the way of equal opportunity.

1. Home background is of vital importance in educational attainment. Some children have a home conducive to happy study; some have not. Evidence reveals that a much higher proportion of students in higher education come from middle-and upper-class homes than from working-class homes. Some suggested reasons for this are:
    (a) the majority of working-class parents have more modest aspirations for their children's careers than middle- and upper-class parents
    (b) a higher proportion of working-class homes are less conducive to study than middle- and upper-class homes
    (c) many working-class parents cannot afford to buy books which would aid their children's education
    (d) some people argue that schools have a middle-class outlook or ethos which working-class children find more difficult to attune themselves to than middle- and upper-class children.

2. Some schools are better than others – they have better teachers, smaller classes, or both; or the students who go to them come from homes where study is encouraged, so the teacher-student relationship is a good one. Hence a student going to one of these schools is more likely to do well than if he went to a school where the teachers were poor, the classes large and fellow-students not so keen on study because of parental indifference. In general, within the state system, middle-class areas have better schools than working-class areas.

This criticism also applies to comprehensive schools. Although, on the whole, they help to further educational opportunity, comprehensive schools in middle-class areas will tend to be more 'successful' than those in poorer areas.

Some local authorities spend more money than others on education. How successful a child is can therefore depend, to some extent, on where he or she lives.

Private schools often have better facilities and gain more GCSEs and 'A' level credits than state schools because they have more money to employ more teachers to keep class sizes down and can pay teachers above the normal pay scale in order to obtain well-qualified staff.

Can anything be done to weaken the forces working against equality of opportunity? Only parents themselves can provide a home environment conducive to study, but what already has influenced parents to encourage their children's studies and will continue to do so in the future are higher living standards and the widening of educational opportunity. Higher living standards increase material satisfaction and whet the appetite for more. At the same time, widening educational opportunity makes more parents appreciate that education can be a means of obtaining a higher income and increased material satisfactions because it qualifies, in principle, a young person for a better job. But however enlightened parents become, there will always be inequalities of opportunity because of differences in home background and differences between schools – although a good school can compensate for a poor home background. To help reduce the difference between areas, there developed the concept of Educational Priority Areas (EPAs), which means channelling a greater proportion of resources to the schools in the deprived areas. Extra resources have been made available to some areas but not on the scale as originally envisaged. But the long-term solution is to increase the standard of living of the working class and rebuild deprived environments. This is already taking place, but too slowly. The problem is particularly acute in the inner-city areas of the older industrial towns.

Should private schools perhaps be abolished to equalise opportunity between the most affluent sections of the population and the rest? This, to some people, would be an attack on personal liberty. Why should parents be forced to send their children to a state school if they want to send them to a good private school? Furthermore, there are a great variety of private schools (although admittedly not all are good) and some educational advance has been due to the experimental nature of some of these private schools. On the other hand, there are those who say the state system of education will never be as good as it should be while those in positions of power and influence can opt out of it by using the private system. It they had to use the state system for their own children, they would soon see to it that the state system was very much improved.

The answer here is perhaps not to abolish the private system but to devote more resources to the state system so that differences between two sectors are diminished. In this century much progress has been made in this direction, but much more still needs to be done. The cutting back of teacher-training was perhaps a backward step as there is now developing a teacher shortage. The average class size in the state primary schools varies between local authorities but is now around twenty-two, which is perhaps still too many to ensure that all are properly taught. And it is in the primary school where the foundations of the basic skills – reading, writing and arithmetic – are learnt. About 25 per cent of primary classes have thirty children or more. In secondary schools the average size is sixteen. We should perhaps work for more equality of income so that all parents have a more equal chance of sending their children to a good private school if they wish to.

SUMMARY

Secondary education for all inevitably led to a big expansion of higher education, an expansion encouraged by greatly increased financial assistance to students and higher living standards in general. Because of the problems associated with the economy – particularly the problem of inflation from the mid-70s onwards and the Thatcher government's attitude to public expenditure arising from these problems – education, as with other services, has been under financial constraints resulting in less money for universities, a higher student-staff ratio in polytechnics and inadequate maintenance of many schools – although the Government would possibly blame local authorities for this poor maintenance. More emphasis has been given to gearing education to the needs of commerce and industry and, arising from this, it is hoped more and more money will go into education from the private sector. In line with the Government's belief in the efficacy of market forces for ensuring the most effective use of resources, the finance of education is to be much more influenced by consumer demand.

The 40 per cent of school leavers who leave school with virtually no qualifications has led the Government to be critical of the way education has been handled by local authorities and so schools can opt out of local authority control and the heads and governors of all local authority schools have more autonomy in the running of their schools with parents having greater representation on their governing boards. But whilst the Government has encouraged more local autonomy in the administration of education, it has tightened central control of its content. Apart from losing opted-out schools, local authorities are to lose further education in April 1993 (they are no longer involved in higher education). Britain still lags behind some of our industrial competitors in the development of post-school education for the less academic type of student – an education which could include English, a foreign language and vocational subjects. However, all parties are aware of the problem and have published proposals for improving the situation.

Side by side with the state system of education, the private system of primary and secondary education for the richer members of the community has continued to flourish. When egalitarian ideas were more fashionable, much thought was devoted to finding ways of integrating the private and state systems but nothing has come of it. Like one's attitude to comprehensive schools, how far one thinks this is necessary, even if possible, depends, to a great extent, on the sort of society one thinks we should be aiming for.

The need for an efficient labour force and pressures from a more educated and affluent electorate are still the main factors in the development of education over the years.

ASSIGNMENTS

1. Make a list of the independent schools in your district or county local authority. How far do you think independent schools should be an essential part of our education system?

2. What do you understand by 'equality of educational opportunity'? To what extent is there equality of educational opportunity in Britain? What factors have contributed to greater equality of educational opportunity since 1945?

3. If possible, obtain from your local authority the average class size in its primary schools and secondary schools. Also, what percentage of its primary schoolchildren are in classes of thirty of more?
4. Discuss how the student intake at your college has been affected (if at all) by government policies in the last few years.

READING

Rodney Barker, *Education and Politics 1900–1951: A Study of the Labour Party* (Oxford University Press, 1972).

Central Advisory Council for Education (England) *Reports*:
  Crowther Report, *15–18* (HMSO, 1959).
  Newsom Report, *Half Our Future* (HMSO, 1963).
  Plowden Report, *Children and Their Primary Schools* (HMSO, 1967).

John Clare, 'Schools of Scandal: the Failure of Britain's Education System', *The Listener*, 31 July 1986.

C. B. Cox and A. E. Dyson, *Black Paper 2: The Crisis in Education* (Critical Quarterly Society, 1969).

'Debate on schools', *Hansard*, vol. 165, no. 36, 24 January 1990.

Education: A Framework for Expansion, Cmnd 5174 (HMSO, December 1972).

'Higher and Continuing Education', *Hansard*, vol. 100, no. 136, 25 June 1986.

HMSO, *Better Schools*, Cmnd 9469 (HMSO, 1985).

HMSO, *The Curriculum Reform 5–16* (HMSO, 1985).

HMSO, *The Development of Higher Education into the 1990s*, Cmnd 9524 (HMSO, 1985).

HMSO, *Education for Adults: A Review by HM Inspectorate of Schools* (HMSO, 1991).

HMSO, *Education and Training for the 21st Century*, Cm 1536 (HMSO, May 1991).

HMSO, *Education for All: a Brief Guide to the Main Issues of the Swann Report* (Cmnd, 9453) *on the Education of Children from Ethnic Minority Groups* (HMSO, 1985).

HMSO, *Higher Education: a new framework*, Cm 1541 (HMSO, May 1991).

HMSO, *Primary Education in England: A Survey of HM Inspectors of Schools* (HMSO, 1978).

HMSO, *Review of Vocational Qualifications in England and Wales: a Report* (HMSO, 1986).

James Report, *Teacher Education and Training: A Report by a Committee of Inquiry* (HMSO, 1972).

William Letwin (ed.), *Against Equality* (Macmillan, 1983).

'Minister's statement on Further and Higher Education', *Hansard*, vol. 191, no. 111, 20 May 1991.

Robin Pedley, *The Comprehensive School*, 3rd edn (Penguin, 1978).

Maurice Preston, 'Higher Education: Financial and Economic Aspects', *Royal Bank of Scotland Review*, December 1985.

Public Schools Commission Second Report, *Report on Independent Day Schools and Direct Grant Grammar Schools* (HMSO, 1979).

Robbins Report, *Report of the Committee on Higher Education*, Cmnd 2154 (HMSO, 1963).

Eric Robinson, *The New Polytechnic* (Cornmarket, 1968).

David Rubenstein (ed.), *Education and Equality* (Penguin, 1979).

Russell Report, *Adult Education: A Plan for Development* (HMSO, 1973).

Stuart Simon, 'Higher Education Solely a Means to an Economic End?', *The Listener*, 6 June 1985.

13 Youth Service

DEFINITION

By 'youth service' is meant the many local authorities and voluntary organisations which provide informal educational and social activities for young people. The official title under which they all operate is the 'Service of Youth'.

HISTORY

Voluntary bodies involved with the welfare of young people were active in the latter part of the nineteenth century. During the First World War the government encouraged local authorities to set up juvenile organisation committees comprising representatives from the local education authorities, voluntary organisations and interested individuals to encourage youth activities. These committees continued to function in many areas in the interwar years – the vast majority of the services were provided by voluntary organisations like the YMCA, the YWCA, Girl Guides, Boy Scouts, etc.

During the Second World War the Board of Education (which became the Ministry of Education in 1944) became responsible for youth welfare, and local education authorities were again reminded of the need to co-operate with voluntary bodies by means of local youth committees in order to promote youth activities – the local authorities providing premises and money. A National Youth Committee was created and later replaced by the Youth Advisory Council, which made reports on youth activities on the assumption that they were an essential part of the education service. During the war the opportunities for helping the war effort stirred the imagination of many young people and the Youth Service expanded rapidly. Under the 1944 Education Act it became an integral part of further education. This meant that local authorities had not only to provide full-time and part-time education for persons over school-leaving age, but also 'leisure-time occupation in such organised cultural, training and recreational activities as are suited to their requirements.'

In the mid-1950s criticisms were made that the Youth Service received inadequate funds from central and local government, and it is true that

166

interest in it had waned. Perhaps one reason for this was that there were all sorts of important developments requiring a great deal of government money. Thus resources were limited and the Youth Service suffered when economies had to be made. In 1958 the Albermarle Committee was appointed: 'To review the contribution which the Youth Service of England and Wales can make in assisting young people to play their part in the life of the community . . . and to advise according to what priorities best value can be obtained for the money spent. Its report, 'The Youth Service of England and Wales' came out in 1960. It stressed that the Youth Service should be concerned with a young person's all-round development and not simply act as a provider of activities to fill a young person's leisure time. Arising from its main recommendations, local authorities gave more help to youth organisations both in money terms and the provision of more adequate premises. A Youth Service Development Council was set up to advise the Minister of Education and a national college for the training of youth leaders was founded. Today certain universities and colleges of higher education provide training courses. Qualified youth leaders are assisted by part-time workers. Qualified teachers are recognised as qualified youth workers. The Youth Service Development Council was disbanded in 1971. The present advisory body to the DES is the Youth Service Review Group.

The 1960s saw a big expansion of the Youth Service after the Albermarle Report but during this decade problems arising from immigration and social deprivation came to the fore. In the 'seventies, problems related to the economy led to financial restraints and the Service seemed to lose its sense of direction. Hence a Review Group looked into the Youth Service. Its report, published in 1982, popularly known as the Thompson Report (Cmnd 8686), stated that the first duty of the Youth Service was 'to help all young people who have need of it'. This help takes three main forms: (i) providing pleasurable recreation; (ii) providing a rescue service for young people who are unhappy and near despair; (iii) providing social education. Social education involves joint activity with other young people which gives greater confidence in personal relationships; participation in decision-making within the group which develops responsibility; community service, which in turn can lead to participation in community affairs and political activities on issues which affect young people, and this can provide greater knowledge of the workings of society and of democratic process.

The Report was very critical of the Youth Service for 'not meeting the social education of young people as fully as it should'. Shortage of money may be a 'contributory factor' but the main reasons are underestimating the importance of social education and not making clear what is meant by it. The Youth Service has failed to take relations with the local community seriously. People do not know 'what the Youth Service is about'. It has failed to co-operate with other organisations and there is 'inadequate provision to meet the needs of the over-16s'. The committee is not just blaming Youth Service workers for these shortcomings – local authorities and central government must also share the blame. Of its many recommendations, one is that staff training should be 'monitored' by a national supervisory panel' and that a minister within the DES should co-ordinate the work of all departments with an interest in youth affairs and that he should speak for the Youth Service within the administration. The Government eventually responded to this critical report by issuing DES, *Circular 1/85*. It stated the Youth Service 'is of immense value to the Nation' and it also praised the voluntary sector – the main provider of the Youth Service. The Government accepted the need for greater co-ordination of the various organisations involved with youth. Hence, arising from the Report, the Government set up a national advisory council for the Youth Service on which sit representatives of youth organisations, including young people themselves. The Government also set up a youth unit within the DES which goes some way to meet the Review's recommendation for a minister within the DES to co-ordinate the work of departments with an interest in youth affairs. It urged local authorities to improve their links with youth organisations to help improve co-ordination of activities and, with the aim of improving training, 'all concerned' should co-operate with the Council for Education and Training in Youth and Community Work, established in December 1982. Local authorities are asked to report to the Secretary of State for the DES their existing arrangements for co-ordination, planning and management of the youth organisations in their area and give their views on how these arrangements contribute to effective training. Voluntary organisations should be encouraged to improve their management techniques and 'grant aid is available for voluntary organisations for short-term experimental projects in managerial innovation'. The youth organisations responded to the DES circular in a joint statement in March 1986. They stressed the need for close links with local authorities which 'have the duty to secure the provision of services for young people'. But they also stressed that 'an effective Youth Service is . . . dependent upon it having adequate finance'. The implication must be that in their opinion youth organisations are not adequately financed, and that some local authorities do not have close enough links with the Youth Service. On the question of finance, the Youth Service is not likely to get any extra cash from central and local government. In its opening paragraphs to its circular, in keeping with its economic philosophy, the Government warned of the limited amount of money available. 'Local authorities will need, in future, to continue to appraise carefully their funding of the Youth Service relative to other claims on their total expenditure.'

In 1988 the Government announced that, in future, there would be periodic national conferences comprising representatives of the voluntary and statutory Youth Service to discuss issues of common concern.

ADMINISTRATION TODAY

Broad policy is laid down by the DES within which local authorities and voluntary organisations must work. Apart from helping voluntary organisation by providing premises, equipment and financial assistance, many local authorities supplement the work of the voluntary organisations by providing youth centres and clubs of their own. Most local authorities have youth councils, advised by full-time, paid youth officers, which comprise representatives of the voluntary organisations as well as the local authority. In spite of local authority financial assistance, the voluntary organisations provide most of the money they need themselves. In England most of them are members of the National Council for Voluntary Youth Services.

There are two main types of youth organisation – those that are linked with a local parent organisation like church youth clubs and those which are not attached to a local parent body. The Boy Scouts and Girl Guides can belong to either type, though they are linked to a national parent body.

Among other bodies representing youth is the British Youth Council which represents all the main voluntary youth organisations and is the main forum of the Youth Service. It also acts as a pressure group. Some other organisations are the Community and Youth Workers Union, the National Association of Youth and Community Education Officers, the National Association of Youth Clubs, the National Association of Boys' Clubs, the Youth Hostels Association, Young Men's Christian Association, the Young Farmers' Clubs, and so on. Acting as an umbrella and helper for them all is the National Youth Bureau, founded in 1973, financed mainly by the Central Government.

Some of the Problems of the Youth Service

Apart from the criticisms made in the Thompson report mentioned above there is still the immediate practical problem of the shortage of good youth leaders. However, there has been some progress. In 1957 there were only 700 full-time staff; in 1988 there were 3500 full-time youth leaders and about 500 000 part-time staff.

The problems of the Youth Service cannot be isolated from the problems of the wider society. We want the Youth Service, apart from providing games and dances and adventure pursuits, to help make good citizens with a sense of community service. But if the society within which the young find themselves exalts material success, and aggressive competition to obtain it, is it any wonder that many young people think of a youth group in terms of what they can get out of it rather than in terms of what they can contribute? It is significant that, during the Second World War, when Britain had a cause worth fighting for and fought for it, the Youth Service had its most rapid expansion. However, a hopeful trend in recent years, both within and outside the Youth Service, has been the growing number of young people who give up their spare time to help the elderly, the sick and the handicapped. The young people doing such voluntary work in the community are often members of such organisations as the International Voluntary Service, Task Force and Community Service Volunteers, which receive financial help from the DES and a number of grant-giving foundations. At the same time, schemes like the Duke of Edinburgh's Award Scheme, which operate through various organisations and firms, help to develop in young people a sense of challenge and purpose in life. A DES discussion paper produced in 1975, *Provision for Youth*, is relevant. It raises the question as to how far the Youth Service should keep to its primary educational function of developing activities for leisure time, or how far it should co-operate with workers in other social services in helping the disadvantaged. This also applies to delinquents. For example, young delinquents under the supervision of a social worker or probation officer may be given 'intermediate treatment' when, under a supervisor, they are given constructive activities to help them become good citizens. Various sections of the Youth Service have been encouraged to accept people on 'intermediate treatment' into their midst. Unfortunately youth groups have not always co-operated and, in certain areas, the probation and after-care service has had to expand its own 'intermediate treatment' activities.

The underlying assumption of the Youth Service is that it helps to develop in a beneficial way young people's characters. But some people see a danger here. Thus a youth club might become an end in itself. It may actually segregate the young people from the community around them and, within it, young people might develop their own code of right and wrong which may not be the community's code and may be harmful to a young person's development. This is especially true in the inner-city areas, where a shabby environment and an exceptionally high rate of unemployment results in many young people feeling cut off from the mainstream of society. While young people need to work things out for themselves in their own groupings, they also need the experience and guidance of adults. One has to strike a balance between the two. The youth organisation should be separate from and yet part of the larger community.

SUMMARY

The Youth Service effectively dates from the Second World War. It comprises mainly voluntary organisations assisted by local education authorities who often supplement the work of the voluntary organisations by running youth clubs of their own. All are linked under the umbrella of a local authority youth council, advised by full-time youth officers, operating within a framework of regulations laid down by the DES. The aim of the Youth Service is to help young people broaden their interests and become good citizens. To some extent, therefore, it complements the work of schools. But the Youth Service can only marginally affect the good-citizenship aim; the main influence in this connection is the total environment in which the young person finds himself, and the Youth Service is only a small part of this environment. In recent years greater recognition has been given to this; and while the Youth Service still has an important role in catering for the individual needs of the young, it is much more concerned today than it used to be with social and political issues, though the 1982 Report of the Committee of Inquiry into the Youth Service found its involvement in such issues not very widespread. It should, however, be remembered that the Youth Service is responsible for only a relatively small proportion of youth provision.

In 1990 there was published a survey of the Youth Service by H. M. Inspectorate which gave a more detailed insight into the work of the Youth Service. It sees the Youth Service as providing social education by offering young people a range of experiences from which they can learn how to cope with many of the problems with which they may be confronted. At the same time the Youth Service 'endeavours to respond to urgent social needs'. Thus the Youth Service helps young people acquire skills for work by giving them support on training and vocational courses; it can help a young person in finding a home; it can teach respect for the law and help young people resist drugs. This necessitates youth workers working with volunteers from 'the local communities' and 'skilled professional staff' operating in other fields and hence, from the centre from which they operate, having a 'team approach'.

The Inspectorate does, however, imply the Service is inadequately funded. It 'has a good record in stretching its modest resources a long way'. And 'often youth workers operate in discouraging circumstances in poor buildings with inadequate facilities'.

ASSIGNMENTS

1.   If you were running a youth club, what sort of activities would you organise? Give reasons for your choice.
2.   Go to the reference library and ask for the *Report of the Review Group on the Youth Service in England*, Cmnd 8686 (1982). After studying it, choose what you consider are two of its more important recommendations. Then discuss their significance.
3.   Find the names of five organisations in your area which cater for young people. Give the name and address of their secretaries and write a short paragraph on each, outlining their main activities.
4.   'Effective youth work seeks to foster young people's personal and social development and to respond effectively to those who have pressing social needs.' (H. M. Inspectorate). Discuss making use of knowledge you have gained from contacts with a youth organisation.

READING

A Joint Statement on DES circular 1/85 (National Youth Bureau, March 1986).

Albermarle Report, *The Youth Service in England and Wales*, Cmnd 929 (HMSO, 1960).

Annual Report of the Duke of Edinburgh's Award Scheme.

Experience and Participation: Report of the Review Group on the Youth Service in England, Cmnd 8686 (HMSO, October 1982).

Provision for Youth, Discussion Paper (Department of Education and Science, 1975).

Tony Jeffs and Mark Smith (eds), *Youth Work* (Macmillan, 1987).

National Youth Bureau, *Year Book of the Youth Service in England and Wales*.

The Youth Service and urgent social needs – a survey by H. M. Inspectorate (HMSO, 1990).

14 Employment Services

ORIGINS

The 1909 Labour Exchanges Act created the first national system of labour exchanges, later called employment exchanges and now called jobcentres. They were the first government offices to be built to provide a service for the people and they began business from February 1910. Their purpose was to reduce unemployment. They could not create work, but unemployment was often due to lack of knowledge – workers not being aware of jobs available perhaps only a few miles away and employers not being aware of the labour available locally. Before the 1909 Act, some local authorities and voluntary organisations had set up bureaux to put workers in touch with employers. At first the trade unions were suspicious of the labour exchanges fearing they would supply workers willing to accept less than the trade union rate of pay. Originally run by the Board of Trade, they became the responsibility of the newly created Ministry of Labour (now called the Department of Employment) in 1917.

EMPLOYMENT SERVICES TODAY

The 1973 Employment and Training Act removed direct responsibility for employment and vocational training services from the Department of Employment to a newly created Manpower Services Commission (MSC) which operated through an Employment Services Agency and a Training Services Agency. The employees of the MSC remained civil servants and the Department of Employment retained responsibility for manpower strategy and industrial relations. In 1988 the MSC was abolished and the employment services, since April 1990, have been run by an executive agency as the Employment Service. There is a separate Training Agency. Both agencies are still part of the Civil Service.

There are now many executive agencies, each covering a particular sphere of a Government department's work. Presumably the Government feels that this kind of administrative set-up within the Civil Service gives more scope for initiative by giving greater freedom to the administrators in their aim to meet Government targets.

For example, the head of the Employment Service is 'personally responsible to Ministers for achieving agreed results'. Employment services operate through jobcentres which give advice on jobs available, job and training opportunities and, in the main centres, there are occupational guidance units which help people with special problems and needs. There used to be at some centres a Professional and Executive Recruitment section but this has now been privatised. There are, of course, other private employment exchanges.

Unemployment benefit offices of the Department of Employment pay unemployment benefit through the post on behalf of the DSS. But the aim is to eventually bring these offices and jobcentres under one roof as, at the moment, many people have to visit both a jobcentre and unemployment benefit office in order to claim benefit. In 1986 a scheme called 'Restart' was introduced. Anyone unemployed for over six months is called for interview with a Restart counsellor and at six-monthly intervals afterwards if still unemployed. Problems relating to the unemployed person's search for a job are discussed. One of the following options may then be offered: a job, a place on a training scheme (see below), a place in a jobclub where job-hunting skills are taught and where facilities are available to help the unemployed in their job applications, or help, under the Enterprise Allowance Scheme, in starting a business. Under this scheme the unemployed person must have at least £1000 to put into the business but receives £40 a week for one year.

Another option could be a scheme called Jobstart where the unemployed person is offered an allowance of £20 a week (taxable) for up to six months if they accept a job paying less than £90 a week gross. However, after the Government's £20 a week finishes, the employee is left with a low wage and if he or she leaves the job unemployment benefit cannot be claimed for 13 weeks. The Government expects unemployed people who cannot get a job at a wage they have normally received, to accept a lower paid job if offered one. One might argue that the aim of Jobstart is to push the unemployed into low-paid jobs and, while Restart does help many unemployed to get a job, one of the reasons for introducing it was the Government view that many unemployed people were not genuinely seeking work.

Careers Service

Under the 1973 Employment and Training Act all local education authorities much provide a careers service for young people attending schools and colleges. (Universities and independent colleges of higher education, including polytechnics, have their own service). Careers officers, or teachers acting as careers officers, give help and advice in choosing a career and help in finding employment when the young person has completed his or her full-time education and, if necessary, making a check on how a young person is getting on in the early years of his career. The Department of Education has a Careers Service Branch which gives guidance on employment trends. But perhaps the main value of the careers service is not simply in finding young people jobs but, hopefully, helping them to make the best use of their talents. As far back as the 1910 Education (Choice of Employment) Act, local authorities were empowered to give advice on careers, if they so wished, to young people under 17. Many of the labour exchanges first set up in 1910 had juvenile departments to help young people find a job. In the inter-war years some local authorities ran their own juvenile employment service. The 1973 Act abolished the dual system.

Unemployment Statistics

In 1986 unemployment was at its peak – just over 3.1 million. Five years later, it had reduced only to around 2.5 million, roughly 6 per cent of the workforce. There are critics, however, who argue that there have been significant changes in the way that unemployment has been counted, and suggest that although there has been a downward trend in the stated numbers of the unemployed since 1986, the figures do not give an accurate measure of the total of unemployed people.

Whereas, previously, all who registered as unemployed were counted, only those unemployed who claim social security are now counted as unemployed and many previously employed people, particularly married women, do not claim benefit. People on training schemes are not counted as unemployed and 16- to 17-year-olds are now normally denied social security benefit if they refuse to go on Youth Training. Under the 1989 Social Security Act an 'actively seeking work' instead of the previous 'available for work' test has been introduced which, in many cases, denies people unemployment benefit because they are unemployed 'without good reason'. The reason, however, could be that the jobs offered were not considered suitable by the applicant, bearing in mind his or her experience and qualification. Hence many people in these circumstances do not bother to claim unemployment benefit. Those who need the money accept low-paid jobs they dislike. Many part-time workers who are not counted as unemployed would like a full-time job if they could get one.

Vocational Training

Technological progress means that at any given time some industries are declining and some expanding and the problem is to move workers from the declining industries into those that are expanding. This often necessitates a worker undergoing a course of training to learn new skills. For the training of skilled workers there was and still is, though now on a reduced scale, a system of apprenticeship which originated in the medieval craft guilds. Apprentices are recruited direct from school and were normally apprenticed to a trade for five years but now the apprenticeship is usually three to four years. They do their training on the job under supervision, often supplemented by the employer giving day release to the apprentice to attend a course related to his work at a further education college, although not all employers give day release. Previously there was the notion of an apprentice 'serving his time' but now standards of competence are usually the rule. Young people going into administrative work learn on the job and many attend day release courses to obtain a professional qualification but are not considered apprentices in the same way as those going to learn a trade or craft. The effectiveness of training depends mainly on employers; some take training seriously but, for many others, the young worker is expected to pick up the necessary skills as he or she goes along. And less than a third of young workers receive day release.

Government and Training

The Government itself has been responsible for a certain amount of training in what are now called skillcentres but previously called government training centres, originally set up after the First World War to re-train servicemen for civilian employment. But it was not until the 1970s that a significant expansion took place in the provision of skillcentres, although in recent years about a third of them have been closed down because of under use and much of the work taken over by a mobile training agency. The sixty skillcentres that remained were privatised in 1990 – forty-six being sold to Astra Training Services Ltd which also took over the Mobile Training Service. The skillcentres were administered by civil servants and many are now concerned about their employment prospects under private ownership.

Training provided by skillcentres has been supplemented over the years by a variety of other Government training schemes (see below). In the meantime the 1964 Industrial Training Act was an attempt to get employers themselves more involved in training. It gave the then Ministry of Labour power to set up Industrial Training Boards (ITBs). Twenty-three were created – one for virtually each of all the main industries. There are now only seven – the record of the remainder was not very satisfactory. The boards are financed, subject to the approval of Parliament, by a levy on firms within the industry (small firms exempted). But the employers receive back a percentage of the levy for each employee they release for training and for firms meeting specified training standards the levy is waived and the boards can give grants for training. Other bodies providing suitable training and sponsored by industry can receive financial help. At the time of writing, the Government intends that these 7 remaining boards should become independent statutory bodies supported by employers. Meanwhile Non-Statutory Training Organisations (NSTOs) have been set up on a voluntary basis by employers which carry out much the same work as ITBs. For small and medium sized firms there is a scheme called Business Growth Training introduced in April 1989. It gives Government financial help in obtaining professional assistance in the setting up of training schemes for employees.

Fresh efforts to get effective training schemes began in the 1980s. They were geared to two main groupings. One, the Youth Training Scheme (YTS) introduced in 1983 (now replaced by Youth Training which is an improved YTS – see Commons *Hansard*, 20 February 1990) is geared to 16-year-old school leavers who are unemployed. Originally a twelve month voluntary scheme, it was extended in 1986 to two years for 16-year-olds and one year for 17-year-olds but, under Youth Training, duration times of programmes have been made more flexible. The training is job-related and can lead to a recognised vocational qualification. There is a training allowance and training is provided by private employers, nationalised industries and local authorities which receive a grant from the Training Service. In September 1988 the Government decreed that 16- and 17-year-olds who were unemployed and who refuse to go on Youth Training will receive no social security benefit unless they can claim 'severe hardship'. This weakens the voluntary nature of the training scheme.

Another development in vocational training for young people is the Technical and Vocational Education Initiative (TVEI), which also began in 1983 with pilot schemes and which allows 14- to 18-year-olds to study a more vocationally orientated course at school and college to help them to be better prepared for working life. The National Council for Vocational Qualifications (NCVQ) organises the national system of defined levels of achievement for the various courses covering the various industries.

The white paper 'Employment and Training for the 21st century' outlines proposed further development for the vocational training of young people.

For young people leaving full-time education before the age of 18 there will be a training credit worth on average £1,000 to spend on training towards National Vocational Qualifications at a level broadly equivalent to GCSE. It is hoped this scheme will be fully operative by 1996. For those staying on at school there will be new qualifications to aim for geared to the world of work. In addition two new diplomas – one Ordinary and one Advanced – will combine academic and work-related qualifications, hopefully helping to promote equality of status between academic and vocational studies. The Compact scheme introduced in 1988 will be extended. This scheme for inner-city areas provides for compact agreements between employers, local education authorities and training providers whereby young people supported by the school or college work to achieve agreed targets. The great majority of school leavers will have a folder recording their achievements in education and training. This scheme began in the spring of 1991.

The other main grouping – adults and long-term unemployed – are now catered for by the Employment Training Scheme (ETS) introduced in September 1988. It replaced a number of training schemes for the long-term unemployed (i.e. anyone unemployed for over six months) including the Community Programme. Skills taught range from basic skills to those needed for the high-technology industries. As with Youth Training, ETS is supervised by the Training Agency of the Department of Employment which has the general aim of promoting vocational training and getting more employers involved in it. A training manager directs the actual training but training managers do not necessarily give the training themselves. They arrange suitable placements with employers who receive a grant from the Training Agency. Trainees receive an allowance equal to any social security benefit they may be receiving plus a training premium, travel expenses and, where necessary, a lodging allowance and special clothing and, for single parents, a child-care allowance. For those who do not get a job after training, a course of further training can be taken or entry to a jobclub. The average duration of training is six months although a trainee can remain on it for twelve months.

A new programme called 'Employment Action', operative from 1992, gives skilled workers who are unemployed work experience to help them keep up with their skills. They would work in the inner cities 'reinforcing the existing activities of voluntary organisations'.

Another government-funded training scheme is the Open College which began providing course from September 1987. There are fees for courses but unemployed people are not charged. Apart from Government money, the College raises money from corporate sponsors and others. Over 600 companies are associated with the College. Its courses are also transmitted on TV.

Training and Enterprise Councils (TECs)

The aim of the Government is to reduce its role in training and increase that of commerce and industry. In 1990 local Training and Enterprise Councils were introduced which, the Government hopes, will eventually take over the work of the Training Agency. Their job is to 'assess skill needs' in their areas, develop a 'training and enterprise strategy and manage existing training schemes'. At the same time they are to encourage local employers to be concerned about the training of their employees. Each TEC has a board of directors mainly comprised of top executives of the major companies at local level. About a third of the directors are drawn from education, trade unions, voluntary organisations etc. Civil servants are seconded from the Department Employment to do the administrative work. On a wider canvas the TECs will, hopefully, tackle skill shortages and strengthen the local economy. They receive Government money but are set annual targets by the Training Agency and rewarded for good performance. They are accountable to the local community as well as the Training Agency and publish annual reports. Eventually, it is hoped, 82 TECs will be operating. To assist in the formation of TECs a National Training Task Force was set up in 1990. It is also an advisory body to the Secretary of State for Employment on training matters and its general remit is to promote training to employers. TECs are to be represented on the governing bodies of further education colleges and sixth form colleges when these colleges are taken out of the hands of local government from April 1993. This is outlined in the white paper 'Education and Training for the 21st century' which also envisages the Careers Service being taken away from local Government and managed by TECs.

THE DISABLED

The shortage of manpower during the Second World War underlined the importance of getting servicemen and factory workers back to work after injury and was one of the main reasons for the development of services for the disabled. The first major scheme for training and resettlement of the disabled started in 1941 under the auspices of the then Ministry of Labour working in co-operation with the Ministry of Health. Its object was the rehabilitation of war casualties.

The present services to help disabled people find jobs are based on the Disabled Persons (Employment) Acts of 1944 and 1958. These acts were based on the finding of two committees – the Tomlinson Committee which reported in 1943 and the Piercy Committee which reported in 1956. A register of disabled people in the area is kept in the jobcentre. Registration by the disabled is voluntary although under the 1970 Chronically Sick and Disabled Persons Act local authorities must seek out the disabled and make known to them the services available.

Disablement Resettlement Officers (DROs)

Jobcentres have DROs. They give advice to disabled people on jobs and, when necessary, on rehabilitation and training. He or she is advised by a local disablement advisory committee now known as the Disablement Advisory Service (DAS) and others including the disabled person's family doctor. The Secretary for State for Employment is advised by the National Advisory Council on Employment of the Disabled.

Employment Rehabilitation Centres

Some disabled people can be found jobs alongside able bodied people without special training. Others need rehabilitating and the Employment Agency runs 26 rehabilitation centres where disabled people can adjust themselves gradually to normal working conditions. There are also mobile assessment teams. They are not taught new skills but given confidence and vocational guidance. The staff at the rehabilitation centre includes doctors, occupational psychologists, social workers, DROs and workshop supervisors with a knowledge of industry. The DRO at the centre and the DRO at the jobcentre co-operate when the time comes to find the disabled person a job. In more recent years mentally disabled people have been accepted at the centres. A few rehabilitation centres are run by voluntary organisations and receive financial help from the Department of Employment.

Sheltered workshops

For those disabled people who will not be able to work under normal conditions there are sheltered workshops run by Remploy, a non-profit-making company mainly financed by the Department of Employment. Its board is appointed by the Secretary of State for Employment who is the minister responsible for it. Some local authorities and voluntary bodies run sheltered workshops with the help of grants from the Department of Employment.

Blind people

There are special services for blind people and some jobcentres have blind persons resettlement officers. The Department of Employment gives financial assistance to those local authorities and voluntary organisations which provide sheltered employment for blind persons.

Other training opportunities
Where possible disabled people make use of the training facilities the non-disabled use – the Employment Training Scheme for example and Youth Training for the young disabled. Some go to skillcentres, some to further education colleges for training and some are trained for a professional career. Some employers are prepared to give training in skilled or semi-skilled work to the disabled and some voluntary organisations give training aided by grants from the Training Agency.

There is still criticism, however, that many employers discriminate against the disabled. For example, under the 1944 Disabled Persons (Employment) Act employers of more than 20 persons must normally employ a quota of disabled people – three per cent of the workforce. Many ignore this law but the projected fall in the number of young people over the next decade may make them think again about the recruitment of the disabled.

EQUAL OPPORTUNITIES

In 1951 women comprised 31 per cent of the labour force. In 1989 they comprised nearly 50 per cent. Half of all graduates are women. While many women are in secure, full-time jobs with pay and conditions comparable with men's (in central and local government, for example), most women workers are found in low-paid jobs – distribution, textiles, clothing and footwear and nearly half of them are clerical workers. But, even in the professions in relation to their numbers, they appear to be underrepresented among the most senior posts. To help reduce inequalities in employment between men and women, two acts were passed in 1975 – the Sex Discrimination Act and the Equal Pay Act. The Equal Opportunities Commission keeps an eye on the operation of these acts. At the same time it has called on TECs to provide more opportunity for women in employment and training not only to help women seeking employment but also to help reduce skill shortages. The Government is encouraging women, including married women with children, to go out to work. One reason for this is the estimated fall of over a million young people in the population during the next decade. However, the Government is not prepared to fund nurseries although it would welcome employers to provide them. This is what the Midland Bank has done and, according to its Personnel Director, is now saving £10 million a year. Previously the Bank lost 1000 women in management posts each year, leaving to start a family. Now the bank provides 400 creches (*Guardian*, 9 February 1990). There are many people, however, who feel women with young children below school age should not go out to work. Some mothers go out to work because they say they need the money, others because of their interest in a professional career.

DISCRIMINATION

Sometimes it is difficult to prove discrimination. Thus, if a woman or coloured person applied for a job and did not get it, it may be a case of discrimination but how can it be proved? The law, however, has helped to change attitudes. There is criticism that where discrimination has been proven, compensation to the complainant or the fine imposed on the employer has been too small to deter the bad employer. The 1989 Employment Act removed nineteenth century legislation which, in the field of employment protection, discriminated against women. They can now work underground in mines or work in quarries and clean machinery in factories! The Act also provides for women to receive statutory redundancy payments up to the age of 65 in line with men.

Employment Protection

The acts mentioned above under Equal Opportunities give a certain amount of employment protection in their attempt to reduce discrimination but there is an Employment and Protection Act passed in 1975, consolidated in 1978, which set up an Advisory and Arbitration Service (ACAS) to improve industrial relations and included the requirement that firms should consult appropriate trade unions about proposed redundancies. However, the trade union legislation of the Thatcher government weakened the bargaining position of the trade unions but there are those who think that certain trade unions had become too powerful. Employees are now normally entitled to receive from their employers written details of their conditions of employment. Employees with a minimum period of service of two years are entitled to lump sum redundancy payments if their jobs cease to exist and employers cannot find them suitable alternative employment. Employees can complain against an employer for unfair dismissal. Industrial tribunals set up under the 1964 Industrial Training Act, arbitrate between employer and employee on these and other matters.

The abolition in 1986 of wage protection for young people under 21 can give rise to their exploitation by bad employers. And the proposed abolition of all wages councils set up to provide minimum wages in trades and industries subject to low wages might seem contrary to spirit of good industrial relations. But lower wages, argues the Government, gives people a chance of getting a job by making firms more competitive.

Health and Safety at Work

Concern for the health and safety of workers began with the Factory Acts in the nineteenth century to protect workers in the textile trade and was extended, in the latter half of the century, to workers in other industries. The first legislation to protect miners was the 1842 Mines Act. Under Public Health Acts, local authorities can enforce sanitary standards in places of work. The 1961 Factories Act is the last in a long line of factory acts. The 1963 Offices, Shops and Railway Premises Act at last gave protection to office workers. The 1954 Mines and Quarries Act protects underground workers and there are special acts to protect farm workers, railway workers and seamen. The 1974 Health and Safety at Work Act (operative from 1 April 1975) strengthened the enforcement procedures of previous acts and extended their scope. Eventually it is intended to provide one comprehensive set of rules covering health and safety at work which will mean the gradual replacement of existing acts covering health and safety. Under the 1974 Act responsibility for health and safety at work was hived off from the Department of Employment and given to a Health and Safety Commission responsible to Parliament via the Secretary of State for Employment. It has seven advisory committees, covering toxic and dangerous substances, genetic manipulation and safety at nuclear installations. The 1974 Act set up a Health and Safety Executive responsible for enforcement but working in co-operation with local authorities. There is also an Employment Medical Advisory Service set up in 1973 with the job of identifying health risks at work and since 1975 it has operated within the Health and Safety Executive. It took over from the Medical Services Division of the Department of Employment. General practitioners and the advisory service must work closely together. Many employers, of course, voluntarily maintain a medical service for their employees. Other divisions within the Health and Safety Executive do research and give specialised advice on health and safety topics. Enforcement of the law on health and safety at work is carried out by inspectors who give no advance warning of their visits to firms. Since 1979 their numbers have fallen yet their role is vital in the prevention of injury and death – a role important both on humanitarian and economic grounds.

Some Problems

A high level of employment is important for social welfare. It provides income and reduces claims on the social services. On the other hand, unemployment leads to a greater demand on the social services because it often leads to illness, poverty, housing neglect, family breakdown, crime and even suicide. In addition, there is the financial cost to the nation arising from benefits paid to the unemployed, taxes foregone, output lost and the extra financial burden placed on the social services both statutory and voluntary. Yet, today, the high level of unemployment raises very little public outcry but, in 1979, although the amount of unemployment was much less, it was considered by all parties as unacceptable. The apparent collapse of the Keynsian system of demand management, with its aim of maintaining full employment, has perhaps led to the belief – held over a long period by many non-Keynsians – that for the market system to work efficiently unemployment is inevitable, though compensated for by a more dynamic economy and a higher growth rate which increases the wealth of the vast majority of the population and, it is argued, even the poorest are better off because of what is called the 'trickle down effect'. Therefore, the unemployed can be looked upon as sacrificial subjects on the altar of economic efficiency. If that is really the case, then they should at least be adequately compensated by the social security system.

In spite of the greater emphasis on training during the past decade, there is general agreement that we still have skill shortages and that we lag behind our industrial competitors in the provision of good vocational training for school-leavers and the long-term unemployed. In 1988 only half of our 17-year-olds stayed on in full-time education compared with two-thirds in most other major industrial countries. Roughly two-thirds of our labour force have no vocational qualifications. Some historians account for our skill shortages in terms of complacency generated by our being the first industrialised country and the centre of a great Empire; others argue that owning land gave greater status than running a business, and that bright children were encouraged to go into a profession rather than industry or trade, since professions commanded greater social prestige.

Of the Youth Training programme there is criticism that much of the training is at a low level and not sufficiently monitored by the Training

Agency and that many young people leave before completing their course. However, about 60 per cent who finish the course find jobs, albeit at low wages for many of them. There are training providers (voluntary organisations and firms) which provide training for the ETS and receive a grant from the Training Agency for each trainee on their books. But, after two years, there is still criticism that the courses are under-funded, leading, in many cases, to lack of adequate equipment for teaching purposes; and some employers have complained that the Government grant per trainee is too low to make the ETS an economic proposition for them. Since then, further cuts in Government funding have been made because of the reduction in unemployment. This will affect the recently created TECs spending plans. The Government feels employers should contribute more and the TECs are a means of getting more money from employers. In 1990 the drop-out of ETS was 70 per cent and, of the 30 per cent who finished the course, only half of them got a job – some firms being reluctant to accept trainees from the course. However, it is quite true, as the Government points out, that the ETS has upgraded the skill of many unemployed people making them more employable. But, say some critics, the courses are not demanding enough in spite of the NCVQ which monitors standards and do not give trainees the skills to meet international business competition. As with Education and Health, when criticism is levelled at under-funding the Government produces figures to show how much more money is being provided in real terms than previously but the providers of the services on the ground still complain of a shortage of resources.

The current emphasis on strictly vocational skills might seem to devalue the importance of humanistic studies. But the entrepreneurial flair which Britain seems to lack – if the exploitation of her inventions by other countries is anything to go by – is just as likely to be found among students of the humanities as among any other kind of student.

The development of a skilled workforce necessitates co-operation between employers, teachers and the Government. Employers, however, may expect only those skills to be taught which they consider strictly relevant to the job. But teachers, while accepting the importance of these skills, are also concerned with the all-round development of their students and their role not just in the firm but also in the wider society.

SUMMARY

Responsibility for Employment and Training was removed from the Department of Employment to the Manpower Services Commission by the 1973 Employment and Training Act. This devolution of direct responsibility for Employment and Training by the Government has continued with the abolition of the MSC and the setting up on an Employment Agency called the Employment Service and a Training Agency. These are now two of a number of agencies seen by the Government as giving a more flexible and perhaps more enterprising administrative system than that of a traditional government department. For Training, the Government, through the newly created TECs, seems to be passing the whole of the responsibility for Training on to employers – the Training Agency simply carrying out the aims of the Government on funding and the overall supervision of quality to ensure public money is not wasted.

The Government still gives the impression that it considers many claiming benefit cannot be genuinely seeking work. Thus, although the Restart programme can and has been of help to many of the unemployed, it can also be a means of keeping a look-out for the abusers of the social security system who, according to the Government, comprise as many as 20 per cent of the unemployed. It is perhaps significant of the Government's priorities that it does not give the same publicity to income tax fiddlers. The making of social security for 16- and 17-year-olds dependent on the acceptance of a training course introduces an element of compulsion which some see as the beginning of what is called 'workfare' where all unemployed people will be required to do some kind of work or accept training in order to qualify for social security benefit. To some this is a form of conscription to be deplored, to others a means of giving the unemployed self-respect. The ETC, however, is still voluntary. To the layman it must seem odd that we spend a billion or so pounds on training, which helps the unemployed from despairing but, then, when so many important jobs need to be done for the well-being of the country and are not being done or not done adequately, we cannot give all who are fit and willing to work a regular job at the proper rate of pay.

ASSIGNMENTS

1. What services are there to help disabled people find employment? The local jobcentre or voluntary bodies can perhaps help you with this assignment.
2. Why do you think most women workers are found in low-paid jobs?
3. When you are working, either for a private firm or in the public service, what laws are there to try and ensure that you are treated fairly by your employer and that you come to no physical harm?

4. Show the connection between unemployment and the cost of the social services.
5. Briefly outline the help given to the unemployed to find jobs.

READING

Albermarle Report, *The Future Development of the Youth Employment Service: Report of a Working Party* (HMSO, 1965).

W. H. Beveridge, *Full Employment in a Free Society*, 2nd edn (Allen & Unwin, 1960).

Child Poverty Action Group, 'Influence of Government policy on pay and working conditions', *Poverty*, Winter 1989–90.

'Debate on Training', *Hansard*, vol. 185, no. 50, 6 February 1991.

Education and Training for the 21st Century, Cm 1536 (HMSO, May 1991).

Employment News (free from 1D2, Department of Employment, Caxton House, Tothill Street, London SW1H 9NF).

Employment News, Training Enterprise Councils (October, 1989).

Health and Safety at Work Commission, *Occupational Health Services: The Way Ahead: A Discussion Document*, 2nd edn (1978).

'Minister's statement on Education and Training', *Hansard*, vol. 191, no. 111, 20 May 1991.

K. Purcell (ed.), *The Changing Experience of Unemployment* (Macmillan, 1986).

Robens Report, *Safety and Health at Work*, Cmnd 5034 (HMSO, 1974).

Jim Tomlinson, *Monetarism: Is There an Alternative?* (Basil Blackwell, 1986), ch. 2, 'Reducing Unemployment'.

Nathan Rosenberg, 'Adam Smith as a social critic', *The Royal Bank of Scotland Review*, June 1990.

15 Housing

HISTORY

It was the danger to public health from slums which led the state to take an interest in housing. Acts of Parliament in 1868 and 1875, and strengthened in 1879 and 1882, gave local authorities powers to deal with insanitary property and areas, even if they were privately owned. But they were permissive acts; compensation had to be paid, so little was done, except in Birmingham under the leadership of Joseph Chamberlain. The 1875 Public Health Act permitted local authorities to make bye-laws laying down minimum standards for new housing. The 1980 Housing Act consolidated previous legislation, made it mandatory for local authorities to deal with insanitary property and areas, and strengthened the laws relating to minimum standards for new housing. It also made it clear that local authorities could build new houses themselves, but, before 1914, only a few did – the vast majority of new houses before 1914 were built by private enterprise and some private-enterprise housing bodies had built homes for working-class tenants. Local authorities concentrated on demolishing insanitary houses, but progress was slow because of the opposition of vested interests. But, by 1914, new housing was sanitary, some progress had been made on slum clearance, there was a little local authority housing and, of interest for the future, housing schemes, deliberately planned to be aesthetically pleasing, had been completed by private enterprise – Bourneville (1879), Port Sunlight (1888) and Letchworth Garden City (1903).

It was not until after the First World War that a housing shortage was officially acknowledged. One reason for this was the growing acceptance in government circles that decent housing was a basic human need and leaving its provision to the free play of supply and demand had left many people without decent housing.

The core of the housing problem was and still is this: if housing is a basic human need, what can be done for people who cannot afford to buy a house or rent a decent dwelling? The first attempt to tackle this problem was the coalition government's 1919 Housing and Town Planning Act (Addison Act). It mandated local authorities, with the aid of a government subsidy, to build houses for letting below the economic rent. Rent control, introduced during the war on certain private houses to stop profiteering, was continued.

In 1923 the Conservative government introduced a new policy. Both local authority and private-enterprise housing was subsidised by the government, but local authorities were only permitted to build for rent if private enterprise could not do so. But under the first Labour government, which came to office in 1924, the Wheatley Act once again allowed local authorities to build houses for letting at subsidised rents irrespective of what private enterprise was doing. The Wheatley Act also increased the government subsidy but, for the first time, the rate fund had to share part of the subsidy. Under this policy many local authority housing estates were built. Unfortunately, low-income-group families could not afford even the subsidised rents so the council houses benefited mainly the better-off working-class people. Differential rent schemes were made permissible by the central government but few local authorities operated them. Even under the Wheatley Act the vast majority of houses were built by private enterprise mainly for sale.

A new housing policy was inaugurated by the National government in 1933. Local authorities were to concentrate on slum clearance (started by the Labour government's 1930 Housing Act) aided by government subsidy, while private enterprise was to build, without subsidy, houses for rent and for sale for all classes. This policy inaugurated a great era of slum clearance and house-building which helped Britain to get out of the inter-war slump.

By 1939 many working-class people had local authority rented houses and a fair number had bought their own homes from private developers. But the vast majority of working-class people lived in private rented accommodation built before 1914 and much of it sub-standard.

HOUSING POLICY SINCE 1945

Subsidised local authority housing has provided rented housing. Until 1949 local authority housing had been for working-class families, but in that year the Labour government, in order to encourage mixed social groupings on council estates, abolished the rule. Unsubsidised private enterprise housing has provided houses for sale and some rented accommodation, mainly flats.

Rent control was abolished in 1957 on all houses except those with very low ratable values, the assumption being that there was enough accommodation for everyone. The abolition of rent control would, it was claimed, cause a shake-out and all would eventually be in accommodation suited to their pocket, if not their needs. Rented accommodation, which since 1945 had disappeared, would again be on the market as landlords would be able to increase rents and make enough money to keep their property in good repair. But it did not work out that way, mainly because the supply of houses in relation to demand was overestimated. As a result, the 1965 Rent Act reintroduced rent control for all furnished and unfurnished accommodation, except that at the luxury end of the market. Part of the 1980 Housing Act provided a much more modest step to help bring more rented accommodation on to the market. It allows 'shorthold' lettings whereby tenants have security of tenure at a 'fair' rent for an agreed period of between one and five years. A rent assessment committee can reduce a rent not considered fair. This does not affect existing regulated tenancies. Furthermore, in England and Wales, under a system of 'assured tenancies', houses can be built and let by approved bodies at market rents outside the provisions of the Rent Acts but they give the tenant long-term security. At the Conservative Party Annual Conference, October 1986, the Housing Minister committed the Party to relaxing rent controls in the private sector should it win the next general election. It did and the 1988 Housing Act abolished rent control for new tenancies.

Slum clearance has continued but on a diminishing scale (see below).

Improvement grants to encourage home improvements were introduced in the 1949 Housing Act.

There are three types of statutory assistance to poorer people to help them pay their rents: (a) rent rebate for council tenants; (b) rent allowance for private tenants both of which come under the general name of housing benefit; (c) since 22 November 1982 under the 1982 Social Security and Housing Benefits Act, people on income support living in council houses have had their rents and rates paid by the local authority instead of receiving an allowance for housing in their income support. Similarly, from April 1983, those on income support living in private accommodation have had their rent and community charge paid by the local authority and, if owner-occupiers, their rates paid. The cost to the local authority is refunded by the DSS. This should be of great benefit to those local authorities owed millions of pounds in rent arrears.

However, under the 1986 Social Security Act, operative from April 1988, all households, even the poorest, have to pay a percentage of their rates, now replaced by a community charge (poll tax). Thus even people on income support must pay 20 per cent of their poll tax.

There is a poll tax rebate scheme for owner-occupiers and those who pay rent which includes poll tax if their income is below a certain level. Owner-occupiers of less expensive properties receive tax relief on mortgage repayments.

Under the 1980 Housing Act it is now obligatory for local authorities to sell their houses at a discount on the market price to sitting tenants who wish to become owners. The percentage discount depends on the length of tenancy. But local authorities can only spend 20 per cent of the money raised on council house sales.

A housing corporation has been set up to promote the growth of housing associations and give them financial help and guidance in the building of homes. Housing associations are non-profit-making.

The 1977 Housing Homeless Persons Act made it obligatory for local authorities to provide accommodation for defined groups of homeless people. The 1980 Housing Act has given tenants of council houses security of tenure and more freedom in the planning of their homes, including subletting and taking in lodgers. No tenant can be evicted without a court order. Tenants of private accommodation already had a high degree of security of tenure.

Under the 1988 Housing Act tenants of council houses can vote to be privatised, that is, cease to be tenants of the local authority. Non-voters are counted as supporters of privatisation. But most of the new landlords are expected to be housing associations. Legislation going back to 1975 and reaffirmed in the 1988 Act permits tenants to run their estates as housing co-operatives. Under the 1989 Local Government and Housing Act rents received for local authority housing must be used solely for improving the local authority housing stock.

Some comparative statistics
In England and Wales between 1919 and 1923 about 65000 houses a year were built, between 1923 and 1932 about 200000 a year, and between 1932 and 1939 about 300000 a year. The 300000 mark was not reached again until 1964. Over 400000 a year were built in 1967 and 1968 but the number has declined since those peak years. In 1974, for example, only 278000 dwellings were completed in Great Britain, and in 1984 198400, in 1988 225000 but in 1989 numbers fell away again.

In 1914 there were 8 million dwellings in England and Wales while in 1982 there were over 18 million. In December 1989 there were 23 million in the United Kingdom. The number of dwellings has more than doubled, yet the population has only increased by just over a quarter. In fact there is actually a surplus of homes over households, but because they are unevenly distributed there are towns where there is an acute housing shortage.

In the interwar years most houses were built by private enterprise. From 1945 to around 1977 public enterprise – that is, local authorities housing associations and new town development corporations, built about two thirds of the housing stock. In the 1980s the majority of houses were built by private enterprise and, in 1989, private enterprise built 85 per cent of all dwellings. With higher living standards house ownership has greatly increased. In 1914, 90 per cent of the houses were rented from private landlords; in 1980 just over 50 per cent were owner-occupied.

In 1989 the total housing stock for Great Britain was divided as follows:

Owner-occupied	66 per cent
Public rented	24 per cent
Private rented	10 per cent

THE ADMINISTRATION OF HOUSING

Housing policy is the responsibility in England of the Secretary of State for the Environment and elsewhere in Britain by the Secretaries of State for Northern Ireland, Wales, and Scotland.

The minister has no direct control over private builders except in the matter of minimum standards of building construction for new houses and their location. Such controls are enforced by local authorities. But the minister may influence private builders during the course of normal contact with their representatives on the advisory committees and elsewhere. The private builders themselves have set up the National House-Building Council in an attempt to set standards and controls by inspection and certification. It has government support but many private builders have not joined it.

The minister exercises a great deal of control over local authorities' housing policies. To build houses, local authorities must borrow money but first must get the minister's approval for doing so and, at the same time, submit their housing plan to his department for approval. Although rents and rates help to finance local authority housing, the central government gives substantial financial help. Local authorities therefore have a certain degree of discretion but must work within a fairly tight framework of regulations laid down by central government. The 1957 Housing Act imposes a duty on local authorities to assess not only housing conditions but also housing *needs*. It permits local authorities to build, convert, acquire, enlarge or improve property to meet housing needs.

SUBSTANDARD HOUSING

By 1986 the number of dwellings lacking amenities in the United Kingdom was 543 000 – a fifth of the 1971 figure. But the number of unfit dwellings and those in serious disrepair has changed little since 1971. It is over 1 million.

What is being done about substandard housing?
Local authorities can provide grants to private owners for home improvements, such as putting in a bath or inside toilet, and for necessary repairs. Local authorities can also provide grants for general improvements to large houses or for converting them into flats.

Under the 1969 Housing Act and subsequent acts local authorities can also designate 'general improvement areas' and improve the environment and encourage house-owners to improve their homes with the aid of grants. The increase in owner-occupation plus higher interest rates on mortgages has resulted in a fair number of privately owned houses falling into disrepair as the owners cannot afford the repairs even with the aid of grants. Under the 1974 Housing Act local authorities can declare 'housing action areas', where they have powers to compel landlords to make improvements to their property to enable a whole area to be improved. At the same time there are government grants to local authorities towards the improvements to a particular area.

Under legislation going back to the nineteenth century, landlords can be compelled by the local authority to do repairs necessary for the health of the occupant.

Under the 1968 Rent Act a local authority can issue a certificate of disrepair on a house, and this entitles the tenant to a reduced rent until the repairs have been carried out.

A tenant can request a local authority to make the landlord install standard amenities, but improvements would normally mean an increase in rent which some tenants may feel unable to meet.

Finally, slum clearance continues but now on a much reduced scale as there is more emphasis on repairs and modernisation. The central government gives a great deal of financial support to local authorities for all aspects of their housing activities. Relatively more money is given to those authorities with greater housing needs.

Although good progress has been made in slum clearance, high-rise flats, in which many people from the slums were housed, have been found unsatisfactory for families with children.

Because of cuts in the central government grant for housing, local authorities have found it difficult to keep their housing stock in good repair. One attempt to mitigate this problem is the 1986 Housing and Planning Act which makes it easier for local authorities to sell off housing estates to private developers or private trusts. This is of particular interest to local authorities in the conurbations where the unpopularity of certain housing estates and, in some cases, faults in their construction, have led to their general deterioration aggravated by vandalism. The act also provides for a bigger discount on the market price for local authority tenants wishing to buy their rented house.

A further development of the above is the setting up in England and Wales of Housing Action Trusts, under the 1988 Housing Act, to take over local authority housing in areas plagued by social problems and housing disrepair. But the majority of tenants must approve being taken over by the Trust. When the Trust has done its renovating work and provided community facilities it will pass the housing on to other owners and managers – housing associations, tenants co-operatives or even back to the local authority – but the Housing Corporation must approve any new landlord.

Since 1985 a Government Estate Action programme has been involving local authorities, tenants and the private sector in England and Wales in the aim of improving run-down areas and encouraging tenants to become more involved in managing their estate.

The 1972 Housing Finance Act laid down a fair-rents procedure to enable landlords to obtain bigger rents and thus have a greater inducement to keep their houses in good repair.

SUMMARY

The housing shortage, officially recognised after the First World War, is still with us, for, despite housebuilding and slum clearance there is still much substandard housing and therefore we still have a long way to go before everyone is in, what by today's standards we call an adequate home. Even worse, there are still people without a home and their numbers are increasingly aggravated now by some owner occupiers not being able to keep up with their mortgage repayments because of the very high interest rate. The big drop in the numbers of houses built in recent years and the financial difficulties in maintaining the housing stock in the local authority sector might well result in a serious worsening of the housing situation.

Private rented housing is still scarce, though housing associations do meet some of the need for rented housing. In recent years housing has suffered greatly from public expenditure cuts.

More investment in housing is obviously needed but, in view of the constraints on public expenditure arising from the government's economic theory, how to do it? One suggestion is to abolish mortgage tax relief and use the money saved for housing investment. But when the numbers who benefit from such a subsidy outnumber those in need of adequate accommodation, will a political party risk losing votes by supporting such a policy? On the other hand there are those, even in the Conservative Party, who believe that public expenditure should be increased, even at the expense of tax cuts, and invested on the infrastructure, including housing.

In the past great emphasis was placed on new housing. Not only were slums demolished but so was older property that was still adequate and often substantially built. In recent years the knocking-down policy has been modified and much more emphasis had been placed on rehabilitation of older property, aided by the concept of 'housing action areas'. This change in official policy is due to a number of reasons: it is cheaper (in the short run at any rate); it retains housing variety; and, most important, it preserves community life. Many older properties are now in much better shape than they were about thirty years ago. Another reason for this is the big rise in house prices leading to a bigger demand for the older but, initially, cheaper houses.

But even if we have enough adequate houses we have to ensure that everyone can afford to move into one. In this connection, the rent rebates should have helped many poor families to take advantage of local authority housing or move into more adequate private accommodation. However, in certain urban areas there is an actual housing shortage in that there are less dwellings than families.

By law, local authorities have to borrow the money to build their houses but they also receive financial help from the government. But the loan charges are a great burden in view of continuing high interest rates. In addition, there is the cost of repairs and management, so that despite higher rents local authorities suffer a big financial loss on council housing, whereas before 1940, when loan charges were small, they actually made a surplus on council housing. This is one factor which has led many local authorities to welcome the Government's policy of encouraging the sale of council houses to sitting tenants. It is argued that not only will this save money for the local authority but it will also give the former tenant new pride in his home, and greater mobility. On the other hand, some people argue that to reduce the housing stock of a local authority where there is a waiting-list for council houses will only make it more difficult for some families to get a home. However, it is all part of the Government's strategy of reducing the housing role of local authorities. Other policies furthering this strategy are the encouragement of housing associations for rented public housing, encouraging the privatisation of council estates and the Housing Action Trusts and the Estate Action Programme referred to above.

Under-use of housing is another problem. There are houses standing empty, there are large houses with few people living in them and there is homelessness.

There are those who say that council housing should be only for those who cannot afford to buy a house and the aim of housing policy should be to have as many owner-occupiers as possible. Owner-occupation is seen as a means of fostering individuality and self-reliance and as something people would prefer anyway. The Conservative Party is the supporter of this viewpoint; and the Labour government in 1977 issued a Green Paper which came out in support of owner-occupation – however, the Labour party, in line with its support for a more equal homogeneous society, has at the same time supported council housing for all who want it. With so much council housing being sold to sitting tenants and with the possibility that much of it will be hived off to private landlords, there is the danger that what council housing is left will be a kind of ghetto for the poor.

Another problem which has been given publicity of late is the growing concern at the high cost to those local authorities which house homeless families in hotels, hostels and other private accommodation. Much of this accommodation is in a very run-down condition and it would seem that some tenants and some local authorities are being exploited by unscrupulous landlords.

ASSIGNMENTS

1. Discuss the view that council houses should only be available to those who cannot afford to buy a house.
2. Find out from your local authority the following:
    (a) the number of council houses it has
    (b) the number of council flats it has
    (c) what proportion of its housing stock it has sold to tenants.
    How far do you agree with the sale of council houses?
3. What policies have been developed to help low-income families obtain and retain adequate housing? How effective do you think these policies have been?
4. Why, when there has been so much house-building in the last sixty years, are there still people without a home? The organisation Shelter might provide you with material for tackling this question.

READING

Marian Bowley, *Housing and the State 1919–1944* (Allen & Unwin, 1945).

John Burnett, *Social History of Housing*, 2nd edn (Methuen, 1986).

Cullingworth Report, *Council Housing: Purposes, Procedures and Priorities* (HMSO, 1969).

Duke of Edinburgh Report, *Inquiry into British Housing* (National Federation of Housing Associations, July 1985).

Michael Fleming and Joseph Nellis, 'A New Housing Crisis?', *Lloyds Bank Review*, April 1982.

R. Forest and A. Murie, *Selling the Welfare State: The Privatisation of Public Housing* (Routledge & Kegan Paul, 1988).

Stella Lowry, Housing and Health, *British Medical Journal*, Tavistock Square, London, WC1H 9JR (1991).

Peter Malpass and Alan Murie, *Housing Policy and Practice*, 3rd edn (Macmillan, 1990).

National Audit Office, Homelessness (HMSO, 1990).

New Society, Special Housing Issue, 25 July 1986.

H. Rose, *The Housing Problem* (Heinemann, 1968).

Various pamphlets from 'Shelter', 86 The Strand, London WC2.

David Webster, 'A "Social Market" Answer on Housing', *New Society*, 12 November 1981.

16   Planning

HISTORY

Town and country planning had its origins in the public health legislation of the nineteenth century. From legislation to create sanitary
conditions, it was a logical development to legislate on the layout of
towns. The first Housing Town Planning Act was in 1909, and permitted
local authorities to prepare schemes for land under development or
likely to be developed. The 1932 Town and Country Planning Act
extended local authority planning powers to all land, but local authorities
could please themselves whether they used them or not, and, for those
that did, parliamentary approval was necessary, which often took over
three years to obtain and, in the meantime, it was difficult to prevent
unwanted development in the planning area. By 1939 only 3 per cent
of Britain had official planning schemes. Thus planning in the interwar years was, in practice, limited to public health and house-building
standards.

The main planning of the interwar years was the attempt, made under
the 1934 Special Areas Act, to attract new industry into those areas of
the country worst hit by the Great Depression and known as 'depressed
areas'.

The 1945 Distribution of Industry Act changed their name to 'development areas' and enlarged them, but the policy remained the same and is still
in operation, though modified by the 1960 Local Employment Act and the
1972 Industry Act.

The depressed areas gave rise to the Barlow Committee Report, published in January 1940, on the geographical distribution of population.
It criticised the concentration of population in the London area and
supported greater diversification of industry to the regions. To apply this
policy it recommended a central planning authority. In 1941 the Uthwatt
Committee on Compensation and Betterment and the Scott Committee
on Land Utilisation were set up. The three reports of Barlow, Uthwatt
and Scott, plus the interest in rebuilding towns arising from bomb
destruction during the war, were mainly responsible for the 1947 Town
and Country Planning Act, which laid the foundations of the modern
planning system.

PLANNING ADMINISTRATION

The 1947 Act set up a central authority – the Ministry of Town and Country Planning. All land development had to be officially approved to try to ensure the best use of the land, bearing in mind all its various uses – for industry, agriculture, roads, houses, parks, airports, recreation and so on. The ministry laid down the broad planning framework, but the actual planning authorities to whom one wrote for permission to build were the local authorities – county councils and county borough councils, (now called metropolitan borough councils) though county councils could delegate planning to the larger district authorities. If planning permission were not granted, or if planning permission had been given for a project to which there were objections, an appeal could be made to the minister and, if need be, a public inquiry could be set up conducted by one of his inspectors to hear all viewpoints and then a report would be made with recommendations for the minister to consider. Furthermore, all planning authorities had to submit development plans to the central government for approval and all building had to conform to the development plan. From time to time development plans were brought up to date. The 1947 Act thus brought in compulsory, creative planning and the administrative procedure it created is more or less the same today, but the Department of the Environment is now the central authority.

The 1968 Planning Act replaced the development plan system of the 1947 Act. Local planning authorities now submit structure plans to the Department of the Environment for approval which set out the principles on which a whole planning area is to be planned, and include possible transport developments and the plan's possible economic consequences. Within the broad policy laid down by the structure plan, local plans are drawn up. The minister is not normally concerned with the local plans, and planning appeals in connection with them are decided by independent inspectors who report to the local authority and who can in fact be appointed by the local authority. Plans may be altered from time to time.

The 1968 Act also provides for public participation in planning in line with the Skeffington Report of 1969, *People and Planning*. Thus individual members of the public and representatives of voluntary organisations can give their views in the formative stage of the structure and local plans. County councils are responsible for the structure (i.e. strategic) planning and district councils for the local plans. Local plans give guidance on development over a period of ten years and all plans are subject to revision and amendment. In January 1989, the Government issued a White Paper, Cm 569, 'The Future of Development Plans', which explains the changes it hopes to see implemented in planning procedures to help speed up the planning process. Counties would still make planning outlines for their respective counties but they would be called 'Statements of County Planning' and, unlike structure plans, would not be subject to the approval of the Minster. Local plans would still be formulated by district authorities but would be called development plans. The proposed new system is called a 'single tier system' as the districts' plans would cover the whole area of the county – under the present system some local plans are prepared by the county council. The Secretary of State would continue to give 'national policy guidelines' and have reserve powers of intervention. Some policies need a regional dimension and counties must, therefore, have regard for regional plans just as district councils must have regard for county plans. The National Parks have developed plans for their areas. Provision for public consultation would be maintained. Local authorities have wide powers for undertaking development, including compulsory purchase. The Town and Country Planning Acts of 1971 for England and Wales and 1972 for Scotland have consolidated the 1947 Act but have retained its essential features.

One of the problems of planning is that it changes the pattern of an area. Some landowners gain because new development enhances the value of their land, while other landowners suffer compulsory purchase and often feel unfairly compensated. Town and Country Planning Acts of 1953, 1954, 1959 and the 1976 Development Land Tax Act were mainly concerned with this problem of compensation and betterment.

New Towns

The 1946 New Towns Act, consolidated by Acts of 1965 and 1968, provided for the building of new towns after consultation with local authorities and objectors. One of the aims of new towns is to stop the outward sprawl of existing towns, particularly London. Certain areas outside of towns are designated as 'green belts' and no development is allowed on these except in special circumstances. The first new towns were built on land beyond the designated green belts.

In more recent years new towns have been seen as growth-points for the economy and some new towns have been built around existing towns – the first was Peterborough in 1968. One of the advantages of building a new town around an existing one is that an established administration structure already exists.

The building of new towns was entrusted to development corporations financed by the government. Originally the intention was to hand the new towns, when completed, to local government, but the New Towns Act 1959 ruled the development corporations should be dissolved and the new towns be eventually handed over to a Commission for New Towns. It was established in 1962. In 1990 nearly all the development corporations had been transferred to the Commission. In Wales a new town was taken over by the Development Board for Rural Wales. Local authorities provide the normal local authority services although much of the local authority housing, originally owned by the development corporations, has been transferred to housing associations and in some towns the Commission itself owns rented housing. In 1979, when the Conservative Government took power, the Commission was instructed to privatise (i.e. sell) the commercial and industrial assets of the new towns (see The New Towns and Urban Development Corporation Act, 1985). By 1990 over £1 billion had been raised in this way in 19 of the 21 new towns in England. But the new towns from the beginning have been a financial success.

The experiment in mixing the social classes in certain of the new towns by having houses for the professional people next to houses for, say, factory workers failed due to the class consciousness of British people.

The expansion of new towns has been challenged on the grounds that they help to speed the decline of older towns which are within their sphere of influence. It is true that many of the older towns, including London, are declining in population, due partly to demolition in the inner-city areas and due partly to firms moving to less congested areas. This, of course, is not all due to new towns – it is mainly due to the great exodus to suburbia which has been going on for decades.

Urban Renewal

This is a relatively new concept embracing the total environment of a town with the purpose of renewing it and improving it. A series of programmes have taken place, initiated by different governments, with this end in view. Slum clearance, begun before 1939, continued apace after 1945, linked with new housing projects and rebuilding bomb damaged areas. The 1952 Town Development Act encouraged local authorities to co-operate on such problems as congestion and over population. For example, one authority may have little or no land for housing while a neighbouring local authority may have a surplus. Many housing sites have developed from co-operation between local authorities. Local authorities co-operate on building plans where development in one local authority may affect the build-up of traffic in another local authority. Special attention is given to traffic, especially since the 1963 Buchanan Report (Traffic in Towns) – the first report to emphasise the need, when planning buildings, to take into consideration their possible effect on traffic patterns. The Clean Air Acts of 1956 and 1968, consolidated by the 1974 Control of Pollution Act, permit local authorities to establish smoke-control areas where the emission of smoke from chimneys (except in special circumstances) is an offence. Planning Acts lay down that lists of buildings of architectural or historical interest should be compiled by the Secretary for the Environment and the Secretaries of State for Scotland and Wales. To demolish such a building requires special consent from the local planning authority or appropriate Secretary of State. The Secretaries of State also give financial assistance for the repair and maintenance of buildings of outstanding interest. Certain cathedrals are now to be considered for a Government grant (normally paid through English Heritage) to help restore crumbling facades.

A parallel development is the 1967 Civic Amenities Act which requires local planning authorities to designate 'conservation areas' of special architectural or historical interest and buildings within such an area may not be demolished or their character changed without permission. The Historic Buildings and Monuments Commission for England, known as English Heritage, (there are similar bodies for Scotland and Wales) manages ancient monuments and gives grants to local authorities for the maintenance of historic buildings in conservation areas. Local authorities can also make grants or loans to help preserve buildings of architectural or historical interest. Voluntary organisations also play an important role in campaigning for the protection of buildings of historic and architectural interest.

Much of the housing development which has gone on in the inner cities and some of the outer suburbs has been the tower-block type of development and has not been successful because it does not suit family life. Planners and architects have been blamed for not being in close enough contact with the human problems inherent in housing policy. In many cases, the new building technology for this type of development has been applied in such a way that faulty constructions have been erected, causing much inconvenience to residents and local authority housing departments. However, many tower blocks have become unsuitable not because of faulty construction but because of vandalism and, in some cases, tenant neglect. Some tower blocks run by local government have once again become desirable places in which to live thanks to the introduction of concierges and adaptations which provide more privacy and security for tenants.

Unemployment is aggravated in the inner cities, especially in the northern industrial towns, because of the high proportion of the unemployed who are unskilled. Since the passing of the 1969 Local Government Grants (Social Need) Act there has been an urban programme specially geared to deprived inner city areas, the first major public spending programme of its kind. The Government gives money to local authorities in addition to the normal grant system and housing subsidies to provide facilities in deprived areas which, without the extra money, would not normally be available – day nurseries, centres for the elderly, community centres, language classes for immigrants, etc. Local authorities pay about a quarter of the cost of any approved project; the rest is covered by Government grant. Voluntary organisations are also involved. The 1978 Inner Urban Areas Act increased resources for urban aid and laid more emphasis on encouraging economic activities. Thus aid has been since increasingly used to strengthen the local economies by fostering business projects and private investment. Since 1982 private interests can qualify for a Government grant if they work with a local authority on a sizeable project of benefit to the area.

The administration of urban aid at local level takes different forms. In severely deprived large city areas, there are inner city partnerships where there is a co-ordinated approach between central and local government. In other deprived areas, local authorities make their own programmes and a project may be carried out by the local authority or a voluntary organisation. In some areas projects are initiated by voluntary organisations – community groups, for example, with money allotted to them by the local authority. Since 1985 City Action Teams have been set up by the Government for certain local authorities to encourage joint projects between the public and private sectors.

A much more radical attempt at urban renewal was attempted by the creation of two urban development corporations for the London and Merseyside docklands respectively. Both these docklands have been transformed, financed by government money and private investment. In 1987 five new urban corporations were created – Trafford Park in Greater Manchester, Tyne and Wear, Teeside, the West Midlands and Cardiff Bay. Four more were set up 1988–89 – Bristol, Leeds, Central Manchester and Sheffield.

Another response was the concept of task forces and on 6 February 1986 the Government announced the launching of eight new inner city task forces. Each would be allotted £1 million, which might seem a modest sum, but aid would be concentrated in a small area of the city. There are now (1991) sixteen of them. Each has its own fund with the main aim of encouraging enterprise and training, working closely with the local people. The idea was that they they should spend money in new ways outside the Government programmes.

A successful example of co-operation between public and private enterprise took place in the eastern part of Glasgow, where industry had virtually disappeared and where housing had been knocked down and not replaced. In this area, over a period of ten years, 250 new factories and workshops have been opened and 150 000 houses rebuilt or modernised and an area where nobody wished to live is now a desirable residential area. The renovation of the area was the work of the government-funded Scottish Development Agency, a task force, private investment and the local community. Under the 1982 Derelict Land Act the Government gives grants to both the public and private sector for restoring derelict land to beneficial use. At the time of writing the Central Manchester Development Corporation is in the process of regenerating vacant and under-used land so as to make it productive by building homes and offices and, at the same time, making improvements to Manchester's rivers and canals.

Since 1981, enterprise zones have been set up with an expected life of ten years. In these zones firms can carry on business free of rates and development tax plus concessions on income tax and corporation tax. Also in the zones the planning procedures are much simpler. There are also what are called Free Port Zones located at certain airports and seaports where goods entering the zone can be processed, stored and manufactured without payment of duties although duties must be paid when the goods are sold on the domestic market. To help small businesses develop successfully in the inner cities the Department of Trade and Industry gives financial help towards the cost of obtaining advice from a consultancy on all aspects of marketing. This help comes under the heading 'The Enterprise Initiative'.

A further campaign called 'Action for Cities' was launched in 1988 to give further impetus to urban regeneration. Its emphasis is on the need to get more effective co-ordination between local and central government, private business and voluntary organisations in the promotion of enterprises and training. When considering all the various projects to further urban renewal, it would be unfair not to mention the financial aid given to certain of them by the European Regional Fund – the G-Mex centre in Manchester for example.

Critics of the urban aid programme accept that it has slowed down urban decline but feel much larger amounts of public money are needed in the inner cities. They point out that although expenditure on urban aid has been maintained in real terms overall, money provided by the central government for local authorities has been reduced because of cuts in the rate support grant. In the meantime the Government might argue that public expenditure has to be kept under strict control and the urban aid programme is a means of concentrating expenditure where it is most needed. The Government might also argue that it has been successful in finding new sources of financial help from the private sector and stimulated local authorities to plan, if possible, developments with the private sector. But urban development corporations, task forces, and the changes in the control of schools and colleges including the new city technology colleges and the encouragement given to the schools by the Government to opt out of local authority control do seem to imply a lack of confidence by the Government in local government.

The Countryside

Access to and preservation of the countryside have been of great interest to many people in the last 150 years, especially with the rapid advance of enclosures, including the enclosure of common land from around 1740. The 1949 National Parks and Access to the Countryside Act was the first major Act to deal with the problem. Large areas of land were designated National Parks, looked after by a National Parks Commission. It also empowered county councils to prepare maps showing public rights of way which must be preserved. Local authorities can also create paths. The 1968 Countryside Act set up a Countryside Commission for England and Wales (a 1967 Act set up one for Scotland) which took over the functions of the National Parks Commission. Its main job is to encourage facilities in the countryside so people will get the maximum pleasure from it – for example, the establishment of camping sites, picnic areas and long-distance footpaths. The actual provision of the sites is mainly the work of local authorities working together to form country parks. By 1985 there were in England and Wales, in addition to the National Parks, 200 country parks and 236 picnic sites. In addition the Forestry Commission (established by the Forestry Acts of 1919 and 1945), which is concerned with the conservation of trees and woodland, has opened seven of its forest parks to the public, four of which are in Scotland. Voluntary bodies also play a large part in preserving the amenities of the countryside. For example, the National Trust owns and protects much land and many historic houses for the benefit of the public. In addition, there are approximately 350 national nature reserves in Great Britain supervised by the Nature Conservancy Council, set up in 1973. However, under the 1990 Environmental Protection Act, the Council is to be dismembered into three separate agencies – one each for England, Scotland and Wales.

A new programme recently launched is the creation of nine community forests, with the idea of bringing town and country closer together and providing pleasing recreation for the nearby town dwellers. Each will cover an area of 40 to 80 square miles. Three have already started – East London, Staffordshire, Tyne and Wear. The Forestry Commission and the Countryside Commission, backed by Government money, in partnership with local authorities, private landowners and farmers are responsible for the development of the forests. Most land will come from landowners and farmers and some from local authorities and they will be compensated. Some farmers are, however, sceptical of the economic benefits to them of turning over fields to forestry.

The central government gives substantial grants to local authorities to get rid of objects disfiguring the countryside. In spite of planning legislation there has been increasing concern over the years about the changing face of the countryside. Since 1945 farmers have been encouraged, aided by subsidies, to grow more food. So successful have they been that today we produce three-quarters of our food supply compared with roughly one-quarter before 1945. But the cost, in certain parts of southern England has been the destruction, in a matter of only thirty years, of the traditional country landscape which had existed for centuries. Thus, in order to make the best use of modern farm machinery, fields have been greatly enlarged necessitating the destruction of miles of hedgerows. Thousands of farm workers have been displaced by the machines. Hence many villages, which were once bustling communities, are now peopled by commuters who have bought the empty cottages left by departing farm workers. The original villagers who are left naturally miss the old community life. This type of modern farming has also led to the destruction of certain types of wild life and areas of special scientific interest. Thus the 1981 Wildlife and Countryside Act aims to preserve sites of special interest from destruction but for it to be effective farmers and conservationists must work harmoniously together.

Pollution of the Environment

From early times there has been some concern about the environment, especially when towns began to grow in size. Londoners in Elizabethan times grumbled about smoke in the atmosphere from the burning of coal fires. The nineteenth century saw the rapid development of a modern industrial society and environmental problems became more acute and public health legislation was enacted to help mitigate some of these problems. Now that industrialism has spread to many parts of the world environmental problems are on a much bigger and more threatening scale. They range from litter and dog dirt in the streets (in England at any rate) to a threat to the planet itself from global warming brought about by what are called greenhouse gases – methane, nitrous oxide but particularly carbon dioxide. Trees absorb carbon dioxide and give out oxygen, so that the destruction of the tropical forests in South America aggravates the greenhouse effect by reducing the exchange of carbon dioxide for oxygen. In between these two extreme examples of pollution are the problems of the disposal of nuclear and industrial waste; the problem of acid rain, caused, it is claimed, by sulphur dioxide emissions from coal burning power stations. There is the problem of polluted beaches due to untreated sewage and other waste being dumped into the sea and river pollution from industrial waste. Some of these problems are common to many countries and so there are international bodies to help control them and near home the European Commission issue guidelines for remedial action.

Until 1990, legislation to protect the environment was piecemeal with different acts of Parliament to deal with specific problems. For example, the 1971 Dangerous Litter Act and 1974 Poisonous Waste Act strengthened the provisions for the control of dangerous litter, much of it dumped in the countryside. The 1974 Control of Pollution Act gave wide powers to local authorities and water authorities to control industrial waste and protect water supplies as well as to ensure clean air and the control of noise. Some of this legislation arose from reports of the permanent Royal Commission on Environmental Pollution. But, following a Government white paper on the environment, there was enacted the 1990 Environmental Protection Act which deals in a comprehensive way with all kinds of pollution from emissions into the air, into water and on to the land. The Act gives Britain 'the first system of integrated pollution control in Europe' (Environment Secretary, Mr Chris Patten – see Commons *Hansard*, 15 January 1990). It embraces people who drop litter in the streets as well as the 'large industrial polluter'. It encourages anti-pollution techniques in all stages of production. Much will depend on the Inspectorate which must have sufficient resources and expertise. Many people would say that in the past there have been too few inspectors for an effective control system. However, there is now a new enforcement policy which is seen to be the answer to this sort of criticism. It is based on economic incentives. Those who pollute will have to pay a pollution charge; those who do not, pay no charge. As an example, companies and farmers are to be charged by the National River Authority for the amount of effluent they pour into rivers. It will pay to obey the law.

REGIONAL PLANNING

Under the principles first laid down by the 1934 Special Areas Act, financial inducements are offered to business people to set up business in depressed areas (called 'development areas' under the 1945 Distribution of Industry Act) in order to help reduce unemployment and obtain balanced economic development nationwide. Increasing aid to development areas led to political pressure for aid to other areas, and following the Report of the Hunt Committee of 1969 (*The Intermediate Areas*) the government designated seven 'Intermediate areas' to qualify for financial aid.

Since joining the European Economic Community help for these areas also comes from the European Regional Development Fund and the European Regional Social Fund. The term 'assisted areas' is now used for three different types of areas, which, because of their long-term structural problems, are able, with government help, to offer financial incentives to attract firms. They are – in order of priority – special development areas, development areas and intermediate areas.

In spite of all the acts of Parliament to encourage the more depressed areas of the country to become more prosperous relative to other areas, the disparities between regions are greater than ever. The only consolation is that without these acts (the 1960 Local Employment Act which replaced the 1945 Distribution of Industry Act which, in turn, superseded the 1934 Special Areas Act), the problem might have been much worse. The 1972 Industry Act and urban renewal policies are later attempts to lessen economic imbalance between regions, particularly between the north and south of the country.

However, under a free market system, it is accepted that an industry will normally go to the region where it is considered the most profitable to operate. Hence, since 1984, the emphasis has been on directing regional aid towards developing an environment which, in the above sense, is competitive and will attract business firms, rather than to give a grant to persuade a firm to go to a particular region. It is hoped, in this way, to make aid more effective in correcting regional imbalance.

PROBLEMS TODAY

Administration

Over the years there has been continuing criticism of the long time it takes for decisions to be made on planning applications. It is hoped that by the changes outlined above and by giving publicity to the number of applications received by the Department of the Environment and local authorities and the time it takes to deal with them, planning procedures will be speeded up. However, it must be remembered that it is very important for the *right* decision to be made.

The problem, however, lies not only in the length of time some inquiries take but also in their cost. For example, the public inquiry to decide whether to build a nuclear power station at Sizewell lasted 2½ years and the estimated cost to the Central Electricity Generating Board (CEGB) was £50 million; the cost to the Friends of the Earth who opposed the building of the power station was £140 000. The Commons Select Committee on the Environment in a report published September 1986 proposed a two-tier system of inquiry in appropriate cases for the purpose of speeding up inquiries. There would be a first hearing at which national policy issues would be discussed and this would cover the need for the project. At the second hearing only local issues could be discussed. The Committee felt that this system of two hearings would avoid much repetition of the same argument. And an important recommendation to give objectors a fairer crack at the whip was that objectors, who had been asked to give evidence, should have their costs paid by the State.

In the past it has been felt that the professional planners have imposed their ideas on the public. The reason for this, it has been suggested, is that often planners see themselves as servants of the developers. It is now much more appreciated that planners must make decisions the community at large supports. And this implies taking into consideration all the social implications of the plan. To this end, consultation with the public is very necessary. The trouble is that, while everyone supports democratic consultation in theory, comparatively few members of the public participate in it in practice, and the vocal minority does not necessarily reflect the views of the 'silent majority'.

The procedure of public inquiries has been changed to give objectors a fairer chance. One example is that at motorway inquiries objectors can challenge the *need* for the motorway and not just the proposed route, as was previously the case.

However, in recent years, there has developed in central government circles the viewpoint that, for certain large projects, the public inquiry procedure is not suitable because these projects are what the Government considers to be in the national interest which must take precedence over regional and local interests. Hence the guardians of the national interest – the democratically elected Government and Parliament – must decide these projects. According to this view, the decision as to what type of power station to build at Sizewell – whether nuclear or non-nuclear – should be decided by the CEGB, subject to the approval of the Government and Parliament. All the public inquiry would have been concerned with would have been where to put the power station.

Green belts

In recent years controversy has arisen over the future of green-belt land, particularly in south-east England. House prices are exceptionally high in London and what aggravates the situation is that land for housebuilding is scarce. Many a young couple wanting to set up a home cannot afford to buy a house in London but can afford one in areas beyond the green belt where land is considerably cheaper and where many housing estates have developed. But they then have the problem of travelling a long distance to their work in London. High house prices in London also contribute to inner-city decay because, like the young couple, many people move out to areas where houses are cheaper. Private housebuilders want to build new villages in the Essex green belt arguing that there will be a housing shortage in the south-east unless new homes are built (see John Herington, 'The Outer City Problem', *New Society*, 9 August 1985). In other areas of the country there is pressure from builders to build on green-belt land and this is also causing concern. In an address to leaders of the construction industry the Prince of Wales is reported to have said (*Guardian*, 29 October 1986) that farmland was being lost at a rate which would see its disappearance in 200 years.

A similar dilemma in planning housing policy for the more rural areas is whether to build the houses around existing communities or whether to go for completely new settlements.

SUMMARY

Planning is the responsibility of local government supervised by the central government.

Planning arose from the need to mitigate the problems of bad sanitation and unhealthy housing created by the rapid growth of towns (especially industrial towns) in the nineteenth century. It later became concerned with the layout of towns from an aesthetic point of view.

In spite of legislation for land development going back to the first Planning Act of 1909, only 3 per cent of Britain had planning schemes before 1939, but a start had been made with regional development under the 1934 Special Areas Act.

The big advance in planning came after the Second World War with the 1945 Distribution of Industry Act, the 1946 New Towns Act and the 1947 Town and Country Planning Act.

Today planning is not just concerned with land use but with the protection of the environment against all forms of pollution.

The new towns have been, in general, a success, though to begin with there were problems in connection with the development of community life. Some people, especially older people, missed the homeliness of their old environment even though its physical side was perhaps not very attractive.

Urban renewal, particularly in the inner cities, offers perhaps the biggest planning problem. There are, especially in the industrial towns, still vast areas of drab, shabby housing and industrial and commercial premises that need replacing. Paradoxically land is often expensive in these inner-city areas, even though it is derelict, making it often more economical for an industrialist to build a factory or plant on the more virgin and cheaper land outside the town. The enterprise zones and the urban development corporations might partially remedy this. The motor-car has also made the problem of urban renewal even more difficult. Some people argue that regional inequalities are inevitable because under an economic system based mainly on private capitalist enterprise businesses will locate where costs are lowest. In a market-orientated economy, it will always be a problem to reconcile the drive for business profit with the wider needs of a civilised community life.

Policies to integrate the countryside and the urban areas for planning purposes continue and the local government structure introduced in 1974 should speed up this integration and ensure the countryside is developed, bearing in mind the needs of both the country people and the people in the towns.

ASSIGNMENTS

1. Think about the town in which you live (or your nearest town). Discuss whether it is well planned and, in doing so, make suggestions for improving it. If possible, consult the development plan of the local planning authority.
2. What provisions exist for protecting the beauty of the countryside? Include in your answer not only the work of statutory bodies but also the work of voluntary bodies. Obtain literature on the work of one of these voluntary bodies. For example, you could obtain information

on the work of the National Trust by writing to its Director-General
at the Trust's headquarters in London.
3.   Discuss the purpose of new towns. Write to the Commission for New
      Towns to try to find out what new towns have to offer for residents
      and commercial and industrial interests.
4.   Why in some towns is there what is called an 'inner-city problem'?
      What is being done to resolve the problem? If you write to the
      Department of Environment, you might get assistance with this
      question.
5.   Why are people worried about the environment?

READING

Audit Commission, *Urban Regeneration and Economic Development: the
local government dimension* (HMSO, 1989).
Britain 1992: An Official Handbook (HMSO).
John Blunden and Nigel Curry (eds), *A People's Charter? Forty years of the
National Parks and Access to the Countryside Act 1949* (HMSO, 1990).
Gordon C. Cameron (ed.), *The Future of the British Conurbations* (Longman,
1980).
Michael Burke and James Cutler, 'Green and Poisoned Land?', *New States-
man and Society*, 6 April 1990.
Gordon E. Cherry, *The Evolution of British Town Planning* (Leonard Hill
Books, 1974).
Countryside Commission, *Annual Report*.
W. Harvey Cox, *Cities: The Public Dimensions* (Penguin, 1976).
J. B. Cullingworth, *Town and Country Planning in Britain* (Allen & Unwin,
1976).
David Donnison and Paul Solo, *The Good City – A Study of Urban Develop-
ment and Policy in Britain* (Heinemann, 1980).
Martin J. Elson, *Green Belts: Conflict Mediation in the Urban Fringe*
(Heinemann, 1986).
The Future of Development Plans Cm 569 (HMSO, January 1989).
Greenpeace U.K., *Why Britain Remains the Dirty Man of Europe* (Greenpeace,
30 Islington Green, London N1 8XE).
John Herington, 'The Outer City Problem', *New Society*, 9 August 1985.
House of Commons, Second Reading of the Environmental Protection Bill,
Hansard, vol. 165, no. 29, 15 January 1990.
Lionel March, 'Why Have New Towns?' *New Society*, 8 June 1972.
E. J. Mishan, 'Economic and Political Obstacles to Environmental Sanity',
National Westminster Bank Quarterly Review, May 1990.
Reports of the Royal Commission on Environmental Pollution (HMSO).
Frank Schaffer, *The New Town Story* (Paladin, 1972).

This Common Inheritance: Britain's Environmental Strategy, Cm 1200 (HMSO, 1990).

Colin Wren, 'Regional Policy in the 1980s', *National and Westminster Bank Quarterly Review*, November 1990.

Margaret Thatcher, address to the United Nations General Assembly on the threat to the global environment (edited text), *Guardian*, 9 November 1989.

17 Probation and After-Care Service

HISTORY

Probation – that is, the release of an offender providing he or she promises to be good – is a legal procedure which has been used for centuries. In the more formal language the offender enters into recognisance to be of good behaviour. This means the probation order requires the offender's consent. The recognisance procedure was increasingly used in the nineteenth century, especially for young offenders, reflecting a growing humanity in the treatment of law-breakers. Unfortunately very few offenders had someone to keep a parental eye on them during recognisance, though by the end of the nineteenth century there were a fair number of voluntary workers for this work – part of what was called the Police Court Mission.

The first Act to provide for statutory provision and guidance of offenders outside the penal institutions was the 1907 Probation of Offenders Act. It covered offenders of all ages and a wide range of offences. It provided for the appointment of probation officers by the courts to be paid out of public funds. It laid down a maximum period of probation of three years, which still stands, but no minimum. The present minimum is six months (Scotland 12 months).

Although put on probation, an offender might be made to pay compensation for damages or injury. Since the passing of the 1907 Act there have been periodic reports followed by legislation which have extended the role of the service, but the 1907 Act still forms the basis of the service today. But since 1971 probation orders have been abolished for persons under 17 (Scotland 16) and replaced by supervision orders (see p. 116).

If the probationer (offender) fails to comply with the terms of the order, the probation officer may bring him or her before the court to be dealt with for the original offence. The terms of the order may require attendance at a day training centre or a stay at a probation hostel or other place of residence, or willingness to accept psychiatric treatment. For offenders who have committed more serious offences which would normally mean a prison sentence, a community service order may be made, though community service is also a sentence in its own right (see p. 217).

The terms may also require the offender to report to the probation officer and notify any change of address. Failure to comply with the probation order may result in a fine or the requirement to attend an attendance centre, in which case the probation order may still continue but, if some other sentence is given, probation terminates. The probationer may also be dealt with for the original offence if he or she commits a further offence while on probation. But if the probationer responds well, he or she may be discharged early.

The growing humanity towards law-breakers was also reflected in prison reform. The Report of the Departmental Committee (the Gladstone Committee), published in 1895, recommended that reformation as well as deterrence should be the purpose of prisons. The 1895 Prison Act implemented its main recommendations – unproductive labour was abolished, prisoners were able to earn money, and so on. In more recent times the 1948 Criminal Justice Act abolished penal servitude, hard labour, corporal punishment and extended the possibilities of non-institutional treatment. It underlined again that the penal policy should be reformation and restoration of prisoners to a normal life. The 1967 Criminal Justice Act abolished corrective training. Since 1965 capital punishment has been abolished for murder. However, the overcrowding and degrading conditions in many prisons do not encourage reformation.

Offenders whose punishment is a fine, whether paid by instalments or not, can be sent to prison if they default on payment. The 1914 Criminal Justice Act gave the court power to put such a person, if between the age of 16 and 21, under supervision until the fine was paid, in an attempt to reduce the number of young persons sent to prison for non-payment. Legislation was eventually passed (the latest being the 1952 Magistrates Act) which laid down that courts should consider supervision before sending defaulters under 21 to prison, and also gave the courts authority to use supervision for adult offenders if they wished. At the same time, probation officers were designated by the Home Office as suitable supervisors.

The after-care service was mainly confined to young people before the Second World War, particularly to those leaving borstals, but arrangements for supervision were made locally with various (including voluntary) agencies. Since 1945 after-care has been extended to older offenders and compulsory after-care now covers, among others, those leaving youth custody centres and detention centres, and those released from prison on licence (parole), young prisoners and those released from life imprisonment. Since the mid-1960s any prisoners on leaving prison can, on a voluntary basis, seek the help of the probation officer in the first year of their release. The probation officer must 'advise, assist and befriend' these ex-prisoners in the same way as he or she must, by statute, 'advise, assist and befriend' any other person needing help. The parole system for prisoners – even those who had committed serious offences – was introduced by the 1967 Criminal Justice Act. The probation service is represented on the Parole Board and local review committees and therefore has some say on the choice of prisoners for parole. But the probation service is responsible for their supervision.

Before sentence is passed on an offender, a probation officer may be asked by the court to make a report on the offender's home surroundings, education, and so on. This only became a statutory duty with the 1948 Criminal Justice Act; previously the reports had been made on a voluntary basis. These probation reports often influence the sentence passed by the magistrates. Under the 1982 Criminal Justice Act a social inquiry report must normally be considered by the court before a custodial sentence is given on an offender under 21.

Since 1966 probation officers can act as prison welfare officers.

Marriage counselling goes back to pre-1914 days and arose from trying to get husbands and wives to settle amicably those matrimonial disputes they were bringing to the courts. It was not until 1937 that statutory authority was given to probation officers to do this work.

Apart from marriage counselling, which the service is now rarely called upon to provide, probation officers may be asked by the magistrates courts or divorce courts to report on the circumstances of the parties and their children in cases of divorce where access to or custody of the children is in question. In adoption proceedings the court can nominate a probation officer (more usually it nominates a local authority social worker) to act as *guardian ad litem* and, under the 1975 Children Act, which is concerned with adoption, the duties of the *guardian ad litem* are extended.

Under the 1969 Children and Young Persons Act the aim is to keep children and young people out of the juvenile court but if, in spite of everything, they have to be brought before one, the court may make out a supervision order under which the child will remain at home under the supervision of the local authority or probation officer. But for a child under 14 the probation officer is not normally involved. The intention of the Act was that probation officers would not look after children under 17 – they would be dealt with by local authority social workers. A supervision order may involve 'intermediate treatment' where, under supervision, the delinquent is given constructive activities. Private organisations, particularly youth groups, are encouraged to provide 'intermediate' treatment facilities and are helped financially to do so (see Chapter 13). But the probation and after-care service has 'intermediate' treatment facilities of its own.

Under the 1969 Act it was intended to raise the age of criminal responsibility from 10 to 12 but it still remains 10.

A child over 10 and under 17 can have a criminal prosecution made against him or her but cannot be sent to prison. This has applied ever since the 1933 Childrens and Young Persons Act. But a custodial sentence may be given for serious offences, including murder. Normally no young person under 21 is sent to prison unless the Court is satisfied no other option is suitable.

ADMINISTRATION

Although the probation and after-care service is a local one, it is not run by local authorities. The country is divided into probation and after-care areas, and each area has a probation and after-care committee of magistrates appointed by the courts in the area. It is these probation and after-care committees that are directly involved in the running of the service, with chief probation officers acting as advisers and administrators. The committees are required to co-opt non-magistrates with knowledge of prisoners and after-care. The committees are autonomous and not accountable to the courts. There is a Central Council of Probation and After-Care Committees.

The central authority is the Home Office, which has a Probation and After-Care Department. It is advised by an advisory council for probation and after-care. There is also a National Association of Probation Officers, formed in 1912. The Home Office also has an inspectorate for the service.

Problems Today

In the last two decades new duties have been imposed on the Probation and After-Care Service – voluntary after-care, parole and prison welfare. The 1972 Criminal Justice Act introduced community service orders and suspended sentence supervision orders. In addition there has been a big increase in the number of requests for court reports and other reports. The workload is likely to increase as crime continues to rise and while, at the same time, the Home Office and the criminologists who advise it see the development of non-institutional care for less serious offences as a means of keeping down crime in the long run, quite apart from it relieving the pressure on overcrowded prisons. In the last ten years in order to cope with this increased workload there has been a '40 per cent increase in staff' (probation officers and ancillaries) and 'expenditure has grown in real terms by more than 50 per cent' (Cm 966). In the Government's view, these developments have made necessary an urgent review of the Service. Already the Government has reformed the Social Security system, the Health and Education systems and introduced new policies for Training and Housing. Underlying all these reforms is the Government aim of making the services more cost-conscious, and where appropriate more sensitive to market forces and more willing to co-operate with the private sector. The Probation and After-Care Service is the last to be looked at.

Thus, from 1984 onwards, a series of Government papers have been published on the Service (see Reading). The Government in its latest paper, Green Paper Cm 966, 'Supervision and Punishment in the Community', published February 1990, sets out in some detail its proposals for the development of the Service drawing upon much of the work in previous papers. (A Green Paper outlines Government proposals on an issue and asks for comments before the Government finalises its intentions which are then published in a White Paper).

The main Government criticism from the public's point of view is the implication that in 'advising, assisting and befriending' offenders, the Service has taken a too soft attitude towards them. Thus the Green Paper wishes to see a better balance between helping offenders and concern for their victims and the public in general. 'Probation work has never meant an exclusive commitment to the interests of offenders.' In keeping with this sentiment, the Government emphasises that the Service is an agency of the courts and how it deals with offenders during a probation period 'must seem credible to magistrates and judges'. And again, the Service must concern itself more with crime prevention. And, rather ominously, the Government in its Green Paper adds that 'probation officers must show they can produce results to justify the extra money being spent on the Probation Service'. This has special relevance in view of the government policy to place more reliance on non-custodial treatment for non-violent offences, as outlined in its White Paper Cm 965.

Having stressed the need for the Service to be 'responsive to criminal justice policy' and to have 'the confidence of the sentencers' the Green Paper then makes suggestions for improving the management of the Service. Thus, in line with the Government's belief in the value of making use in the public service of the managerial experience of businessmen from the private sector, it suggests reducing the number of magistrates on probation committees to make way for people with business experience. In fact, it states that senior managers need not have been probation officers but could be brought in from other professions. In keeping with this, the

Government feels it should have more say in their appointment. In fact the Government favours much more central control of the Service. In the long run, it argues in the Green Paper, a national service is better, because there is a better chance of good practices receiving the attention of all probation committees, standards would be more consistent throughout the Service as all probation committees would follow the same 'clearly defined objectives' with 'clear lines of responsibility'. And to improve links with the judiciary, a circuit judge could sit on a probation committee or, alternatively, there could be set up a probation liaison committee with the crown court.

The Government would like to see a widening of the involvement of the voluntary and private sector in the work of the Service. Much of the work does not require 'professional probation skills'. Probation officers should concentrate on 'managerial oversight' of the work. At the present time day-to-day supervision of offenders on community service schemes is provided by ancillary workers in the Service, by voluntary organisations and individual volunteers, with probation officers providing the managerial role. Ancillary workers also do such things as court and escort duties, maintaining registers of employers and lodgings. Volunteers who are given training, apart from helping in community service schemes, also do such duties as taking wives by coach to visit their husbands in prison or helping families with visits to long-term prisoners.

But the Government considers that other work within the Service could be carried out by people who are not probation officers – for example, the counselling of young people who have been cautioned and charged and supporting the parents of these young people; finding accommodation for defendants on bail to avoid their having to go on remand or in custody; helping offenders to find a job, to fight drug addiction, to read and write; supporting prison staff in their welfare work; taking on much more of the after-care of people leaving prison leaving probation officers to concentrate on those released on licence. All this will mean, states the Government, even closer co-operation with 'the police, local authorities and the rest of the community,' And if organisations in the voluntary and private sector do become more involved with the Probation and After-Care Service, the duties of HM Inspectorate of Probation will need to be extended to cover the oversight of these organisations.

The reaction of the probation and after-care officers to the Government's reform proposals has, in the main, been critical. In the view of the National Association of Probation Officers, the proposals, if implemented, would make them more like 'prison officers in the community'. If the Association's viewpoint is correct, it could make probation officers' relations with offenders less likely to inspire that mutual trust without which the officers' aim of helping offenders to change their behaviour is less likely to succeed.

On 11 April 1991, the Government announced it had decided not to pursue, for the time being, its reform proposals.

SUMMARY

Once a system of supervising offenders as an alternative to prison was introduced, then it was only a matter of time before there developed a variety of ways of supervising to suit the different categories of law-breaker.

The main duties of the problem and after-care service are as follows:

1. *Probation.*
   (a) maintain contact with the offender placed on probation at home (and the offender must contact the probation office when asked to do so)
   (b) 'advise, assist and befriend' the offender, which can include advice with any domestic difficulties, including the finding of lodgings, help in finding a job, and encouragement generally – some offenders placed on probation must attend a day training centre or stay at a probation hostel or do community service.
2. *Reports.* Probation officers may be asked, before sentence is passed on an offender brought before the court and found guilty, to provide the court with a report on the offender's home surroundings, education, health and general social conditions.
3. *Supervision of juvenile offenders aged 14–17 placed under a supervision order.*
4. *Supervision of offenders given a suspended sentence.* Unlike a probation order, a suspended sentence does not need the offender's consent.
5. *After-care.* Probation officers provide after-care for a wide range of offenders and must 'advise, assist and befriend' any discharged prisoners who voluntarily come for help during their first year of release.
6. *Prison Welfare.* Probation officers act as prison welfare workers.
7. *Marriage guidance.* Probation officers were usually asked to meet

those who came before the courts or who applied to the magistrates courts for separation orders. They often acted as marriage guidance counsellors to these people and in fact gave advice on marriage to all who voluntarily approached them. But work in connection with marriage guidance is no longer significant. What has become an important part of probation officers' work in cases of matrimonial breakdown is the preparation of welfare reports on the custody of and access to children.

8. *Children.* Children who come before the courts needing care and protection are normally put in the care of the local authority, but they can be put in the care of a probation officer if aged over 13.

9. *Divorce and family court work* where access to or custody of children is in dispute.

Reliance on non-custodial treatment for non-violent offenders came more to the fore in 1973 with the introduction of community service, an expansion of day training centres, probation hostels for adults and after-care hostels. As non-custodial treatment is extended in line with modern criminology (and also encouraged by overcrowded prisons), the service will continue the expansion which has been going on ever since it was first created in 1907. (Non-custodial treatment is very much cheaper than custodial treatment – see John Harding.) It will continue to need the co-operation of other social workers and the community at large. Volunteers will continue to play an important role in the service.

ASSIGNMENTS

1. Write to the administrator of your local probation and after-care service and ask if you can have a copy of the service's *Annual Report* for the area. From your reading of the report discuss what you consider to be its most interesting contents

2. Why must the probation and after-care officer be involved with the personal social services run by the local authority? Give examples where co-operation with these services may be necessary.

3. How far is the probation and after-care service an agency in the war against crime?

4. 'The Government wants to transform the Probation Service from one which befriends offenders to one which administers punishment in the community.' Discuss this statement.

READING

Britain 1992: An Official Handbook (HMSO).

Paul Cavadino, 'Criminal Justice Act 1982, A Pragmatic Compromise', *Community Care*, 11 November 1982.

Crime, Justice and Protecting the Public, Cm 965 (HMSO, February 1990).

John Harding, 'Probation in the Community: "Twelve Pounds a Week"', *The Listener*, 19 September 1985.

Joan King (ed.), *The Probation and After-Care Service* (Butterworth, 1969).

Mark Monger, *Casework in Probation*, 2nd edn (Butterworth, 1972), ch. 1.

Melanie Phillips, 'Putting the service on probation', *Guardian*, 16 February 1990.

Lord Scarman's Report, *The Brixton Disorders*, Cmnd 8427 (HMSO, 1981).

Supervision and Punishment in the Community, Cm 966 (HMSO, February 1990).

Wendy Taylor (compiler), *Probation and After-Care in a Multi-racial Society* (Commission for Racial Equality, 1981).

18 The Future of the Social Services

Until the beginning of this century the only help for those in need outside that of family and friends was that provided by the Poor Law and voluntary organisations. In this century income maintenance and other services have developed outside the Poor Law. Income maintenance includes a comprehensive system of National Insurance plus child benefit and other miscellaneous benefits, augmented, where necessary, by income support paid for out of taxation – the Poor Law having been abolished in 1948. From a system where most ordinary people, when sick, only reluctantly, because of its cost, sought medical help from an impoverished doctor, there has developed a comprehensive National Health Service paid for mainly out of taxation. There has also developed a wide range of community social services covering health and welfare, many of which were previously the concern of the Poor Law authorities. Parallel with these developments, educational advance has resulted in secondary education for all and higher education for all who want it and who can benefit from it, made possible, for children of poorer parents, by a system of grants and loans. Housing standards have risen, and there has been a big increase in the nation's housing stock, though much of it is substandard.

Since 1945 we have been trying for the first time, under a comprehensive planning system, to make the best use of the land and, more recently, planning has come to include not just land use but concern for the environment as a whole, including its pollution. Finally, the humanising of the penal system has led to a much greater use of probation and after-care for offenders and a corresponding increase in the duties of the probation and after-care service. The black spot is the severe overcrowding in our Victorian-built prisons.

Community care, which involves treatment in the home or neighbourhood instead of an institution – first considered in relation to mentally handicapped people – has been developed on an increasing scale to other categories of people needing help. The concept has been given administrative expression by the creation of a local authority social services department to provide a community-based service in support of the family. Many social problems arise from a bad home environment and the social services department is an attempt to prevent problems arising in the first place by trying to keep the home situation of 'families at risk' as sound as possible. It involves the co-operation of many types of workers from the range of helping services. Community care will continue to develop and the social services department could become the focus of community service. It necessitates the co-operation of the ordinary citizen, as one of the assumptions of community care is that problems cannot be solved by professional social workers alone. Is there enough community spirit to ensure its success? Community spirit will certainly be put to the test when community care is developed on a much greater scale than now for law-breakers. Already the normal treatment for young offenders is rehabilitation, supervision and accommodation, all in the local community, and if these trends continue this will become the standard treatment for grown-up offenders as well, with prison being reserved for a smaller number of hard-core law-breakers. In other words, in the future the community will be asked to accept greater responsibility for all types of people who need help, including criminals.

We tend to assume that all doctors, dentists, opticians, teachers, social workers, planners, and so on, in their own particular sphere, know what is best for us or our children. Greater community participation in the social services, which will inevitably follow from a greater acceptance of responsibility by the community for those in need, will probably make us much more critical of professionals' advice. They will be asked more and more to explain the assumptions and theories which guide their methods of work and influence their conclusions.

The biggest problem affecting the future of the social services will continue to be the problem of resources. There never will be enough money to do all that is needed, and hence it is a question of making the best use of the money available. The reasons for the increasing cost of the services, apart from the paying out of more unemployment benefit, are: improved services due to the use of more equipment and the employment of more workers in the social services; the continuing increase in the proportion of old people in the population; the increasing number of single parents; the increasing proportion of people claiming means-tested benefits, as the official policy of giving more publicity for the service continues; the increasing wage bill, which will be difficult to reduce because the social services rely on people to operate them, and hence, as the wage bill increases, greater use cannot be made of machinery as happens in industry; and finally, an awareness of new needs that had previously been overlooked.

The increasing cost of social services has given rise to the criticism that the welfare state has stimulated private demand and public consumption beyond the means of the economy and hence expenditure on the welfare state must be reduced to what the country can afford.

This has led to one of the main controversies surrounding the welfare state – the degree of selectivity there should be or how far benefits should be given to everyone irrespective of their circumstances. At the present time we have both universal benefits and selective benefits – perhaps far more selective benefits than is generally realised. Nobody has suggested that all benefits should be universal, though there are those who say all benefits should be selective. Selectivity is an easier policy to put across than the defence of the universal principle mainly because it seems so obvious – why give benefits to people who do not need them? Not to give benefits to those who do not need them would reduce government expenditure and allow more to be given to the needy. This seems a difficult argument to counter. One practical point against any extension of selectivity is, of course, that the take-up will be nothing like 100 per cent – it will perhaps be as low as 60 per cent in some cases – and many are still left in need. But the real arguments for and against selectivity are political. They centre upon the kind of society we want and what we think the aims of the social services should be. The supporters of more selectivity tend to see the social services simply as a means for helping the weaker members of the community. The richer we become, the more the riches will go to those in work and hence the state must step in to help the old, the sick, the unemployed and the large family, in order to redress the balance. On the other hand, the defenders of the universal principle see the social services as a means to a more homogeneous and egalitarian society. They see selectivity as a divisive force in our society. In any case selectivity imposes burdens of form-filling and feelings of humiliation on people who have already had a poor deal, while the more fortunate ones are free from this. The change in government thinking from Keynesian demand management to a form of monetarism, combined with a high rate of inflation, strengthened the hand of those who wanted more selectivity.

A system of negative income tax is seen by some as a means of making the universalist-selectivist argument obsolete, but is a comprehensive system administratively and financially feasible?

Within the present system of universal and selective benefits there is room for manoeuvre without going to one extreme or the other. It is possible to introduce bigger selective benefits for special categories of poorer people, bigger child benefit, greater reliance on private insurance and perhaps a more modest scheme of negative income tax.

But how the social services will develop in the future will depend (apart from the economy) on which of the political parties happens to be in power, because of their contrasting political philosophies. However, with the change of leadership in the Conservative Party and its leader's commitment to a 'classless society' that would ensure 'a better quality of life for all our citizens', and the Labour Party's conversion to a more modest role for the State, the contrast in outlook between the two parties is not as great as when Mrs Thatcher was Prime Minister. What further lessens the contrast between them is that the Labour Party is more sensitive to the financial constraints within which, if it gained power, it would have to operate when working out policies for helping the poorer members of the community. This leads to a seeming paradox. Although a market system appears to be better for producing wealth and satisfying consumer needs than a State organised system, it creates great inequalities of wealth leaving about a third of the population relatively poor and a sizeable section of that third very poor. Thus the Welfare State has been criticised for its failure to abolish poverty but that may not be the Welfare State's fault but rather the nature of our market (capitalist) society. On the other hand, the dream of a much smaller role for the market with the State having a much greater say in wealth production and distribution in order to ensure a more egalitarian society and good living standards for everyone has faded. However, change of emphasis in both the Conservative and Labour Parties' philosophies in the post-Thatcher period might result in some kind of consensus politics returning, with both parties appreciating that, although the market has a very important role in the distribution of goods and services, there are more areas than previously acknowledged where the market is inadequate for the ends required and it is in these areas the Government must intervene. The difference between the two parties, in the future, will be the degree of intervention required – the Labour Party being more interventionist than the Conservative Party.

Below are some of the ways the two main parties may perhaps differ in their future attitude to certain of the social services. Whilst a Labour government will admit a role for the private sector in the running of social services, it will almost certainly be more limited than envisaged by a Conservative government. And whilst the Conservatives stress the importance of voluntary action in social care, the Labour Party do not want greater reliance on the voluntary sector at the expense of the statutory services.

A Conservative government will continue to support the development of private health care and the Labour Party fear the effect of its development on the NHS. Hence, under a Labour government hospitals are not likely to be encouraged, even if permitted, to opt out of district health authority control – this being seen as a move to a kind of privatisation of the Health

Service. Similarly, the Labour Party, with its greater emphasis than the Conservative Party on the need for a more egalitarian society and hence more homogeneous society will continue to favour comprehensive education and be less sympathetic to an assisted-places scheme or schools opting out of local authority control if it is seen as a threat to comprehensives. On the other hand the present Conservative Government expects most schools to opt out of local authority control and those that are left will control 85 per cent of their budgets. The Conservative Party is not as deeply attached to comprehensive schools as the Labour Party. In fact, both private health and private education are seen by the Labour Party as a divisive force in our society but it is unlikely to seriously challenge them because of the charge that it would be restricting freedom of choice. Like the Conservative Party it will aim to improve the Health Service and the public sector of Education. The Conservative Party will continue to put greater stress on the expansion of owner-occupation of housing than the Labour Party – the Labour Party fearing that local authority housing will more and more become a kind of ghetto for the poor. Both in employment training and environmental protection a Labour government would be more likely than a Conservative government to use the compulsion of statute law to enforce certain of its policies – a Conservative government relying more on voluntary action.

On its past record under Mrs Thatcher (and this is perhaps an unfair way of judging it), a Conservative government is likely to be less generous in its social security payments to the poor than is a Labour government. In the Conservative Party there is a greater willingness than there is in the Labour Party to blame the individual for his or her misfortune whilst in the Labour Party there is too great a willingness to blame society. But, whatever the future, the state of the economy will be the limiting factor to whatever a government wishes to do.

ASSIGNMENTS

1. Give the main advantages and disadvantages of the following agencies for the administration of social services:
    (a) local authorities
    (b) central government departments
    (c) voluntary bodies.
2. 'The future of the social services depends more on the economists than the professional people in the social services.' Discuss.
3. Write to the headquarters of each of the main political parties asking

for the party's policies for the future of the welfare state. From the replies, which may include party literature on the welfare state, make your own summary of the views of the respective parties.
4.   'Giving choice always means those with more money have better choice.' Discuss in relation to one social service.

READING

Robert Bacon and Walter Eltis, *Britain's Economic Problem: Too Few Producers* (Macmillan, 1978).

Muriel Brown and Nicola Madge, *Despite the Welfare State* (Heinemann, 1982).

The Citizens' Charter, Cm 1599 (HMSO, July 1991).

Peter Donaldson, *A Question of Economics* (Penguin, reprint 1986).

Frank Field, *Poverty and Politics* (Heinemann, 1982), chs 11 and 12.

George Gilder, *Health and Poverty* (Buchan & Enright, 1982), ch. 11.

Ian Gough, *The Political Economy of the Welfare State,* reprint (Macmillan, 1981).

David Graham and Peter Clarke, *The New Enlightenment: the Rebirth of Liberalism* (Macmillan, 1986).

John Hills, (ed.), *The State of Welfare: The Welfare State in Britain since 1974* (Oxford University Press, 1990).

Norman Johnson, *Reconstructing the Welfare State – a Decade of Change 1980–1990* (Harvester Wheatsheaf, 1990).

Martin Loney, *The Politics of Greed: the New Right and the Welfare State* (Pluto Press, 1986).

Robert Pinker, *Social Theory and Social Policy* (Heinemann, 1971), ch. 5.

Arthur Seldon, 'Thaw in the Welfare State', *Lloyds Bank Review*, July 1972.

J. F. Sleeman, *The Welfare State* (Allen & Unwin, 1973).

G. Bernard Shaw, *The Intelligent Woman's Guide to Socialism, Capitalism, Sovietism and Fascism* (Penguin, 1937).

R. H. Tawney, *The Acquisitive Society* (G. Bell and Sons, Ltd., 1921 and later reprints).

R. M. Titmuss, *Essays on the Welfare State*, 3rd edn (Allen & Unwin, 1976).

Jim Tomlinson, *Monetarism: Is there an Alternative?* (Basil Blackwell, 1986).

Appendices

1 Some of the Main Social Security Weekly Benefit Rates (beginning 8 April 1991)

Unemployment Benefit (leaflet NI 12)	(£)
Over pension age	
single rate	52.00
adult dependency addition	31.25
Under pension age	
full rate	41.40
adult dependency addition	25.55

Sickness Benefit (leaflet NI 16)	
Over pension age	
single rate	49.90
adult dependency addition	29.95
Under pension age	
full rate	39.60
adult dependency addition	24.50

Severe Disablement Allowance (Leaflet NI 252)	31.25
Adult dependant	18.70
higher rate	11.10
middle rate	6.90
Lower rate	3.45

Retirement Pension (leaflet NI 46)	
On own insurance	52.00
On spouse's insurance	31.25

Widow's Benefit (leaflet NP 45)	
Widow's payment	1000.00
Widowed mother's allowance	52.00
Widow's pension – standard rate	52.00

Invalid Care Allowance (leaflet NI 212)	31.25
Adult dependency addition	18.70

230 *Appendices*

Invalidity Benefit (leaflet NI 16A)
    Invalidity pension   52.00
    Invalidity allowance
      higher rate   11.10
      middle rate   6.90
      lower rate   3.45

Maternity Benefit (leaflet NI 17A)
    Maternity allowance
      full rate   40.60
      adult dependency addition   24.50

Child dependency additions
    For each child with:
      retirement pension, widows benefit,
      invalidity benefit, invalid care and
      severe disablement allowance, higher
      rate industrial death benefit,
      unemployability supplement and sickness
      or unemployment benefit if beneficiary
      over pension age   10.70

Child Benefit (leaflet CH 1)
    for only or eldest child   9.25
    for other children   7.50
    (from October 1991)

One-parent Benefit (leaflet CH 11)   5.60

Income support (leaflet IS 1)
    Personal allowances
      Single person (over 25)   39.65
      Couple (both over 18)   62.25
      Single people (18–24)   31.15
      Single people (16–17)   23.65
(For details of premiums in addition to the above amounts,
see DSS leaflet NI 196)

dependent children (from October 1991)
    over 18   31.40
    16–17   23.90
    11–15   20.00
    under 11   13.60
(The scale for blind people is slightly more than the above rates.)

Family Credit (Claim)

Single parent or couple	38.30
plus for each child aged:	
under 11	9.70
11–15	16.10
16–17	20.05
18	27.95

SOURCE: House of Commons *Hansard*, 24 October 1990, DSS and COI leaflets. (For comprehensive listing of benefits See DSS and COI leaflet NI 196.)

2 Expenditure on Social Security Benefits for Great Britain 1988–9 and Estimated Number of Recipients 1988–9

	Expenditure (£ million)	Recipients (000s)
National insurance benefits		
Pension benefits		
Retirement pensions	19237	9710
Invalidity benefit	3359	1100
Industrial disablement benefit	451	325
Widows benefit and industrial death benefit	909	400
Lump sum payments to contributory pensioners	109	10900
Other benefits		
Unemployment benefit	1107	600
Sickness benefit	192	105
Statutory sick pay	898	365
Maternity allowance	27	15
Statutory maternity pay	250	80
Non-contributory benefits		
Pension benefits		
Non-contributory retirement pension	36	35
War pension	610	265
Attendance allowance	1003	730
Invalid care allowance	173	100
Severe disablement allowance	316	270
Mobility allowance	675	560
Lump sum payments to non-contributory pensioners	9	900
Other benefits		
Supplementary pension	1178	(1986–7) 1180
Supplementary allowance	6784	(1986–7) 3285
Income support	7575	4310
Child benefit	4515	12010
Family Income supplement	161	(1986–7) 215
Family credit	394	280
One-parent benefit	179	705
Housing benefit – rent rebates and allowances	3489	4090
Social Fund	149	
Administration and miscellaneous services	2163	

SOURCE: *Social Trends, 1991* (HMSO).

3 Manpower in the National Health Service in the United Kingdom in 1979 and 1989

	Thousands	
	1979	1989
Regional and District Health Authorities		
Medical and dental (excluding locums)	45.3	55.0
Nursing and midwifery (excluding agency staff)	449.2	509.0
Professional and technical (excluding works)	74.1	99.7
Administrative and clerical	121.8	149.4
Other staff (including ancillary, works, maintenance, and ambulance)	272.4	186.9
Total Regional and District Health Authorities	962.8	1000.0
Family practitioner services		
General medical practitioners	28.5	31.5
General dental practitioners	14.4	18.4
Ophthalmic medical practitioners, ophthalmic opticians and dispensing opticians	8.8	9.9
Total family practitioner professionals	51.7	59.8

SOURCE: *Social Trends, 1986* and *Social Trends, 1991* (HMSO).

4   National Health Service Hospital In-patient Waiting Lists by Speciality for the United Kingdom

					Thousands
	1976	1981	1986	1989	1990
Speciality					
General surgery	200.5[1]	169.1[1]	180.3[1]	173.0[1]	172.5
Orthopaedics	109.8	145.1	160.5	153.0	155.9
Ear, nose or throat	121.7	115.4	132.2	123.2	127.5
Gynaecology	91.8	105.6	106.6	96.4	98.0
Oral surgery	26.5	35.5	56.3	50.4	53.7
Plastic surgery	44.7	49.2	46.1	46.8	45.3
Ophthalmology	41.2	43.4	64.6	88.9	92.7
Urology	22.0[2]	29.1[2]	42.7	47.1	47.2
Other	42.5	44.2	41.3	48.0	48.8
All specialities	700.8	736.6	830.6	827.0	841.6

1.   Includes the Northern Ireland figures for 'Urology'.
2.   Great Britain only.
SOURCE: *Social Trends, 1991* (HMSO).

5 Number of Beds in England in the Private Health Services

					Thousands
	1971	1981	1986	1987–88	1988–89
NHS beds authorised for private in-patient care	4.4	2.7	3.0	3.0	3.0
Registered private nursing homes, hospitals and clinics					
Total available beds	25.3	33.5	62.1	78.2	94.5
Percentage of available beds in premises with an operating theatre			14.5	11.8	10.0

SOURCE: *Social Trends, 1991* (HMSO).

6   Education: Numbers of Students in 1989 in the United Kingdom (in thousands) for Nursery, Primary and Secondary Education and in 1988 for Higher and Further Education.

Nursery Schools		
Public sector	100	
Primary schools		
Public sector	4792	
Secondary schools		
Public sector	3551	
Assisted and independent schools		
(nursery, primary and secondary)	641	
Special schools (full-time)	118	
Higher education (full-time)		
Universities	284.5	(In addition 65.1
Other higher education	294.6	overseas students)
Higher education (part-time)		
Universities	50.1	
Open University	85.3	
Further education advanced courses		
Part-time, day	185.5	
Evening only	64.6	

In addition to the above there are students at further education colleges taking courses up to 'A' level and intermediate professional level. (W. E. B.)

SOURCE: *Social Trends, 1991* (HMSO).

7 Class Sizes as Taught by Type of School in England in 1989

Primary schools	
Percentage of classes taught by:	
One teacher in classes with:	
1–20 pupils	14
1–30 pupils	62
31 or more pupils	17
Two or more teachers	7
Average size of class (numbers)	26
Number of classes (thousands)	145

Secondary schools	
Percentage of classes taught by	
One teacher in classes with:	
1–20 pupils	47
21–30 pupils	44
31 or more pupils	4
Two or more teachers	4
Average size of class (numbers	21
Number of classes (thousands)	137

SOURCE: *Social Trends, 1991* (HMSO).

8   Public Expenditure on Education for the United Kingdom, 1988–9

	£s million
Current expenditure	
schools	
Nursery and Primary	5290
Secondary	6474
Special	888
Further and adult education [1]	3187
Training of teachers: tuition	197
Universities [1]	1966
Other education expenditure	1003
Related current expenditure	2401
Total current expenditure	21 406
Capital expenditure	
Schools (nursery, primary, secondary and special)	477
Other education expenditure	435
Total capital expenditure	912
Total government expenditure	22 317
Of which, expenditure by local authorities	19 123

1.   Includes tuition fees.

SOURCE: *Social Trends, 1991* (HMSO).

9   Pupils in Secondary Education in 1989 in England, Wales, Scotland and Northern Ireland

	Percentages and thousands
England (percentages)	
Maintained secondary schools	
Middle deemed secondary	6.3
Modern	3.9
Grammar	3.4
Technical	0.1
Comprehensive	85.9
Other	0.4
Total pupils (=100%) (thousands)	2945
Wales (percentages)	
Maintained secondary schools	
Middle deemed secondary	NIL
Modern	0.2
Grammar	0.2
Comprehensive	98.9
Other	0.7
Total pupils (=100%) (thousands)	192
Scotland (percentages)	
Public sector secondary schools	
Selective	NIL
Comprehensive	100
Part comprehensive/part selective	NIL
Total pupils (=100%) (thousands)	312
Northern Ireland (percentages)	
Public sector secondary schools	
Secondary intermediate	87.8
Grammar	12.2
Technical intermediate	NIL
Total pupils (=100%) (thousands)	103

SOURCE: *Social Trends, 1991* (HMSO).

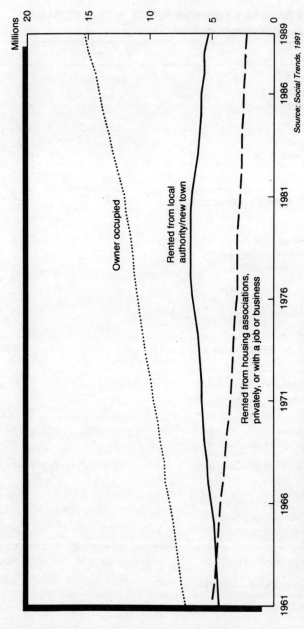

Figure 1   Stock of Dwellings in the United Kingdom: by Tenure

Source: Social Trends, 1991

Source: Social Trends, 1991 (HMSO).

Figure 2   Housebuilding Completions in the United Kingdom: by Sector

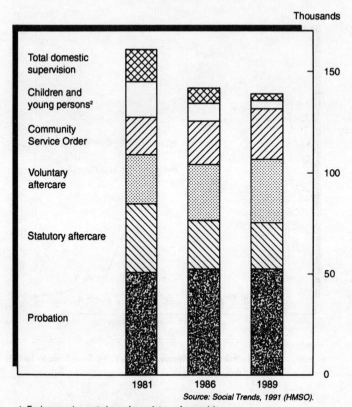

Thousands

Total domestic supervision

Children and young persons[2]

Community Service Order

Voluntary aftercare

Statutory aftercare

Probation

1981   1986   1989

150

100

50

0

Source: Social Trends, 1991 (HMSO).

1 Each person is counted once for each type of supervision.
2 Supervision under the Children and Young Persons Act, 1969.

Figure 3   Persons Supervised by the Probation Service: by Type of Supervision in England and Wales, 1981, 1986, 1989

Index

149, 151, 166

General Certificate of Secondary
Education (GCSE) 178
GCE 'A' level 154, 155
General Improvement Areas 193
General Medical Council 67
Gingerbread 111
Gladstone Committee Report, 1895
(on prisons) 215
grammar schools 125, 126, 127, 128,
129, 130, 132, 133, 135, 152,
153, 154
Green, Thomas Hill 12
Green Belts 200, 210
Gregory Commission 17
Griffiths NHS Management Inquiry
Report 1983 79
Griffiths Report, Community Care,
Agenda for Action, 1988 103

Hadow Report, 1926 (on education
and the adolescent) 129, 133
handicapped children 113–14
Harris, Dr. Drew 41
Health Care Planning Teams 71
Health Centres 74, 94, 108
Health and Medicines Act 1988 81,
82
Health and Safety at Work 183, 184
Health and Safety at Work Act,
1974 183
Health and Safety Executive 183
Health and Safety Commission 183
health inequalities 92
Health Insurance 15, 16, 17,
18, 60, 64
Health Service Commissioner 96
health visitors 73, 94, 108, 121
high rise flats 193, 202
higher education 137–8, 139, 140,
143–8, 151, 160, 162, 223
Higher Education Corporations 138,
148, 175
home helps 75, 94, 121
Home Improvement Grants 193
homeless 191, 194, 196
home nursing 72, 121

Hospital Patients' Association 97
hospitals 11, 13, 58–9, 62, 69–71,
80, 82–4
households below average income 46
housing 2, 223
Housing Act, 1930 189
Housing Act, 1949 190
Housing Act, 1957 192
Housing Act, 1969 193
Housing Act, 1974 193
Housing Act, 1972 194
Housing Act, 1980 188, 190, 191
Housing Act, 1988 190, 191, 194
Housing Action Areas 193, 195
Housing Action Trusts 194, 196
Housing administration 192
Housing Town Planning Act,
1909 199
Housing and Town Planning Act,
1919 188
Housing and Planning Act, 1986 193
Housing Associations 191, 194,
195, 201
housing benefit 1, 21, 26, 31, 40,
42–4, 47, 190
Housing Finance Act 1972 43
Housing Corporation 191, 194
Housing Homeless Persons Act,
1977 191
housing officer 94
housing statistics 191–2
Hunt Committee Report, 1969 (on
intermediate areas) 208

Improvement Grants 190
Income Guarantee Scheme 50
Income support 1, 20, 21, 23,
26, 28, 29, 30, 31, 33, 34–6,
37, 39, 40, 41, 43, 44, 46,
47, 48, 49, 53, 54, 110, 118,
190, 223
Independent Living Fund 118
Independent Schools (private) 137,
158–9, 161, 162, 163
Industrial Revolution 4
Industrial Inquiry Advisory
Council 27
Industrial Training Act, 1964 151,
176–7, 183